Truth,
Knowledge,
or just plain bull

Truth,
Knowledge,
or just plain bull

How to tell
the Difference

A Handbook of
Practical Logic
and Clear Thinking

Bernard M. Patten

59 John Glenn Drive
Amherst, New York 14228-2197

Published 2004 by Prometheus Books

Inquiries should be addressed to
Prometheus Books
59 John Glenn Drive
Amherst, New York 14228–2197
VOICE: 716–691–0133, ext. 207
FAX: 716–564–2711
WWW.PROMETHEUSBOOKS.COM

08 07 06 05 04   5 4 3 2 1

Library of Congress Cataloging-in-Publication Data

Patten, Bernard M.
    Truth, knowledge, or just plain bull : how to tell the difference / Bernard M. Patten.
        p. cm.
    Includes bibliographical references and index.
    ISBN 1-59102-246-0 (pbk. : alk. paper)
    1. Critical thinking. I. Title.

B809.2.P37 2004
160—dc22
                                                        2004011546

Printed in the United States of America on acid-free paper

TO HER

SINE TE NIHIL

Because the real is out there, we must effectively with it, else it may deal effectively (and harshly) with us.

Yes, that's the problem, your problem and mine, the crux of our existence, for the real brings many revenges. The real has a sneaky habit of finding us and, eventually, making us trade with it as an intractable fact. It's sad but true: reality haunts us and punishes us for not dealing with it correctly. I am sorry to have to tell you that fact, but that is the way things are. That is the nature of nature. That is the reality of reality.

Not convinced? Don't get it? Don't agree? Thinking, "So what?"

Wishful thinking doesn't work and may be dangerous.

Permit me to illustrate the point: I would love to flap my arms and fly to the moon. And sometimes I would like it to rain beer. Those things are not possible. To fly, I must stick to the reality-based technologies of zeppelins, helicopters, and airplanes. If I tried my fantasy idea, if I flapped my arms and jumped off a building, I would suffer. Chances are, if I did that from the top of a tall building, I would suffer greatly. And to get a beer, I have to purchase one at the local supermarket or bar or bum one off a friend or neighbor. If I waited for it to rain beer, I would wait forever.

Aye, there's the **rub**.[2]

Wishful thinking might give a kind of warm, cozy, fuzzy, happy feeling. But when it comes to operating in the real world, wishful thinking presents handicaps—handicaps that range from the inconvenient to the fatal.

What can happen when reason leaves and wishful thinking takes over? Aviation gives some of the clearest examples. Consider an aviation case in point: You are piloting a jet plane. Momentarily, you look away from that beautiful blue vista in front of you and glance at the fuel gauges. Uh-oh! The gauges are approaching empty. What to do?

That's the question. What to do? Often, it is the most important question that we have to deal with our whole life long. And as usual, there are multiple answers, multiple choices, some good, some bad, and some ugly.

Some choices will work, some will not. Others will keep you safe. Some will lead to disaster. Which should you choose? How will you know that you have made the right choice? How will you know that you are right? How will you know that you are reality based and safe?

Consider one option: Assume the gauges are wrong and keep flying. This line of thinking assumes that you have fuel, that the gauges are not measuring the fuel you have, that assumes the gauges are wrong. The action that follows from this line of thinking is keep flying. Don't worry.

What's wrong with that line of thinking? What's wrong with the action that followed from that line of thinking? Pause for fifty microseconds and think. Why won't that approach work?

That won't work because it is highly likely that the gauges are right. Therefore, it will be highly likely that you will run out of fuel and run out soon. Because fuel is needed to keep an airplane aloft, it is highly likely that when you run out of fuel, you will fall out of the sky, tumble back to Mother Earth, and get hurt. Without fuel, it is predictable that your plane will come down under emergency conditions.

I hope you don't crash. If you do crash, there will be a consolation: There will be no explosion. There will be no fire. There will be no explosion and no fire because there is no fuel.

Another option: Just don't pay any attention to the problem. Deny its existence. Forget it. Go back to dumb contemplation of the beautiful blue limitless dome of the sky, with its fleecy white clouds drifting by. This approach is known as the ostrich approach after the dumb bird of the same name. The ostrich, when danger comes, hides its head in the sand. The ostrich thinks it has solved its problem because it no longer sees the problem. The problem, however, continues to see the ostrich and does not go away because the ostrich no longer wants to see it. The problem is still there. Reality doesn't go away just because the ostrich wants it to. Instead, the problem stays, often stays to cause trouble, sometimes even eats the ostrich. If the danger were real, the ostrich would have been better off running away, fighting directly, or doing almost anything but what it did.

When you choose to ignore a danger, the danger may not go away. Often it continues and causes trouble, lots and lots of trouble. That is why your consideration of and perception of the reality is so important.

Another option: Assume that the gauges are correct but that airplanes don't need fuel to fly. Or worse—assume that your plane is special and doesn't need fuel the way other planes do. In which case, continue flying, and prove, once again to yourself, and to everyone else, now and forever, that planes *do* need fuel to fly. Prove again that when a plane, any plane, regardless of make and model and of who is at the controls, runs out of fuel, it topples out of the sky.

Yup, that's the reality principle. That's the law that governs the situation. There is no way around it. Never has there been an exception to that rule, not for you, not for anyone. You either know the rule, or you don't. You either follow it, or you don't. But if you don't know it, or if you know it and don't follow it, as the night follows the day, trouble follows you. You run out of fuel. When you run out of fuel, you might crash.

Option four: Do the reasonable thing. Take action based in reality. Land. Refuel. Live to fly another day.

Let's carry the aviation analogy one step further—into your private life. What's the lesson? Is it possible that unacknowledged conditions, unknown and unintended consequences, self-deception, and other obstacles limit your ability (and mine) to understand fully and react appropriately to the complex situations that we discover in our everyday lives? Were it otherwise, there would hardly be a point to studying clear thinking, **logic**, or science. Were it otherwise, there would hardly be a point to your reading this book.

Deal with your problems intelligently, reasonably, and realistically. So don't crash your life away because you don't know how to deal with reality. Don't wreck your chances for success with wishful thinking. Take the reasonable approach. Deal with the problem directly and rationally. Know the truth, the reality situation, and deal with it as the real situation requires. Act reasonably. Plan your actions on the basis of what is reasonable and expected. That's the best way of handling the unreasonable and the unexpected and the unexpectable, things that have a sneaky habit of coming your way. The plane analogy shows us the obvious answers. That's why I selected it. Not much thinking is involved in solving a fuel deficiency problem. In general, you either fuel or your engine stops. It's that simple.

An airplane needs fuel the way human beings need food.

The fuel problem applies to human beings. Either you eat, or you die.

Xenophon, in his famous book the *Anabasis*, tells us that there was one, and only one, cure for the hunger sickness that was causing the Greek troops to collapse on the side of the road. That cure was food. As soon as they were fed, the hunger sickness disappeared, and the troops were able to move again. If the troops were not fed, they continued to languish and subsequently died. Xenophon concluded that the hunger sickness, without food, was fatal. It still is.

Fuel problems and hunger problems have similar solutions. They have similar solutions because they are similar problems. Engines need fuel the way the human body needs food.

Most reality-based problems are not as simple as fuel or food problems.

Believe me, I wish there were simple answers to the other problems that we must face and solve. If there were simple answers, we could all be out on our boats having fun or playing in the garden, swimming in the pool, or enjoying a good book or movie. Unfortunately, that is not the reality. The reality is quite the opposite. Most of the time, there are no simple solutions.

All of which brings us to the first important principle to keep in mind when working on the solution to any problem. Memorize this principle now. Recite it often to yourself in front of the mirror. Recite it every day. This principle will serve you your whole life long:

> *Principle:* Simple answers? Forget it! Usually, there are no simple answers because there are few simple problems. On the contrary, most of the problems we must face—the problems that are important to us—are quite complex.

Not only are there usually no simple answers, but as civilization progresses, the issues we have to deal with become more and more complex and the answers become more and more complex, too.

The progression to complexity isn't all bad. It probably fuels our creativity in all fields. If we reached the end of the line, the human spirit would shrivel and die. No worry about that. We and the things around us—our human creations and our understanding of reality—will increase in complexity, if not in depth, and will remain the cornerstone of our rising powers, as long as we continue to think and act rationally and solve the problems as they arrive on our doorstep.

> *Lesson:* Because there are no simple answers, a simple answer is likely to be wrong.

Yes, wrong!

Therefore, don't accept at face value *any* simple answer; especially don't accept any simple answer to any complex problem.

Recently, investors have learned this lesson the hard way. The moral as applied to investing is that any approach to moneymaking in the stock market that can be easily described and followed by a lot of people is by its very terms too simple and too easy to last. Benedict de Spinoza's concluding remark to his *Ethics* applies to Wall Street as well

Why is that?

Besides the confusing mix of hype and hope, most of the ideas out there in the public domain are simple and therefore likely wrong. The reason for this sad state of affairs is straightforward: Simple ideas are easily remembered, easily explained, and easily disseminated—all those things that TV audiences seem to want and need.

Don't forget we present our society as being one of free initiatives, individualism, and idealism, when in reality those are mostly words. We are a centralized managerial industrial culture of an essentially bureaucratic nature and motivated by a materialism that is only slightly mitigated by truly humanistic concerns. TV is mainly owned and operated and (through advertising revenues) controlled by big business, the American corporation, that routinely lies to us about the quality of its products and sometimes (as with WorldCom, Dynergy, Adelphia, Tyco, CMS Energy, Reliant Resources, Enron, and Global Crossing) about the soundness of its own business practices.

So watch out!

People who wish to influence you, who want to drive your opinions—whether teachers, advertisers, corporations or, God help us, politicians—those people, the image makers, adjust what they have to say to the intellectual level of their audience. And the larger the audience, the lower the level. That's why you get your news chopped up into sound bites, reduced to its simplest elements, which, in turn, are spun into headlines and slogans, designed to be easily digestible pellets of information—and often misinformation.

Thomas Jefferson said that the man who doesn't read the newspapers knows more than the man who does. The man who doesn't read the papers doesn't have his head crammed with misinformation. If Jefferson thought that about newspapers, what would he have said about TV? Mark Twain, who held a similar opinion, said that it wasn't what he knew that hurt but all those things he knew that weren't true. Jefferson and Twain would have agreed with Buddha, who expressed the same idea in his Noble Truths: There is suffering. Suffering has a cause. The cause of suffering is misapprehension (by which Buddha meant misinformation leading to misconception).

There's the problem. What's the solution? Enter clear thinking.

Clear thinking tells you, better than any other tool, what is likely to be true and what is likely to be false. Clear thinking is a tool that helps us think correctly. Clear thinking even supplies the tools to decode hidden messages so that you get to the truth. Clear thinking tells you when they are handing you rubbish.

My hope is that this little handbook of clear thinking and practical logic will speed you along the correct path to a safer, happier life by introducing you to the much-neglected art of reasonable thinking. My hope is that this little handbook will give you the tools to know the truth. My hope is that this book will give you a chance of adding a very large item to your stock of mental delights. My hope is that you will, along the way, have some fun as I did when I was learning this discipline.

Increasingly, civilization is in a race between straight thinking and disaster. If we don't straighten our crooked thinking soon, we will crash. If we don't start thinking right, God help us.

REVIEW

Time spent in review is never wasted. Neuroscientists have discovered that review fixes our memories by increasing the probability of reactivating previously activated neuronal networks. Repeated reactivation results in actual structural changes in the brain that facilitate recall. Neurons that fire together, wire together.

Therefore (here you should be able to generate your own conclusion from the above mentioned premises).

EXERCISES

1. Reread all the main points in this chapter. When you have done so give yourself a check here ___.
2. Reread all the main points in this chapter aloud. When done, give yourself a check here ___. Rereading aloud fixes the memory better than silent rereading. Rereading on separate days fixes the memory better than rereading twice the same day. The more you reread, the more you will fix the memory. But don't overdo it. Four times should be quite enough. You don't want to acquire the reputation of being a drudge.
3. Tell why logic isn't half as important as love. Give yourself a check mark if you think you are right ___. Hint: The answer to this question is not in this book, but it is in your heart. By

second. This rate was and is always the same for all objects, whether dropped, thrown horizontally, or shot horizontally from a gun.

Newton also concluded that the same force caused water to run downhill and that same force also holds the earth, sun, and stars together and keeps our moon and the satellites of other planets in orbit. In his book *Philosophiae Naturalis Principia Mathematica* (1687), Newton showed that all observations of earth's gravity could be explained by a single law of universal gravitation that attracts every other celestial body with a force described by

$$F = \frac{Gm_1 m_2}{r^2}$$

where G is the universal gravitational constant, m_1 is the mass of object 1, m_2 is the mass of object 2, and r is the distance between them.

Note that Newton reached this conclusion by an extrapolation from his particular observations that he actually made and measured to events and things that he could not actually physically measure. Since Newton did not measure the gravity of all heavenly bodies, at all times past, present, and future, he had to **generalize** from his particular observations that they would follow the same gravitational rules as the objects followed here on earth. By making this generalization, Newton could not possibly predict all future observations on the subject because they had not been made and the results could not be known. Newton opened himself to a possible falsification of his generalization. If someone could show that there was just one single exception to his gravitational generalization, then Newton would be proven wrong.

This is the reason that all inductive reasoning is hypothetical and tentative: A single contradiction would require revision of the generalization. In other words, if I could show that there were objects that were attracted to each other that did not have mass, or objects that did have mass that did not attract each other, and so forth, I could prove Newton wrong.

If I proved Newton wrong, revisions in the Newtonian theory of gravity would be needed because the generalization that Newton propounded would not have described reality exactly. About this particular vulnerability of inductive logic to experimental evidence, more later. Right now, here's the principle:

Principle: A generalization is proved wrong by finding one exception.

From which follows:

Lesson: Prove a generalization wrong by finding one exception to the generalization. Once you have found the exception, the generalization is wrong. Act accordingly.

Albert Einstein proved Newtonian gravitation wrong by finding an exception to Newton's laws of gravity. According to Einstein, gravity is not a force but relates to the geometry of space-time, warped or curved in the presence of matter or energy, the way a mattress sags under a heavy weight.

In 1919, Einstein proved that gravity is not a force and that mass bends space-time around it. Einstein showed this by predicting that photons would bend toward the sun as if attracted by the sun's gravity. Since photons did bend exactly as predicted by Einstein, Newton's laws of gravity had to undergo revision. That revision, among other things, is now called general relativity theory.

Don't feel bad about this. Newton wouldn't have felt bad about it. Why should you? Newton probably would have rejoiced at the refinement proffered by Einstein because it flashes with the steel of reason. Because it—not Newton's theory—predicts the experimental results, it more closely reflects the nature of reality. Einstein's prediction is a remarkable illustration of the sheer force of thought that Newton would have loved. And whether Newton would have loved it wouldn't matter. For despite his or anyone else's personal preferences, that's the way it is. That's the reality. That is the reality of what light does when it passes the sun. And that's the way progress is made. That's the way our knowledge is refined and expanded.

Principle: Good generalizations encompass all examples.

Principle: All scientific principles are tentative and subject to revision in the face of new data.

From which follows:

Lesson: If scientific principles, which have the firmest basis in reality, are tentative, then all general principles are tentative.

If someone can recite the alphabet backward, chances are that he or she can recite it forward. If you can do the hard thing, chances are you can also do the easy thing. If our hardest, most solid, most refined and difficult form of general knowledge is provisional, then our less refined and less rigorous forms of general knowledge must be more so. Therefore, we are required to look for exceptions to any and all generalizations so that our understanding of reality may improve and we can get closer to the truth.

Principle: All general principles are tentative, whether scientific, religious, political, and such. All general statements are fair game for repeated tests of truthfulness and reality. Therefore, no general truth is absolute.

From which follows:

Lesson: The word *all* and that word *never* are too general for intelligent use. People who say *all* or *never* usually do so at their peril.

Wait a second! If all principles are tentative, then the above principle is tentative, too.

You spotted the snag. Don't look at me that way. It's not my fault. Logicians have argued your point for years. It's a problem.

Or is it?

I am not asserting that that principle is an exception to the general principle. I am, in fact, considering that principle as also subject to the discovery method. Right now, I can't think how the principle might be falsified, but someone in the future might be able to discover how to prove it wrong. Thus, until proven wrong, the principle must stand:

Principle: All principles are tentative, including this one.

Work out on the above rule. See if you can use it to prove something. Try to think about the following question: Do women who wear glasses smoke cigarettes? How would you resolve this question? How would you answer it and know that you are right?

When working on such statements, it is helpful to transform them into positive statements (called *hypotheses*) and then try to prove the positive statement wrong. The question then becomes: How would you prove that the following statement is right or wrong?

Women who wear glasses never smoke cigarettes.

Or (which is the same)—Women who smoke cigarettes never wear glasses.

For most of my time as a teenager, I believed that women who wore glasses did not smoke cigarettes and that women who smoked cigarettes never wore glasses. I arrived at that generalization by a series of observations based on the fact that every woman I saw who smoked had no glasses and that every woman who had glasses did not smoke. How could my original hypothesis about this situation be falsified? That is, how could you prove that I was wrong?

Sit back and think about this for two minutes. Time your thinking by the clock. See if you can actually prove something. See if you can prove the statement false. Address the specific question: How would you prove my hypothesis wrong?

OK. Did you come up with anything? Got it? Don't get it?

It's important to understand yourself. "Know thyself" was the motto written on the wall of the temple of Apollo at Delphi. Socrates, too, thought that the beginning of all knowledge: Know thyself. Those who saw the movie *The Matrix* know that the same motto was written on the wall of the old woman's kitchen. Why is it important? Part of knowing thyself is to know what you know and what you don't know. The Socratic questions for his students were part of his general program to get them to know themselves. Here's the Socratic paradox. Socrates said he knew more than others because he knew that he knew nothing. Others didn't know anything but thought they did. Therefore, Socrates was ahead.

Another example: When a scientist does an experiment and it comes out the way he thought it would, he rejoices. When a scientist does an experiment and it comes out differently from the way he thought it would, he rejoices more.

Huh? When an experiment goes wrong, scientists like the idea? Why?

The second experiment exposes ignorance. The second experiment opens things up for the possibility of progress, for the discovery of something new and different. That's what scientists are in business for, the discovery of new knowledge, not the simple confirmation of what is already known. All progress depends on discovering the new.

So if you got the answer to the question above, great. But if you didn't, that is greater still because it indicates you are now aware of your own ignorance. It shows that you are about to make, or at least have the possibility of making, some real progress. It indicates that you need to improve your powers of thinking. It shows that you have the potential for benefits from further study and application.

With that great benefit in mind, let's get back to the women smokers with glasses problem.

It is obviously wrong. What was your answer? Do woman with glasses smoke? Or don't they? How would you prove it one way or the other?

Here's one answer. My theory about smokers and glasses would be proven wrong by finding one woman who wore glasses and smoked. In fact, one fatal day (fatal for my theory, that is), I saw a woman in the park stop walking her dog, pause, and light up a cigarette. Since she was wearing glasses and smoking, the exception to my scientific theory was found. The theory was proved wrong. Soon after that, I saw multiple people violate the rule that I had previously thought inviolate. That's not unusual.

Once a generalization is proven wrong, many similar examples usually follow.

Why when one exception is uncovered, multiple other exceptions surface almost right away is not entirely clear. But it is a common enough observation, even in scientific work. Probably this has something to do with the way we humans view reality. We may have a deep unconscious bias that tends to make us observe the things we expect. And we may have a deep unconscious bias not to observe the things we don't expect. When a rule is proven wrong, we tend to see the light, so to speak, and uncover multiple other examples. Thus might the scales drop from our eyes. Thus might our knowledge of reality take a giant leap forward. The process can be painful, especially for our bruised egos (and our depleted retirement funds). The process illustrates the immensely complex situations with which we are involved as we struggle to draw firm conclusions, to distinguish appearance from reality and truth from falsehood.

Once one accounting fraud surfaced, multiple others were discovered. Once a few accounting frauds at Enron were exposed, multiple other accounting frauds surfaced not only at Enron but also at multiple other companies. Investors became more alert to the problem or were able to read between the lines in the cash-flow statements or something similar, turning over other rocks and finding slimy things beneath.

The Security Exchange Commission started investigating not only Enron but also Global Crossing and ImClone and companies of that ilk. They found an epidemic of frauds. Congress held special inquiries and acted as if it didn't know anything about these accounting sleights of hand, and in many cases it didn't. Now we seem to have a plague of accounting fiascos bursting all over.

The point is that a little discovery of a little nugget of truth often opens the way to a big discovery of a big truth or even truths. In the case of multiple American businesses, the bitter truth is that multiple corrupt practices are rampant.

But what's all this about? Why are we spending so much time and energy discussing generalizations? What's the point? The point is that once the general rule is established, it can be applied to particular situations to make correct predictions or reach correct conclusions about reality. This can become a useful guide helping us decide what action to take. Furthermore, the **deduction** from the general to the particular generates predictions that one can **verify** (show to be true) or **falsify** (show to be false). Verification might tend to confirm the general principle, but falsification refutes the general principle absolutely. In the philosophy of science, this process is known as the hypothetico-deductive method. More than a few philosophers have observed that no matter how many confirming examples you produce, you can't prove any open, universal proposition or generalization with decisive finality. This observation led Francis Bacon (1561–1626) to conclude, "The force of the negative instance is greater." T. H. Huxley (1826–1895) added (probably with tongue in cheek) that "The great tragedy of science—the slaying of a beautiful hypothesis by an ugly fact."[2] Thus, science is, and must only be, a matter of endless striving and of endless inquiry.

For example, let's apply what we have learned to the airplane fuel problem of the introduction.

All jet planes need fuel (general rule). My jet is running low on fuel (particular situation). Therefore, I must fuel the plane (reality-based conclusion derived from and based on the application of the general principle to the particular instance). (Note that the application has the protective effect of preventing disaster.)

The event of going from the general to the particular (that is, the

Unlike most normal human beings, scientists like to have their laws questioned and disproved. They know that upon process all progress depends. Thus, science looks at its own laws rather dispassionately. If a law is proved wrong, a new law is established to take its place. The new law will be a generalization that will have greater accuracy in telling us the real situation and the truth.

This type of thinking not only applies to scientific understanding of gravity and deaf blue-eyed cats; it can apply to our personal lives as well.

As I said, in my youth, I believed that women who wore glasses never smoked. That idea has been proven wrong. Now I know that what I thought was true was not true and that smoking and wearing glasses probably have nothing to do with each other. The association, my mental conjunction "glasses and not-smoking," did not reflect the reality situation. So much for my erroneous idea about smoking and glasses. That is one personal generalization that doesn't work. But what about all the other erroneous ideas I hold that I don't know are wrong? Ouch! Those are the things that can hurt.

Mark Twain said it. Give him credit. "It ain't so much the things I don't know that hurt. It's all the things I know that ain't so."

What you don't know can hurt. Those ideas, the ones you think you know that ain't true, can hurt even more.

All swans are white was proved wrong by finding one black swan. Some years ago, scientists thought that all swans were white. But that generalization proved wrong when the black swans were discovered in Russia.

The speed of light may not be constant but may change with time. The speed of light was considered a constant until recent studies of the light from seventy-two quasars showed evidence that older light seems to travel at a speed slightly slower than more recent light. If that is true, then the scientific law that the speed of light is a constant will be shown not to be true. If the observations are correct, the speed of light will be shown to depend on time: The more time evolves, the faster light moves. Why this occurs is not known, but to know it is true might help us better understand the nature of light and of time. Light and time are two things we need to know a lot more about. Any fool with a watch can tell you what time it is. But who can tell you what time is? We can measure time, and Einstein has told us that time is just another form of space, but really and truly we don't know what it is.

Any fool can turn on a light. But who can say why the light goes on and what exactly makes the electromagnetic wave that we call light appear? We can see light and we can manipulate to our service, but we don't really know what it is.

Scientists can be quite ignorant of the true nature of things.

Physicists tell us there are four forces in nature: the strong force, the weak force, electromagnetism, and gravity. They can measure these forces and make profound predictions on how these forces will interact. But no physicist actually knows what any of the forces really is. To their credit, physicists admit their ignorance. In fact, no one knows what gravity is or what light (an electromagnetic wave) is. Science tends to explain the things it doesn't understand in terms of tautologies or circular reasoning. This makes science appear smarter than it really is. And the fact that scientists can successfully manipulate what they don't fundamentally understand makes science seem even more impressive than it really is. I can always tell a nonscientist because he is the person unduly impressed by science. Real scientists know their limitations. They know how little they really know. And yet with such little knowledge, scientists are able to do so much. The telephone is a trivial application of electricity and magnets, yet its applications are not trivial. If scientists can do so much with so little knowledge, just think of what they will be able to do when they know a lot. The future is bright, bright indeed.

Not all scientists know how little they know.

Of course, there are scientists who don't know how little they know. I met one of them, a professor of astronomy named Don Kurtz from the University of Capetown, South Africa. He was lecturing aboard the *Queen Elizabeth II*.

One elderly woman passenger (a grandmother type) asked Professor Kurtz what holds the galaxies together. He told her, "Gravity."

"But what is gravity?" she retorted.

Kurtz, shocked by this abysmal display of ignorance, said, "You know, Madam, the same force we have here on earth. The force that holds the galaxies together."

Kurtz explained this circular reasoning quite confidently, as if he believed it 100 percent. But I hope he knows, deep in his heart of hearts, that not a soul alive knows what gravity is and that he recognizes how deficient his explanation must appear. The same basic scientific ignorance applies to time, matter, and energy. Sure, we can measure those things, but we don't actually know, all in all, what we are dealing with, what we are measuring.

Isn't that fascinating?

bad, or if you have already had seven pints and are about to drive. Guinness can't be good for you if you fuel your automobile with it or apply it as a hair tonic.

Proverbs, too, are usually half-truths that require qualification. "Slow and steady wins the race" is in some circumstances excellent advice but would not work so well for Olympic athletes attempting to break the world record in the sixty-meter dash. This does not preclude well-reasoned proverbs that remain correct at all times. For instance, Patten's Law of Novel Writing states that novels that never get started never get finished. This is axiomatically true at all times because something must be started to get finished. Or how about Euclid's axiom: Things equal to the same thing are equal to each other. No question about it. If one thing is equal to a second, and a third thing is equal to the second, then all three are equal to each other. In the realm of novel-writing advice, of logic, and of geometry, some things can be absolutely true. That is the reason educators have such an affection for such disciplines. That is the reason such disciplines are overemphasized in the education of our youth. Geometry and mathematics have the additional educational advantage that the problems on the tests have definite and usually single (and simple) answers, giving children the illusion that a similar situation might pertain to their lives.

Think back to your school days. What did curiosity do to the cat? What happened to the kid, like Question Quiggley in *Angela's Ashes*, who was always asking questions? Did you ever hear the teacher say, "We don't have time for all these questions? We have to get through the lesson plan?" Socrates was always asking questions. For his trouble he was forced to drink hemlock.

I don't know about you, but I started my school career with an almost insatiable curiosity. I soon learned that the answers were considered more important, much more important, than the questions. I soon learned that the educational system doesn't like ambiguity, nor does it support question-asking skills. Rather, the skill that is rewarded is getting the "right answer," which, regrettably, is usually the answer held by the teacher who was, regrettably, usually operating under the mistaken belief that there was in fact a correct answer, one right answer, only one right answer.

The authority-pleasing, question-suppressing, rule-following approach will serve you well in getting through grammar school, high school, college, and professional or graduate school. No question about it—follow the dogma works. The same attitude will provide society with fine assembly line workers and bureaucrats, but will it do much to prepare you for the harsh realities of life? Will it do much good to prepare our society for the future?

A closely related difficulty is to think that there is only one cause or only one solution of two possible solutions to a problem. This error in thinking, which I consider part of the overgeneralization error (because it is an overgeneralization), needs a name. Stephen Jay Gould in his book *The Mismeasure of Man* calls this error dichotomization. That's a mouthful to denote our inclination to parse complex and continuous reality into divisions by two (smart and stupid, black and white, good and bad, etc.). We know what he means. But let's help ourselves by calling this error theat of black-and-white thinking.

> *Principle:* Black-and-white thinking is an error because it simplifies a complex idea or situation.

From which follows:

> *Lesson:* Avoid black-and-white thinking.

If people tell you there are only two courses of action or only two possible solutions to a complex problem, don't believe it. If they tell you there is only one course of action, that is wrong for sure. Black-and-white thinking is usually wrong. Black-and-white thinking prevents us from viewing the complexity of a situation and therefore hurts our ability to arrive at alternative solutions.

The Nazis (some Nazis anyway, not all) thought that if they killed the Jews, Germany's troubles would be over. They thought the Jews were responsible for all Germany's problems. Just on the surface, a thinking person would know that that was absolutely impossible. There is no way on earth that all the Jews or any other racial or religious or political group could be responsible for all the problems of Germany or of the world or of anyplace. The Jews or other groups might be responsible for some of the problems, some of the time, but that would have to be proven with evidence involving the specific problems and the specific cases. Evidence, incidentally, is, by definition, any sign that points to the truth. There are many kinds of evidence, but the best kind is physical, which we observe ourselves. That way we know for sure that the evidence is real. As there was no evidence that the Jews were responsible for all Germany's problems, that idea is wrong. Furthermore, the idea is an overgeneralization about the Jews because it assumes that each Jew is exactly like every other Jew. That can't be true. Jews are individuals, as are we all.

Is the gold standard necessary for America's prosperity? Believe it or not, many people thought that America's prosperity depended on the gold standard. Some, despite the evidence to the contrary, still think it does. Others think unemployment would be abolished if welfare were abolished, if jobs were created by the government, if everyone were given short shifts, or if the government made everyone who needed a job work on the road. And so forth.

Juvenile delinquency? No problem. It's caused by lack of religious training. Or does delinquency boil down to our being soft with children? What the kids need these days is a good thrashing. "Spare the rod and spoil the child." What does that actually mean? Does it mean we should spare the rod and spoil the child, or does it mean we shouldn't spare the rod because if we do spare the rod we will spoil the child? What evidence supports what position? Which is correct? Can the statement remain correct for all children under all circumstances?

You get the point.

Sweeping generalizations such as these either/or statements are seductive because they often contain some truth but never the whole truth, for the whole truth requires consideration of the facts and evidence and quite some thinking about complex issues, not thinking about a simplified version of a few of them, or part of them.

> *Principle:* The key to correct evaluation of complex issues
> and problems is analysis of evidence.

What's the evidence? Three little words and a question mark that weigh several tons. What's the evidence? Always say that to yourself (if you want to be reasonable) whenever you hear a quick solution to any general problem. What's the evidence that anything is true? How do we know that for sure? Questions like that usually expose the complexity of the problem and the simplistic nature of the proposed solution. The questions help us understand the need for more thinking and more understanding of the problems before we take action that may be helpful or avoid taking action that may not be helpful.

For instance, concerning the spared rod and spoiled child problem. Some children are spoiled. I have a granddaughter who is, but I love her anyway. Callie Patten is spoiled. So what? There is little evidence to suggest that spoiled children are more likely to commit crimes than those children who are neglected. Spoiled children often feel loved and happy and may grow up to have an entirely happy life. Look at me.

In fact, neglected children may cause more trouble when they become adults than do the spoiled. But that is neither here nor there because we are not interested in the fact per se, but in the reasoning behind the statements from which we can take a step further.

There may be children who respond to no appeal but fear, and the bully, who is at heart a coward, may well benefit from a dose of his own medicine. But to argue that indiscriminate beating would always be effective ignores that some children (boys especially) are quite unmoved by beating, and others are in fact encouraged or trained by it to do the same.

The point is that no punishment can possibly be suitable for all situations and all miscreants. Juvenile delinquency takes many forms and has as many complex causes as Mott's has applesauce. The most that anyone could say is that using the rod might be suitable in some cases. Limited statements like that, however, lack appeal, especially to dogmatists, who think that one must have courage of conviction, even where the evidence warrants nothing but skepticism.

Sometimes overgeneralization is used as a trick to win an argument.

What may happen is that your statement might be simplified and extended by the other side so that it becomes stupid or untenable. Such extended and simplified arguments, as you know, are much easier to refute.

Do you really think that Hitler can be dismissed as a cruel, oppressive, and tyrannical figure, unredeemed by a single compensating virtue, whereas Churchill and Roosevelt were paragons of excellence? Human beings are too diverse and complex in fact to fit into such rigid categories. It defies experience to insist that anybody is entirely without fault or entirely without merit. Furthermore, no person in this wide world is entirely consistent. The murderers at Buchenwald fed starving birds during cold weather. Yes, they were kind to animals, a practice that in no way mitigates their foul crimes. These little remembered acts of kindness and of love nevertheless prove that even the most evil of humans are not utterly without compassionate feelings. Complicated facts do not lend themselves to simple judgments, nor do complicated humans.

Recently, an atomic scientist of Chinese heritage, expressed sympathy for China and the fact that in China the wealth is more evenly distributed. He immediately came under suspicion, was arrested, and temporarily lost his security clearance and his job at the atomic research center at Los Alamos.

Chinese communism is a complex and complicated creed that has, I imagine, something to say about myriad human activities. However perverse, it would be unlikely that the Chinese were wrong on all issues at all times. It would be unlikely they would be wrong about everything. But the question here is more specific: Are the communists wrong about common ownership? And if they are, should we prevent an American of Chinese origin from expressing his admiration for a small part of the Chinese way of things in current practice?

Sharing common things is characteristic of most contemporary American families, a family value so to speak, though many Republicans would not admit it as such. Common ownership is a principle of domestic law in each state that has a common property statute related to marriage. Family ownership and community property are in a real sense communist ideas. Is that wrong? The early Christian Church shared all things in common, too, though some contemporary Christians, especially those on the right wing, would hardly admit the early Church was communist as such. Common property was the rule among most native American cultures. Thus communism, not capitalism, should be considered the original indigenous economic system.

The mere fact that an American scientist expresses sympathy for one aspect of a foreign government's policy does not make that scientist a spy. To treat him as if he were a spy commits the error in thinking called overgeneralization. The overgeneralization would go like this: He said he likes the Chinese, therefore, he is a commie. Because he is a commie, he might be a spy. If he is a spy, he can't keep his security clearance and his job. Fortunately, the courts are more reasonable than the bureaucrats who were in charge of this scientist's security clearance. The man got his job back.

What's the point?

The point is that you should avoid seeing things as black and white. Avoid making a mountain out of a molehill. Avoid undue extrapolations and overgeneralizations.

Reservations and respect for half measures and compromise are not all bad.
Along these lines, we should also avoid despising half measures.

Have reservations. Always have reservations about such personal matters as love, marriage, having children, and so forth. If you need to have reservations about those issues, you certainly have to have reservations about big issues like going to war with Iraq, or changing the constitution, or electing the president, and such. Don't demand and don't expect a straight, simple answer to any complex question. Don't follow the crowd—it might be jumping off a cliff. Simple answers, like the tooth fairy, just don't exist.

> *Principle:* Black-and-white arguments are wrong. Black-and-white reasoning leads to the failure to consider all the possible solutions to a situation or problem.

From which follows:

> *Lesson:* There are many solutions to complex problems, not just one or two.

Try to think outside the conventional wisdom (box) to arrive at viable alternatives to the stock philosophy or rationale. The answer may or may not be there. But just thinking about it will clarify the nature of the problem and the work needed to get close to an adequate solution. Avoid easy solutions. Not many things are "no brainers."

Avoid extending your arguments or overgeneralizing them or believing in them too much yourself.

Yes, our opponents are not the only ones who extend our arguments. Who else extends our arguments? We do. We extend our arguments, simplify them, and make them look better than they are in order to win the argument. This is wrong. Knowing the truth, the complex truth—or admitting your solution is not perfect—is much closer to reality and will serve you and humanity better.

Yes, we may extend and simplify our own arguments—even we who are trying to be reasonable. In the heat of argument, we may exaggerate our case. Eventually our argument becomes so exaggerated that, like an overinflated balloon, whose rubber has been stretched to the limit, thinned excessively, it bursts. At the slightest touch.

> *Principle:* Extreme assertions are easily attacked. Moderate assertions are not.

It is wrong because authorities are often wrong. Authorities are often wrong because they misrepresent or misperceive reality. In that case, respect for the authority becomes a disrespect for reality.

Prestige achieved in one sphere gives no authority in another.

Here, the admirals have achieved their positions through a combination of noble birth, hard work in seamanship, success in fighting at sea, and political connections. That they achieved their positions because of superiority in those spheres gives them little special authority in discussing the iron boat question, which is a scientific and engineering problem, not an admiralty problem.

If you don't get this idea, consider the following: Is a movie star an expert in advising you about where to go for financial advice?

A well-known movie star is unlikely to have much of value to say about the regulation of commodity trading, stock or bond trading, or where to go for financial advice. Ditto a football player about investments. A Catholic priest would be an unlikely commentator on the Rig Vedas (unless he had separate credentials in ancient Hindu religions), the sacred Hindu texts that date from 1500 BCE. Barbara Boxer, senator from California, who doesn't know the difference between a revolver and a semiautomatic pistol, is unlikely to shed intelligent light on the relative safety of either gun.

Yet, Boxer considers herself fully qualified to frame laws on subjects about which she obviously knows little. Boxer is the senator and we are not. Our position (and our ignorance) may force us to rely on her (phony) authority and to take much of what she does and says on trust. But we must always remember that she, like the other authorities operating outside their respective fields, may be wrong. If she is wrong, then we might be the ones who have to pay for her mistake.

> *Principle:* Biased authority is, to the extent of the bias, not reliable. Knowing the source of bias and its intensity gives clues as to its direction and magnitude.

A biased authority is, to the extent of the bias, no authority. Take, for example, the case of Mary Meeker. In April 1999, Mary Meeker (dubbed by Barron's "Queen of the Internet") issued a "buy" rating on Priceline.com at $104 per share. In twenty-one months, the stock sold for $1.50, a loss of 98.5 percent. If you followed her advice, you would have turned a $10,000 mountain into a $144 molehill. Undaunted,

Meeker issued "buy" ratings on Yahoo!; Amazon.com; drugstore.com, inc.; and Homestore.com. Millions of investors followed her advice and lost their shirts. Yahoo! crashed 97 percent. Amazon cratered 95 percent. Drugstore headed south 98.9 percent. Homestore plummeted 95.5 percent. The rapidity and the magnitude of those declines raise the question of why Mary Meeker recommended those dogs in the first place. And why did she stick with her recommendations, even as the stocks declined 20, 40, 50, and 70 percent?

Answer: I don't know.

But I have suspicions that Mary was biased. Each one of Meeker's "strong buys" was paying Morgan Stanley Dean Witter, her employer, millions of dollars to promote their shares. And could it be that Morgan Stanley rewarded Meeker for helping them do it—rewarded her with a mind-blowing salary of fifteen million dollars a year?

So, I figure, while millions of investors twisted in the wind, Mary Meeker and Morgan Stanley, and the lousy companies they were promoting, laughed all the way to the bank. An isolated example? I wish. And you wish.

In 1999, Salomon Smith Barney wanted to sell AT&T on using its underwriting services to take its giant wireless division public. The problem was that Jack Grubman, Salomon's chief stock analyst, had been for years giving AT&T low ratings. When Salomon made its pitch to AT&T, Grubman miraculously changed his low rating on AT&T to a "buy."

The rest of the story follows as the night the day: Salomon was named lead underwriter and made millions. AT&T got the super-successful initial public offering (IPO) it craved and made millions. Grubman got to keep a $25,000,000 salary. The public, when the stock crashed thirteen months later, lost 50 percent of its money.

Individual Investor magazine named Jack Grubman to its "Hall of Shame." In December 2002, Grubman pleaded guilty and was fined $15,000,000. And so it goes.

These were not (in my opinion) honest mistakes. They were an attempt of Wall Street insiders to get rich at public expense. They ate your lunch—and with relish.

Principle: Before taking expert advice at face value, always check for bias.

Principle: Ignorance plays a major role in stupid decisions, particularly those of committees, particularly
those of government committees, and particularly those
of government officials. Not just ignorance, but pigheadedness, which often arises from overconfidence, a systematic defect in many modern leaders who tend to
anchor their opinions on single facts that dominate their
thinking.

From which follows:

Lesson: Although you are not responsible for the ignorance or pigheadedness of others, try to correct such
ignorance when you come across it. And always suggest
objective testing when cherished beliefs or single facts
dictate important policies and actions.

Principle: Failure to consider counterevidence or contrary
positions is an error in reasoning.

The advantage of iron boats would be that, unlike wood, iron boats
would not be subject to wood rot and sea worms, a problem that
plagued the British navy at the time. Iron is stronger than wood, so it
will withstand the actions of wave, wind, and enemy cannon fire better
than wood. Furthermore, iron does not burn as readily as wood.
Clearly, the admiralty did not think about these possible advantages of
iron over wood. Therefore, the committee was not thinking clearly
when it rejected iron boats. It had failed to consider the advantages and
disadvantages of iron and wood and all the possibilities. This failure
means that the admiralty's thinking was black and white: According to
them, iron had to be bad. Wood had to be good. Their analysis was
simple, simplistic, and, let's face it, probably stupid. In fact, their statement, when closely examined, doesn't make sense. It is a non sequitur.
In its simplicity it fails to consider a large body of evidence that runs
counter to the admiralty's received standard opinion.

Iron versus wood? Which is best for boats? Of course, we know
the answer from our modern experience and perspective, but I believe
the answer also could have been figured out at the time that the admiralty issued its ridiculous statement. I believe by clear thinking we

could have figured out at the time that the admiralty statement was probably wrong.

Prospective thinking is often an overgeneralization and therefore can result in erroneous conclusions.

Because of the nature of contingent events, understanding things in retrospect, like the iron boat issue, is easier than understanding the same thing in prospect. That doesn't mean prospective understanding isn't possible. It just means it is difficult and less reliable than retrospective analysis. Because prospective thinking is less reliable, it requires more circumspection, but often, when done properly, it can provide a true view of reality.

For instance, take this statement: "A machine that thinks? That is simply not possible." What do you think about a machine that thinks? Is it possible? Or not possible? Solve this question the way we solved the iron boat question. Solve this question the way the Wright brothers solved the heavier-than-air question. Ask yourself if a thinking machine is possible by restating the question as a statement that makes a definite claim. Then try to prove the claim wrong by finding an exception.

Question restated: A thinking machine is not possible.

If such a thing were not possible, then how come each of us has a thinking machine in the hollow round of our skull? Yes, that and all the other brains on this planet, from the brain in the littlest mite to the brain in the biggest elephant, are electrochemical jellies that think. If those electrochemical jellies are thinking, why couldn't some man or woman of the future make something similar that would also think? Clearly a thinking machine is not only possible; billions of such machines already exist.

Given that, think about this: Isn't it also possible that sometime in the future it would be possible to make a machine that would think faster, better, and more efficiently (that is, use energy better) than the human brain? Who would construct such thinking machines? Humans, of course. If they last that long, humans will make a better thinking machine than the human brain, just as they have made a better flying machine than the human body. By the power of pure rational thought, we can then induce that sometime in the future, the machines made by humans will not only be thinking better than humans, they will feel better, have better moral standards, work better, and play better. This is the future. It has to happen. An authority that said differently would likely be wrong.

Another related error is to attribute authority erroneously and then generalize from that erroneous attribution.

Erroneous attribution of authority is an error that leads to false conclusions.

For example, take this statement: "The official US government policy about the health hazards of smoking must have changed because I saw President Clinton smoking a cigar. If he smokes a cigar, smoking can't be all that bad."

What President Clinton does in his private life has nothing whatsoever to do with the health policy of the US government. To conclude that because Clinton does something, it is OK for us to do it is an error that wears multiple hats: It is a false analogy because we are not him. It is an overgeneralization because it infers that what is OK for Clinton is OK for us. It is an unsupported assumption because it assumes that he and we share certain characteristics that make it OK. And it involves the **Tu quoque** defect in reasoning, which rejects criticism by accusing one's critic of doing the same thing (that is being criticized), diverting the argument to an irrelevant issue, and then extending the conclusion by overgeneralization.

Example: "Clinton smokes cigars. So it must be OK for me, too."

Whether the other party does something or not is not materially related to the conclusion. It is often just a diversion to focus attention away from the real issue. The Latin name for this error in thinking is *tu quoque*, translated as "you (do it) too."

"At your age, you shouldn't be working so hard, Roy. You might get a heart attack."

"Look who's talking."

The questions of age and working hard were not addressed. Instead, it is implied that since the speaker does it too, it must be OK. What others do or don't do, insofar as those actions are not supported by reason, is irrelevant to the implied conclusion that hard work is OK at that age. Even if it were relevant, outside evidence would have to prove that the conclusion could reasonably be generalized to include the particular person or persons cited.

"Allegra hit first." Children should not feel entirely justified in antisocial behavior if they can explain it that way. Because someone else is bad, that doesn't give you general license to be bad, too.

"George, if I were you, I wouldn't smoke so much."

"If I were you, Paul, I wouldn't smoke so much, either."

The respondent knows that the other is not him and that therefore the statement is not only tu quoque, it is also contrary to fact. Contrary to fact statements ignore evidence and are therefore irrelevant.

"Mickey, I don't think you should be drinking. Alcohol tends to dull your senses, reduces your physical control, and may even become addicting."

"Pop, that's not very convincing with you standing there with a scotch whiskey in your hand."

A father has a duty to tell his son his concerns about his son's drinking. The father is under no moral requirement to follow such advice himself.

"You must stop smoking, or you'll get another heart attack."

"Nice of you to say that, Doctor. But I saw you ditch that cigarette just before you came into the room."

The doctor has a perfect right, some say a duty, to advise patients about the adverse health effects of anything. But the doctor is under no obligation to follow that advice himself. In fact, whether the doctor smokes is irrelevant to the issue under consideration, which is clearly stated by the doctor. Even if it were OK for the doctor to smoke, that doesn't mean that conclusion would apply with equal vigor to the patient, especially one who has had a previous heart attack.

Prejudice is a form of overgeneralization.

When we overgeneralize about race, we are bound to make errors and suffer the consequences, as illustrated by the following story told to me by a lawyer friend who lives in Kentucky. The story was front page news for several weeks as journalists tried to figure out what went wrong in the thinking of the police. See if you can figure out what went wrong. How could the police have handled the situation better? How would you have handled the situation better?

Case study: Two cops in a patrol car were on the side of a highway watching traffic. Along came a brand new red Cadillac driven by a black man who was wearing a blue suit, white shirt, and red tie. The Cadillac was cruising at and not above the speed limit. There didn't seem to be anything irregular about the driving, the license plate, or the inspection stickers. Nevertheless, the cops pulled out and followed the Cadillac for a few miles and then pulled the Cadillac over.

"Anything wrong?" asked the black man.

The only reply was, "Driver's license and insurance."

One cop examined the documents while the other covered his partner. They were on condition orange, a police term that means pretty alert for armed attack but not actually under attack.

General conclusions about products have to be based on carefully selected and characteristic samples, not on partially selected and often dubious evidence. In advertising, it is almost never the case that the evidence is scientifically selected and impartially presented.

The real motive behind partially selected evidence is to reinforce prejudice. Watch out for that because there is a real tendency to seize upon facts that are agreeable to us and to ignore those that are not.

Personal preferences should put us on guard against the possibility of erroneous conclusions and overgeneralizations.

If I like to drink wine, I might look favorably on news reports that tell me that drinking wine will be good for me and will prevent me from getting a heart attack or a stroke. If I wish to argue reasonably, I must counter this tendency by searching for conflicting evidence. The confidence that can repose in the generalization that wine is good for me should not depend so much upon a few striking reports from France apparently verifying the statement as upon the thoroughness of the search made for instances disproving the theory. The wine generalization must be based on investigations covering a sufficiently wide field, and the instances studied must be representative of people like myself, not just the French. The French may be eating something else that prevents heart attacks and therefore the benefits of wine drinking are more apparent than real. In fact, wine drinking might be associated with a higher social and economic status and increased consumption of vegetables and less stress, all of which might be the controlling factors reducing the incidence of heart attack and stroke. In view of all that, the wine drinking might be a spurious association or a confounding variable. As discussed, even if the wine statement meets all these conditions, it should be regarded as a working rule or *hypothesis* subject to review and revision in view of new data.

Advertisers have nearly perfected the art of unreasonable thinking. Very few advertisements appeal to reason; most prefer mere assertion, repetition, and tied suggestions, which are themselves irrational overgeneralizations. Virginia Slims cigarettes don't make you thin, though that is what the advertiser wants you to believe. Virginia Slims don't make you beautiful, though that is what—by showing a young, beautiful woman smoking a Slim—the advertiser would like you to believe. Virginia Slims don't bring on the men, though that is what—by showing those shadowy male figures in the background—the maker would like you to believe. Virginia Slims don't make you a free spirit and individual thinker, though that is what—by showing statements like "I look temptation in the face and make my own decisions"—the cigarette maker would like you to believe.

Conclusion: In most cases, advertising = bunk.

From which follows:

> *Lesson:* Have nothing to do with it.

Before we go on to chapter 2, we pause for a brief word about general rules and exceptions.

General rules admit no exceptions, else they would not be truly general.

Do exceptions prove the rule?

Think about this.

How many times have you heard that "the exception proves the rule." This assertion might silence criticism for fifteen seconds, but it is a meaningless statement. General rules admit no exceptions. If exceptions exist, they prove the rule wrong. Incidentally, the word *prove* in this context originally meant "test," and the statement was a way to test the general rule by looking for exceptions. This method of disproving general rules is exactly what we discussed. To test a rule by looking for exceptions is the way to test the rule. If an exception is found, it then proves the rule wrong.

Pseudoscholars like me think that the assertion that "the exception proves the rule" came from a poor translation of the Latin phrase *Exceptio probat regulam*, which means that rules cover every case not (specifically) excepted.

Oh well, into every life a little rain must fall.

To those of you who have made it so far, much thanks. There is one last molehill to climb before we head into the review and then enter the next chapter and start our downhill coast through the rest of this book. That molehill is called **syllogism**, a word from the Greek *syn*, meaning "together," and *logizesthai*, meaning "reason," hence "reasoning together." Syllogism is a form of generalization in which statements, also known as premises, are made and a conclusion is drawn from them.

A syllogism is an argument or form of reasoning in which (usually two) statements—called *premises*—are made and a conclusion is drawn from them.

Example:

1. All mammals are warm blooded. (**major premise**)
2. Whales are mammals. (**minor premise**)
3. Therefore, whales are warm blooded. (conclusion)

1 + 2 + 3 = the syllogism.

Because there are three sentences in each categorical syllogism, and each sentence can be one of four moods (A, E, I, O: universal affirmative, universal negative, particular affirmative, particular negative), that gives sixty-four different categorical syllogisms. Since there are four figures to each syllogism (that is, arrangements of the major term, minor term, and **middle term**), there are 256 known forms of categorical syllogism.

Logicians have distinguished the **valid** syllogism from the invalid. Although valid and invalid are fundamental to most contemporary academic systems of logic, we are not (much) concerned with them here because this is a book of practical, not formal, logic designed to help you know the truth, not to acquaint you with the intellectual heritage of the Western world. However, it is important to mention the most common error in syllogism, which is known as the *undistributed middle*. This example will give you an idea of how formal logic operates and how it is concerned with appraising truth values by studying the interrelations of premises. Consider the following:

1. All mammals are warm blooded. (major premise)
2. Whales are warm blooded. (minor premise)
3. Therefore, whales are mammals. (conclusion)

In this syllogism, the conclusion is true but not logically deducible from the premises. Premise 1 did not say that all warm-blooded animals are mammals. If premise 1 did say that, it would have been dead wrong. In fact, considerable evidence indicates that the dinosaurs were warm blooded (they were animals), and, of course, birds are always warm blooded (they are animals). So premises 1 and 2 as stated above do not logically make conclusion 3, because premise 1, though true, does not include the fact that some warm-blooded animals are not mammals. It is easier to see the reason for this with cars as an example:

1. All Fords are cars. (major premise)
2. I own a car. (minor premise)
3. Therefore, I own a Ford. (conclusion)

In fact, I do own a Lincoln Continental, which is a Ford product, so that conclusion is true. But it is not logical because premise 1 didn't state that all cars are Fords. In fact, if premise 1 *did* state that, it would have been incorrect because there are many kinds of cars besides Fords. I could easily have owned some other kind of car.

In both the whale and the car syllogism, the problem arose because the middle term—that common to both the major and minor premises—did not encompass the whole universe of possible warm-blooded animals (example one) or cars (example two). In technical terms, the middle term of the major premise was not **distributed**, that is, it didn't apply to each member of the mentioned class of warm blooded animals (example one) and each member of the mentioned class of cars (example two). There were other members of the class of warm-blooded animals that were not whales, and there were other members of the class of cars that were not Fords. Thus, the conclusions were actually generalizations that were not true.

A very famous syllogism offers us another view of how reasoning from syllogism can get us into trouble:

1. All men are mortal. (major premise)
2. Socrates is a man. (minor premise)
3. Therefore, Socrates is mortal. (conclusion)

The conclusion is true and was proven by Socrates' death upon drinking the hemlock. But the syllogism is true only insofar as it encompasses all the observations to date. It certainly can't be logically applied to future generations who may someday discover the secret of immortality. One single case to the contrary in the future would refute the Socrates syllogism.

How about this one? Can you find the defect?

1. Other men die.
2. I am not another man.
3. Therefore, I will not die.

REVIEW

Time spent in review is never wasted. Neuroscientists have discovered that review fixes our memories by increasing the probability of reactivating previously activated neuronal networks. Repeated reactivation results in actual structural changes in the brain that facilitate recall. Therefore, you should do it. (Notice that the repetition of this paragraph had the effect of giving you a sense of familiarity that you did not get when you first read it at the end of the introduction. Notice also that I filled in my deduction so that you can compare your deduction with mine.)

EXERCISES

1. Reread all the main points in this chapter. The main points are the principles, lessons, and the topic sentences presented in italics. When you have done so, give yourself a check here ___.
2. Reread all the main points in this chapter aloud. When done, give yourself a check here ___. Rereading aloud fixes the memory better than silent rereading does. Rereading on separate days fixes the memory better than rereading twice the same day. The more you reread, the more you will fix the memory. But don't overdo it. Four times should be quite enough. You don't want to acquire the reputation of being a harmless drudge.
3. How would you prove wrong the statement that women who wear glasses never smoke? Give yourself a check mark if you think you are right ___. Hint: The answer to this question is in the chapter. If you understand the answer to this question, you know how to prove a generalization wrong.
4. Do you really believe that all scientific knowledge is tentative and not known to be absolutely true for all times and all places? Give yourself a check mark if you think you are right ___.
5. Do cats think? How do you know? Give yourself a check mark if you think you are right ___.
6. What is the cause of most incorrect, unreasonable, false, and defective thinking? Give yourself a check mark if you think you are right ___. Hint: This is a trick question in that it was covered in the introduction, not in chapter 1. Hint: If you are not sure about the answer, don't be lazy. Look it up in the introduction.
7. Explain why statements with words like *all*, *always*, and *never* are likely to be wrong. Give yourself a check if your answer seems OK ___.
8. "Smoking pot is always bad." Why is such a statement wrong?

What error in thinking is involved? Why do I call a statement like that an *overgeneralization*? Is it also an example of black-and-white thinking? Give yourself one, two, or three checks depending on how well you feel you answered the questions _____.

9. What is *evidence*? What is the best kind of evidence? Give yourself two checks if correct _____. Hint: The answer to this question was hidden in the text. I defined *evidence* as any sign that leads to the correct perception of the truth. As such, evidence would include facts, intelligent experimentation, clear reasoning, verification, and a host of other signs that include formal and informal logic, which indicate the way to truth.

10. What is unreasonable about blindly following the dictates of an authority? How can following the dictates of an authority lead to trouble? Under what circumstances should you follow the dictates of an authority? Hint: Should you trust yourself to fly a 747 to Tahiti, or should you trust the UTA pilot who has flown the trip many times? How about surgery? Would you consider yourself qualified to repair a leaking aortic valve, or would you let a heart surgeon do the job? Give yourself four checks if you thought about the possible answers to the above questions and your answers seem OK _____.

11. What is unreasonable about the following? "As the author of a book on logic, I can claim to be qualified to diagnose a straightforward case of manic-depressive psychosis. Unequivocally, Andrea Yates was not thinking logically, and her behavior was irrational at the time she drowned her children." Give yourself a check mark if you think you are right ___. Hint: Authority in one field is not an authority in another. An author of a logic book is not a forensic psychiatrist. An explanation of the psychological or irrational mechanisms that led Andrea Yates to drown her five children may explain what happened, but it doesn't necessarily excuse it, much less justify it.

12. Read about the famous Charge of the Light Brigade or study Alfred, Lord Tennyson's poem on the subject. Explain why the English brigade of about six hundred men unflinchingly obeyed an erroneous order though they knew "someone had blundered." Why would military men, at great disadvantage to themsleves, make a heroic but futile charge against Russian

heavy artillery at the Battle of Balaklava in the Crimean War? Is it reasonable to obey an order, even a military order, if you know it is wrong? Why do American military personnel take an oath to obey all "reasonable and lawful" orders, rather than an oath to obey all orders? Give yourself two checks if you had the energy to look up the charge or if you read the poem. Give yourself five checks if you did both _____.

If you feel up to it, check your answers to the questions above by rereading the appropriate sections of the text. If you got most of them correct, stop here and reward yourself in some way with a simple pleasure that will also serve to fix the memories. Rewards for work well done help the brain function effectively.

If you don't feel up to checking your answers, go on to the next chapter and learn about a common source of communication difficulties, vague definition.

NOTES

1. Robert Frost, *The Poetry of Robert Frost: The Collected Poems* (New York: Henry Holt, 1979), p. 17, line 13.

2. Both quotations appear in Anthony Flew, *How to Think Straight: An Introduction to Critical Reasoning* (Amherst, NY: Prometheus Books, 1998), p. 37.

3. Quoted by Louis Rukeyser, "There Is No Magic Key: Only Knowledge and Consistency," *Louis Rukeyser's Mutual Funds* (February 2001).

4. Martin J. Medhurst, *Dwight D. Eisenhower: Strategic Communicator* (Westport, CT: Greenwood Press, 1993), pp. 78, 167. The original quotation comes from a March 27, 1970, *Life* article by John K. Jessup.

5. This quotation is based on Don DeLillo, *White Noise* (New York: Penguin, 1985), pp. 114, 117.

6. In Paul H. H. Schoemaker, "Disciplined Imagination: From Scenarios to Strategic Options," *International Studies of Management and Organization* 27 (1997): 1.

chapter 2

Vague Definition

This chapter discusses the error in thinking called *vague definition*. Correct definition leads to the truth. Vague definition leads to error. By the end of the chapter, you should have a working knowledge of some of the kinds of definition—generic, divisional, and by specific criteria or example—and you should be able to uncover the hidden meanings behind what people say.

Confusion may arise because many words have several meanings. In a given context, the meaning of a word must remain constant, or there will be confusion. Confusion may also arise because individual words have different kinds of meanings—a denotive meaning (the explicit or intensive meaning), a connotive meaning (the more extensive idea or notion suggested or associated with the word), a word history (which suggests a meaning), and a word atmosphere (tone), all of which conspire to give a word shades, intimations, allusions, indications, and refinements of meaning, some of which under certain circumstances can be misleading.

Correct use of words leads to precision of expression, correct thinking, and correct conclusions. Incorrect, sloppy, or deceptive use of words leads to imprecision of expression, incorrect thinking, incorrect conclusions, and sometimes fraud and deception. Attention to definition will help you become acquainted with how to better discover truth and deal with reality. Attention to definition will help you say what you mean and help you avoid saying what you don't mean.

x   x   x

Words are important. Did you have any doubt? Words are especially important for complex human thinking.

As demonstrated in the previous chapter, animals think, probably without words. Animals probably think by crude associations of one concept with another, as in the cow example where in the cow's brain PAIN = ELECTRIC FENCE, ELECTRIC FENCE = PAIN.

Like little animals, very young children probably think without words. Some of us adults know that we sometimes think without words, too. I drove to Houston yesterday, but for the life of me I don't know how I did it. I didn't consciously tell my foot to brake or go when appropriate, nor did I do any serious thinking about keeping away from other cars and avoiding accidents. My brain handled much of my driving at some subconscious level without the use of words. That's OK for small tasks like driving, but to think about more sophisticated things my brain needs words.

The subtlety of human thought owes a lot to language. Soliloquies, of which dramatists are so fond, may appear absurd, but in fact the only thing that makes them ridiculous is that the actors declaim their thoughts aloud. Most of us are always declaiming soliloquies to ourselves, discussing issues, planning what to do, and appraising situations.

How do you address yourself? I usually address myself as "you" when I am unhappy with myself or with what I did, as in "Oh, God, Patten, you really screwed up that time." And I usually address myself as "I" when something good is involved, as in "I want an ice cream." How do you usually talk to yourself?

The process of holding a kind of debate with oneself is an ordinary way of solving problems. That it is so illustrates the dependence of thought on words. Since our thoughts so depend on words, proper thinking requires that the words be used correctly. Otherwise we can't arrive at real significance. The problem is that many words have several definitions or common uses. Confusion can arise if one of the definitions is used by one party while the other party embraces a different definition.

For example: Whether alcohol is a food, a poison, a drug, or part of the sacrament of transubstantiation depends on the definitions of those things and how they are applied to alcohol.

Grain ethyl alcohol has a calorie content of seven kilocalories per gram. If we define *food* as a substance that when ingested is capable of being used to produce heat or body energy, then alcohol is certainly a food. If we define *food* as a substance that when ingested is capable of being converted into body amino acids, proteins, fats, and even carbohydrates as needed, then alcohol is certainly a food.

If we define *poison* as a substance that if ingested may under certain specified circumstances kill a person, then alcohol is certainly a poison. If we define *drug* as a substance capable of altering the function of the human brain, then alcohol is certainly a drug. If we believe that the wine used in the Catholic Church is (despite all evidence and appearances to the contrary) actually changed with its alcohol content into the blood of Jesus Christ, then alcohol under certain specific circumstances is a sacrament. So, alcohol is either a food, a poison, a drug, or a sacrament, depending on how we define those things.

Well, which is it?

How much sense would it make for two people to debate whether alcohol is a food or not, if one of those persons had in mind that alcohol was a poison and the other believed that it was a gasoline additive to protect the environment?

Definitions therefore are crucial to clear thinking and reasoned discussion. If that's true, then to be entirely consistent, we should start off with an understanding of what we mean by *definition*. We should start off with a definition of definition.

Definition divides itself into two main avenues: genus and division. *Genus* sounds academic or biological, but it is really not. A genus definition can usually be spotted by the fact that the definition (meaning) is stated in sentence form. Example: Texas penal code paragraph 1.07: "A firearm is any device designed, made or adapted to expel a projectile through a barrel by using the energy generated by an explosion or burning substance or any device readily convertible to that use."

So if I am caught carrying a pellet gun that shoots 22-caliber pellets powered by a carbon dioxide cylinder, I can't be arrested for carrying a firearm. The pellet gun does not conform to the genus definition of a firearm. A dart gun doesn't meet the definition either. But a zip gun that was not originally a firearm but has been adapted to work like a firearm will fall within the definition and send me to jail for up to ten years.

Note the difference a few words can make. A few words can make all the difference in the world. A few words can decide my fate: whether I am culpable or not, whether I go to jail or don't. Definition is important. No question about it.

Principle: Definitions count and often count plenty.

From which follows:

Lesson: Pay attention to the definitions.

Consider abortion. In the matter of abortion, everything hangs on the definition of the creature subject to the abortion. If we define the object of abortion as a human being, then we condemn abortion as premeditated murder or manslaughter (depending on the definition of *murder* and *manslaughter*). If we define the fetus as something not human, say, a kind of parasite because it can't exert (at the time of the abortion) a human existence independent of the mother, we can shift the ground of discourse to a question of freedom of choice. So, whether we might favor abortion or freedom of choice might depend on what we consider the generic definition of life.

Indeed, for centuries, the Catholic Church permitted abortion up to the time of the quickening (about the end of the first trimester when fetal movement first was felt) because that is when Saint Thomas Aquinas concluded that life for the fetus actually began. Recently, the Catholic Church has changed its position on the issue by changing the definition of when life begins. It now maintains that life starts when the sperm enters the egg at the moment of conception. Since life starts at conception (according to this definition), the Catholic Church has concluded that any kind of abortion kills a human being. As killing a human is wrong, abortion is therefore wrong.

The change in definition looks suspicious because Thomas Aquinas is still considered a doctor of the church and is in fact the patron saint of Roman Catholic schools.

Definition by division is a form of definition that proceeds in bite-sized pieces, usually in a numbered list. The genus definition of a firearm could have been defined divisionally as follows:

A device shall be considered a firearm if:

1. It is made, designed, or adapted to expel a projectile.
2. The projectile is expelled through a barrel.
3. The energy generated to expel the projectile is explosive or by burning a substance.

In divisional definition, further refinements can be made by specifying what things are excluded from the definition. As, for instance, "No part of this statute shall be construed to mean that a BB gun or a dart gun or pellet gun powered by compressed air or other gas as a firearm. Antique and curio firearms made before 1899 are excluded."

Divisional definitions are quite important in the law. Conviction or acquittal often depends on them, on the strict application of a definition.

Texas penal code paragraph 46.035, section 5, says it is unlawful to carry a handgun in an amusement park, even if the person carrying the handgun has a specific state of Texas concealed handgun license.

That seems clear enough until one consults subsection f of the same penal code, which states, "in this section 'Amusement park' means a permanent indoor or outdoor facility or park where amusement rides are available for use by the public that is located in a county with a population of more than 1 million, encompasses at least 75 acres in surface area, is enclosed with access only through controlled entries, is open for operation more than 120 days in each calendar year, and has security guards on the premises at all times."

Wow! If the amusement park where the gun is carried fails to meet just one of those many criteria, the carrying of the gun there by a person holding a license is legal. By the definition of negatives, we find that if the park is not permanent or has no rides, or the rides are not available to the public, or the park is located in a county with fewer than one million people (most counties in Texas), is open for only 119 days a year, is smaller than seventy-five acres in area, or doesn't have twenty-four-hour security, it is not an amusement park according to this statute and therefore is not covered by the penal law section.

Law is like that. It has lots of exceptions and weird turnings and strange twists. Law is full of exceptions. Aristotle said, "The law is reason without passion."[1] I say that law is reason punctuated by exceptions. Others say law is mainly exceptions because it often turns and twists on obscure definitions, the reasons for which were probably known at one time to the legislators who voted for the specific language of the statute. In many cases, the reasons are no longer known even by those who voted for them.

After enactment, law itself, not the goals to be advanced by law, becomes the focus. That is when the lawyers have their field day.

The concealed handgun illustration above shows how precise rules do not close the loopholes. It happens to be the other way around. Loopholes exist only because the rules are so precise. The United States Constitution, a short document of general principles, has few loopholes. That is why it has held up so well and lasted so long.

×   ×   ×

Among the many kinds of definition, we find definition by synonym, example, or specific criteria. For instance, how can we define anxiety?

Anxiety is feeling nervous. This is a definition by the criterion of synonym. Anxiety is what I feel when they take my blood pressure at the doctor's office. This is a definition by example. Anxiety is the subjective feeling of nameless dread associated with increased activity of the autonomic nervous system. This is a definition by psychological and physiologic criteria.

Here are some more illustrations of definition and its application to situations.

1. Property claims were sometimes specified in divisional terms. You owned a property by right of conquest (in olden times), by purchase from the legal owner (notice purchases from nonowners and from illegal owners are excluded), or by inheritance, marriage, or contract, as in the settlement of a gambling debt. If you have lived on a property for twenty years and have had no attempts of the real owner to move you off, you can own a property by right of adverse possession or squatter's right, and so on. That list is the divisional definition of the right of ownership. If you can show you meet one of those criteria, the courts will recognize your property right and the sheriff will come out and arrest trespassers.

2. Lots of medical diagnoses are based on divisional definitions. Consider the diagnosis of systemic lupus:

a. Malar rash
b. Discoid rash
c. Photosensitivity
d. Oral ulcers
e. Arthritis
f. Serositis
g. Renal disorder
h. Neurologic disorder
i. Hematologic disorder
j. Immunologic disorder
k. Antinuclear antibodies

"If four of these are present at any time during the course of the disease, a diagnosis of systemic lupus can be made with 98% certainty and 97% sensitivity," says Harrison's textbook of medicine.[2]

Sounds terribly scientific. Doesn't it? Or does it? What if a patient had only three of the items and yet at autopsy was found to have died of lupus? I had a patient like that. That woman had lupus by one definition (autopsy fact), but she didn't have it by another definition, the standard medical textbook definition. In that case, should we conclude that the patient died of a disease she didn't have? See? This is the old "alcohol is a food, drug, or poison" problem, applied to diagnosis of disease.

How about the generic definition of lupus? Will the generic definition help clarify the diagnostic situation in my dead patient? You decide. When you do, let me know. Generic definition: "Systemic lupus erythematosis (SLE) is a disease of unknown etiology in which tissues and cells are damaged by pathogenic autoantibodies and immune complexes."[3]

No wonder doctors seem to be always arguing about who has what and what should be done. Many of those arguments arise from legitimate differences in understanding the nature of the disease. Many of the arguments arise from legitimate use of different definitions of disease, and many arise from legitimate differences of judgment, experience, or (can this be?) conventions and stylized forms of reasoning or logic (or what they think is logic).

> *Principle:* Some medical terms have little or no real meaning because their relationship or correspondence to reality is dubious.

While we are on the subject of medical terms, I should mention that a surprising number of medical terms that are thrown at patients daily have little meaning. The skeptic might even claim they have surprisingly little meaning by design. The skeptic might claim that they are designed to conceal the doctor's ignorance and befuddle the patient.

But that's another story. The principle is clear:

> *Principle:* Medical diagnosis is often based on highly questionable definitions that may or may not adequately reflect the reality situation.

From which follows:

> *Lesson:* Medicine is not a science. It is subject to large limitations because of, among other things, the vague defi-

nitions, most of which arise from incomplete, inaccurate, and, in some cases, faulty knowledge.

I'm not criticizing medicine or beating up on doctors. Why would I do that? I myself am a doctor. So are my wife and my daughter and my son-in-law. I am just helping you face the facts. The current state of medical knowledge is probably less than you and most people assume.

Whether doctors are arguing about a disease or a diagnosis, or others are arguing about abortion or something else, a surprising number of arguments arise from the failure of disputants to define the terms they use. They believe themselves to be debating questions of fact whereas the real issue is the definition of the words used.

In the controversy about abortions, you can define a human being as possessing the following characteristics: a head, two eyes, two feet, a heart, and so forth, and then you can show that the embryo at the moment of conception possesses none of these things; therefore, it is not, by that definition, human.

On the other hand, if you define a human as a living thing that has a complete lifetime supply of human genetic material and is, genetically speaking, a perfected and independent creature, then any embryo from the instant of conception forward qualifies as human, as does an in vitro fertilized egg, as does a stem cell.

The abortion controversy is a disagreement concerning the social decision about the beginning of life. There is no novel objective fact to be discovered in this sphere, no original biological research to be done. What is needed is a philosophical reflection that resolves the issue to the satisfaction of everyone. That reflection will be a generally accepted decision about where, in the continuous process from fertilization to birth, it would be best to draw the line between merely biological and genuinely human existence. Too much is at stake for this determination to be groundless or arbitrary.

Is the tomato a fruit, a vegetable, or a berry? On a more mundane level, whether a tomato is a fruit or a vegetable depends on the definition used. Certainly it is a question that has encouraged controversy. My mother always considered the debate a matter of fact, but I forget what side of the fence she was on. To me, the problem is merely verbal. If you define *fruit* as the part of a plant that encloses the seed, then the tomato is clearly a fruit. If you define *vegetable* as something edible that comes from a garden, then the tomato is a vegetable. Botanically the tomato is a berry, but according to the United States Supreme Court decision in 1880, for tax purposes, the tomato is not a fruit or a berry but a veritable vegetable. Fruit, berry, or vegetable? Which is it?

Who knows?

It just depends on what we mean. It just depends, as do so many things in life, on definition.

Just because the government or some officer thereof defines something some way, that doesn't make it so.

Ronald Reagan, as I recall, urged school lunch programs to identify ketchup as a vegetable in order to meet federal nutrition guidelines for school lunches. Most of us would identify ketchup as a seasoned sauce of puree consistency, the principle ingredient of which is usually tomatoes but sometimes another foodstuff (like mushrooms). Despite the president's opinion, ketchup is not a vegetable. Reagan got into further trouble over tomato ketchup when he applied it to his cottage cheese, saying that the stuff was awful without ketchup. In consequence, he lost the Wisconsin vote.

Some definitions are culturally conditioned and vary from place to place. A person who lives in Somalia would have a completely different definition of the word *poor* than a person who lives in the United States. In fact, the income level that officially defines *poor* in America would equal a level of income that is considered quite wealthy in Somalia.

Scientific categories of biology are choice-inclusive in character. There is a choice to cut definitions in a certain way and not in others. We could, for example, classify whales by their habitat and method of locomotion, in which case they would be related to the elephant, or by their intelligence, in which case they would belong to the same group as humans and the great apes. Viewed in this light, the current "scientific" classification, based on method of reproduction and the feeding of the young with milk, loses its apparent privilege.

Each aspect of our perception of the nature of whale is reasonable, legitimate, and useful; each focuses on some interesting features of the animals and highlights their significant relation to other animals. To say that one and only one of them captures the way things really are amounts to a defamatory impoverishment of the complexity of the biological world.

What's the point?

The point is not to argue the pros and cons of what is and what is not a firearm. The point is not to discuss the pros and cons of what is or what is not a human. Nor is the point to tell you that a tomato is a fruit or a vegetable or a berry. The point is not to tell you that the word *poor* means a level of poverty in Somalia quite different from that in the United States. Nor is the point to trash the currently accepted biological classification of cetaceans.

The point is to clearly demonstrate and demonstrate clearly how important the definitions are in reaching conclusions. One might even say that some definitions that are accepted will lead to certain conclusions almost automatically.

So watch out. Make sure you know what you are talking about. Make sure you know what the other guy is talking about.

> *Lesson:* Pay attention to the definitions. They can be the
> key to understanding and can make all the difference.

As mentioned, a great number of words have several meanings. Some words have a particular meaning, and no confusion exists when they are used. *Hydrogen* or *quark* or *pancreas* by general agreement refer to a specific element with one proton and one electron, a nuclear particle three of which make a proton or a neutron, or the exocrine-endocrine organ in the abdomen, respectively. No argument about the meanings of those words and no confusion of one with the other. Well, not exactly no argument. Even with these scientific terms arguments can arise. But not many.

The case with other words is quite different. Widely divergent interpretations appear when we use more abstract words such as *law, nature,* and *democracy.*

The trouble with such terms is that they try to say too much by representing concepts of great scope and complexity. Each word may mean different things to different people. Let's talk about *democracy* for instance.

Reading the ancient texts such as the *Anabasis* by Xenophon, we find the Greeks elected their generals and their captains. In fact, the Greek army held a council every day in which the ordinary soldier was free to express his ideas about what should be done and when and who should do it. Furthermore, at these councils the action taken was always that agreed on by the majority of the soldiers there assembled. Those soldiers considered any other way of running the army a form of slavery. These Greek soldiers routinely considered anyone who followed the orders of a nonelected official a slave.

By contrast, the American army has its generals appointed by the president and approved by the Senate. American soldiers do not vote or even express an opinion on the important daily question posed to ancient Greek soldiers: Who do you wish to command your army today?

This being the case, ancients Greeks would not consider the American army a democracy in the sense in which they understood the meaning of the word. And they should know. The ancient Greeks invented democracy. In fact, *democracy* is a Greek word meaning government by the *demos*, the mob.

On the other hand, most Americans have a different definition in mind when they think of democracy. Most Americans would consider the idea of an army democracy silly, stupid, and unworkable. To most Americans, democracy does not mean government of the people. It means something like personal liberty and the ability of the people, if they so desire, to change their government. If that is the definition of democracy, then America is a democracy. If it is not the definition of democracy, then America is not a democracy.

During the cold war, there was a lot of acrimonious debate between communist USSR and capitalist America about which government was truly democratic. The Russians claimed that they were the democracy and that America was not. To the Russians, democracy implied a classless society in which the means of production are owned in common, something they had accomplished and America had not. They thought it irrelevant that the supreme power was wielded by an oligarchy in which opinions were silenced and individual rights suppressed.

Using different definitions, the USSR and America accused each other of being undemocratic. The point at issue is what definition of democracy should be used. If we use the American definition, then America is the democracy. If we use the Russian definition, then the USSR is the democracy.

Well, which is it?

And more important: Should we have gone to war over this issue? Should we go to war over a disputed definition?

See! The question of definition is not trivial. It can't be trivial because war is not trivial. In fact, major wars have been fought over smaller stuff than that. Perhaps both the Russian and American definitions of democracy are deficient. Perhaps we need to apply something different. How about Lincoln's definition at Gettysburg? What kind of definition was it? "Democracy is government of the people, by the people, and for the people."

If you guessed that the above was a divisional definition, you were correct because the definition breaks down, divides itself, like ancient Gaul, into three parts. If you answered a generic definition, you were correct in the sense that the definition was stated in a complete sentence. If you guessed that it was a definition by example and specific criteria, you were right again.

Using Lincoln's definition, let's consider the American government. Is the American government a democracy according to Lincoln's definition?

Item: Government of the people? Of course! How could any government *not* govern the people? (I am only kidding.)

Lincoln did not mean government of the people in the sense of the government controlling the people, telling them what to do, or ordering them about. Quite the opposite. The confusion here arises because the little word *of* has several meanings. In this context, it is the possessive. It means that the people own and control the government, not vice versa. According to Lincoln, legitimate government was a created instrument of the people, lacking any independent existence, and it is the people who tell the government what it was allowed to do, not the other way around.

Whether this is the case in contemporary America is debatable. The fact would have to be decided by the consideration of a large body of evidence. Recent disclosures of the roles of lobbyists (64,000 of them registered as of January 2002!), corporations, and big money in controlling politicians who, in turn, control the government raise serious questions about whether Americans have a government of the people—owned and controlled by the people—as Lincoln meant it. It is possible that selfish business interests own more of the government than the people do.

Item: Government by the people. A problem. In fact, a big problem. Most people feel that the government is something and they are something else. Most people I know feel harassed by the government, controlled by government, not vice versa. Other than once in a while (on election day), real power doesn't seem to reside with the people but with the bureaucracy (government by offices).

Item: For the people? I'll leave this to you to answer. My own suspicion is that most of the evidence indicates the present American government is for particular special interest groups and not for the people as a whole.

Precision and accuracy: Call me at six on the dot; little things mean a lot.

If a little two-letter word like *of* has multiple meanings, you can imagine the difficulties we get into with bigger words. Consider the three-letter word *lie*. My dictionary has ten definitions, including one that is often used with *down* and another, which we discussed previously, that describes *lie* as a deliberate false statement. What would a young woman think if I said to her, "I want to lie about you." Should she sue for slander, for sexual harassment, or both? Should she hop into bed with me or shun me as an enemy? Or should she be preemptive and belt me one in the face?

Sometimes the confusion about the meaning of little words arises from the fact that people are not aware that the word has several meanings. Take the statement "The coffee is cold," in which the word *is* is technically known as a predicative because it exactly describes the current state of the coffee. On the other hand, the statement "There is a God" contains a completely different is; the *is* in that sentence is not a predicative (although it looks exactly the same as the predicative *is*). The *is* in that sentence about God is technically known as the *is* of existential assertion. This dual meaning for the little word *is* leads to a **fallacy**, that of confusing two senses of the verb *is*, which, in turn, reflects two senses of the verb *to be*.

Among many other uses, the verb *to be* can be used both to ascribe a property (the *is* of predication) and to assert existence (the *is* of existential assertion). The later fallacy, the basis of the ontological proof of the existence of God, arises from the fact that the assertion of the existence of a thing grammatically resembles the predication to that thing of some property, so that an assertion of existence, like a predication, appears to presuppose the existence of the very thing whose existence is asserted. This makes positive existence assertions a circular form of false reasoning known as a **tautology**. The process is called *tautological*.

Once I told an attorney who was cross-examining me that he was being Sisyphean. Whereupon the opposing attorney jumped in saying, "and needlessly repetitive as well." That's what tautologies do. They waste our time with needlessly repetitious or trivially obvious observations: They are Sisyphean.

"He's poor because he is always broke." "Our annual report comes out every year." "The homeless are homeless because they have no homes."

Here are some tautological gems from President Bush:

"A low voter turnout is an indication of fewer people going to the polls."

"It isn't the pollution that is harming our environment. It is the impurities in our water and air that are doing it."

"The vast majority of our imports come from outside the country."

After hearing those tautologies, we are left blank. We are not one bit more informed than we were before. Since a tautology doesn't get us closer to the truth and doesn't inform us about reality, I consider it an error in thinking.

"Either George Washington died in 1999, or he did not."

On one level, the linguistic level, some people might regard that statement as true. I think it's just bunk because it doesn't inform us about anything. After we have read it, we remain just as unenlightened as we did before. In fact, the statement is always true and therefore it is a tautology. The formal proof of this is:

Let P equal "died in 1999."

Let not P or ~P mean "did not die in 1999."

Let T = true, F = false, and P ∨ ~P mean "P or not P," with the *or* meaning the inclusive meaning of *or*: one, the other, *or both*.

A statement is a sentence that makes a definite claim. A truth table is a table that shows all the possible combinations of the claims in a given statement with their resulting truth or falsity. Thus, consider statement "p." If "p" is true, then its denial is not true. All possible combinations of p and not p and their truth or falsity can be thus symbolized by the truth table:

p   not p
T   F
F   T

The table conveniently tells us that there are only two cases. Case 1—when p is true, not p is false. Case 2—when p is false, not p is true. There are only two possibilities of p—it can be true, or it can be false. There are only two possibilities of ~p—it can be false, or it can be true. Then, all cases and possibilities would be described by the following truth table:

	P	~P	P ∨ ~P
Case 1	T	F	T
Case 2	F	T	T

Since P ∨ ~P (read as "P or not P") is always true, no new information comes to us by the statement, and the statement is a tautology.

Reporter: "What are you going to do about the current economic situation in the United States, Mr. President?"

President Truman: "Well, we're going to do something. And if that doesn't work, we'll do something else."

Truman has said nothing substantive except that he is predisposed to action.

"Why can't women serve in combat?"

"Because established federal law explicitly prohibits any soldier in the American armed forces, under any command, and in all circumstances whatever, from serving in combat unless he is an able-bodied, adult man."

Complete bull!

The so-called reason is no reason at all—it's merely a restatement of the government's policy. It is a cop out and a tautology. The questioner asked why. All she got was a repeat of the policy itself, not the reason for it. Incidentally, no reason is stated because it would be hard to justify the exclusion of a properly trained female soldier from combat. The rationale at the root of the government's attitude is the overgeneralization "All male combat soldiers are superior to all female combat soldiers." If this generalization is false, then (as women increasingly appreciate) the government has a good reason for altering the policy, which it has. Two women were killed in combat in the Gulf War, and many more were captured.

"Too much caution is not good." This statement seems to repeat what is already contained in the subject. If anything is "too much," the implication is that it is not good. We get the idea, though. We would have gotten the idea better if we were told why too much caution is not good or if we had been given an example proving that under one circumstance too much caution was bad.

Negative existential assertions are contradictory.

The same process that makes positive existential assertions tautological makes negatives ones contradictory, leading to such confusions as nonexistence must exist since it can be the subject of a negative existential assertion. This error in thinking can cause lots of problems—for instance, the argument that the nonexistent exists, since the nonexistent is the nonexistent. That the unknown is known, since the unknown is known to be unknown. Or worse, the unknown is known as one schoolboy told his mother: "It is X!"

Similarly, since the improbable happens, it is probable (given enough time) that the improbable will happen. Hence the improbable is probable (classic false reasoning).

Using such confusions of the meaning of the verb *to be*, it is possible to make weak arguments appear stronger and to delude ourselves and others into error. Languages other than English sometimes try to get around this by having several words that are translated into English as forms of *to be*. *Estar* and *ser* are examples in Spanish, indicating various aspects of the verb *to be*. Tibetan (I am told) has even more.

The confusion we owe in large measure to the officious ubiquity of the little word *is* and its removal to an Italian mathematician and logician, Peano, who recognized the difference between *is* and *is a* and honored the later relation with a special symbol ∈, the Greek letter epsilon. By means of a distinct notation, the relation of class membership may now be clearly distinguished from identity, inclusion, entailment, or any number of other relations named by *is*. Thus, in symbolic logic to express briefly and concisely that Reynard is a member of the class "fox," we can write:

Reynard ∈ fox,

which is read "Reynard is a fox," bearing in mind that ∈ means "is a member of the class." That way, we do not confuse it with other sundry meanings of *is*. With this meaning of *is* in mind, how do you read:

8 ∈ number
castle ∈ fort and home

Let's do a little more work on this little word *is*. See if you can spot the difference among the other meanings of *is* that we mentioned.

What is the *is* in the statement, "God is just"? In that statement, is *is* predicative or assertive? Or both? What is *is*?

We have already seen that if we confuse the one *is* with the other, we might assume the statement "God is just" exactly, precisely, and specifically as true and as matter of fact as the statement that the coffee is cold.

See if your answer matches mine: The statement about God is an item of a different order than a statement about coffee. The statement about God is a mere assertion. As such the statement "God is just" asserts two things: It asserts by assumption that God exists, and it asserts by predication that she is just. We are not required to believe mere assertions unless proven, and we have already learned how to prove general assertions wrong by finding the exception. By showing one instance of injustice that occurred under God's control or supervision, we could prove that God is not just.

Arguments that God exists tend to be weak and the refuge argument that God exists because it can't be proven that she doesn't exist is nonsense. That argument is known as *argumentum ad ignorantiam*, Latin for "argument [as an appeal] to ignorance."

Argumentum ad ignorantiam tries to prove a proposition by asserting that it has never been disproved. That something hasn't been disproved is never an argument that it has been proved. How could it be? Yet the argumentum ad ignorantiam has widespread applications among the ignorant: Ghosts must exist because nobody has established that they do not. UFOs exist because no one has proven that they do not.

By the way, I know UFO abductions exist because I am a victim. Years ago, I was abducted by twenty Venusians, all of whom looked like Marilyn Monroe in her salad days. They took me aboard their space ship and repeatedly subjected me to. . . . Well, you get the picture.

Work on this statement by telling what it asserts:

We are the master race.

The *we* refers to the German people. The statement is Hilter's claim for the German people. He claims that

1. There is a master race.
2. The German people are a race.
3. The German people are the master race.
4. Since there is a master race, there must be a slave race.
5. Since there is a master race and a slave race, the master race may enslave the slave race.

Claims 1 through 3 are part and parcel of the original statement. Claims 4 and 5 follow directly from the first three claims as **subaltern** claims implicit in the statement. Claims 1 through 5 are false. Can you prove they are false?

To avoid ambiguity, as well as a great many other difficulties, symbolic logic replaces the word *is* by arbitrary symbols that are not subject to the vagaries of literary grammar and syntax but present a simplified grammar of logical structure. For instance, consider:

a. The rose is red. In this statement, *is* ascribes a property to an element known as rose.
b. Rome is greater than Athens. In this statement, *is* has been included only as an auxiliary value of asserting the dyadic relation, "greater than."
c. George Bush is president of the United States. Here *is* expresses identity.
d. Bill Clinton is a legendary liar. Here *is* indicates membership in a class, the class of legendary liars.
e. To sleep is to dream. This *is* implies entailment because it says that dreaming entails (implies) sleeping.
f. God is. As we noted before, this statement has an *is* that asserts existence.

So we see that a and b have an *is* that is only part of the verb. It serves to assert a relationship, which is otherwise expressed. But in the remaining cases—c, d, e, f—the *is* expresses a different relation in every case. These *ises* really name a relation that would appear to have a common form but would wear the badge of their distinctions plainly in view, signaled in symbolic logic by special signs so that the relation is clear:

c. George Bush = president
d. Clinton ∈ legendary liar
e. To sleep ⊃ to dream
f. E! God

Shades of meaning and word atmosphere—*Le mot juste*.
The wealth of words that are nearly synonymous yet embody subtle shades of difference in meaning makes language more precise and helps us capture a precise tone and sense by providing exactly the right word. For example, deciding between the words *paternal* and *fatherly* in the following sentences involves sensitivity to a distinction that few languages other than English make:
The judge's decision rested on Tom's _____ rights.
Pop gave Marge a _____ smile and went back to reading his newspaper.
I would have put *paternal* in the first sentence and *fatherly* in the second. *Fatherly* and *paternal* share the same basic meaning or denotation, and I could have used *fatherly* in the first sentence and *paternal* in the second, but the opposite choice is preferred because of matters of

connotation, the secondary associations of a word. *Paternal* is more formal and more appropriate to a legal context, while *fatherly* is less formal and more appropriate to a home situation. *Fatherly* implies by extension the idealized qualities of fatherhood, personal warmth, love, caring protection, and so forth.

In addition to denotation and connotation, words tend to have an atmosphere and a history that also confer meanings. *Paternal* comes from the Latin *pater* and *father* comes from Old English, which, in turn, was derived from the ancient Indo-European word *patre*, probably originally from baby talk meaning papa. We don't have time or space to go into this, but the history and atmosphere of a word can be just as important in communication or thinking of anything as strict dictionary meaning. Style, mood, and level of familiarity plus emotional coloring may come through or influence our thoughts without our conscious awareness. For instance, I can't help but think of the Arabs when someone mentions coffee. Nor can I help thinking of American Indians when someone mentions tobacco. What images come to your mind when you read words like *landscape, yacht, algebra, holster, avocado, shampoo* (one of the few Hindu words in English), *pantaloons* (where our word *pants* comes from), *asparagus, daisy* (condensation of *Day's eye*, the old term for that flower), *weenie, black out, beat, booby trap* (originally a bucket of water over the entrance), *allomorph, affricate, pancration*?

Notice if you don't know the word—and lots of people don't know allomorph, affricate, pancration—nothing comes to mind, or just puzzlement, confusion, and self-doubt. When you see an unfamiliar word, what should come to mind? Think for a second. What action should be suggested by your encounter with a word that you don't know?

Answer: The desire to head to the dictionary and look it up.

Take, for example, a quotation from pages 5 and 6 of Lewis Carroll's *Alice in Wonderland*: "Let me see: that would be about four thousand miles down, I think—. . . yes, that's about the right distance—but then I wonder what Latitude or Longitude I've got to?" (Alice had not the slightest idea what *Latitude* was, or *Longitude* either, but she thought they were nice, grand words to say.)

> *Principle:* Words have meanings. Some words have many meanings and many shades of meaning. Some meanings you may know, and others you may have to look up.

From which follows that Alice should look up *longitude* and *latitude*, and you should abide by this lesson:

> *Lesson:* When you are unclear on a word's meaning, look it up. And for heaven's sake, avoid using a word that you don't know.

I keep an index card in my pocket and use it to write down the words I come across in my daily life that I am not sure of. You do the same. Write the word down and look it up that night. Pay attention to the word's denotation and connotation. Study the word's atmosphere and history. Try to discover if the word has any hidden meanings, which brings us to the next topic.

Hidden meaning is an important topic. At this point before you tackle it, you may wish to prepare by getting a cup of java, getting up to stretch, or taking a short walk to refresh your soul. What you are about to read should have a major influence on your life and prosperity. You want to be maximally alert to benefit maximally from what you are about to learn about hidden meanings.

> *Principle:* Every statement has two meanings: overt and covert.

Almost every statement you hear has at least two meanings, the obvious meaning and the hidden meaning. These meanings are known as the *overt meaning* and the *covert meaning*, respectively. The overt meaning is easy to understand just from the literal interpretation of the statement. The covert meaning is not open or as easily understood and often depends on the hidden implications of the overt statement.

"There are two things I can't stand: Prejudice against other cultures and the Dutch." The overt meaning of that prejudicial statement from the movie *Austin Powers: The Spy Who Shagged Me* is clear and so is the covert meaning that Austin's father is in fact prejudiced against the Dutch. Since he claims he doesn't have a cultural prejudice and actually does, Austin's father is also telling us that he is a hypocrite.

Why hidden meanings exist is not entirely clear. I believe it is some primitive attempt of the unconscious mind to tell the truth. I believe hidden meanings reflect the innate goodness of the human spirit, the unconscious assertion of a kind of natural law, like the second law of thermodynamics, with a vector pointed in one direction, toward truth and away from falsehood. I believe that is why the hidden meaning can be so helpful to those interested in knowing the truth.

Psychoanalysis uncovers hidden meanings.

Long ago, in an attempt to help hysterical Viennese housewives get over their neuroses, Freud uncovered the unconscious mind, the ideas of which often surfaced in disguised form in dreams and in slips of the tongue. While all that is interesting, it won't concern us here. We will not have to use the tedious techniques of psychotherapy to figure out the hidden meanings of what people say to us. Instead, we will just have to think and think clearly.

Analyze this: "I hate going to parties where most of the other guests are unfamiliar to me." What's the overt statement? What does she mean? The overt meaning is easy enough to understand and is to the point. She doesn't like to party with strangers. But what is the covert meaning? What does she mean covertly? What is the hidden meaning behind the overt statement?

Without actually saying it, the woman has told us that she doesn't find it easy or pleasant to strike up a conversation with people she does not know. She has said covertly, "I am shy."

How about this one? "I am calm. I *am* calm. *I am calm!*"

If a young woman says she is calm and says it in a calm, detached voice, then we might believe her. But if she repeats herself in a crescendo and ends up shouting it, she is trying to convince—us and herself—of something that probably isn't so. How she says what she does contradicts the literal interpretation of what she said. Also, people who repeat that they are calm are less likely to be calm than those who don't repeat. Emphasis, especially undue emphasis, suggests the speaker is trying to convince. If she is trying to convince, it is possible that there are (justified) doubts. Perhaps she has doubts herself. For that reason, "I am calm" is more likely to be true than "I am perfectly calm."

How about this one?

"Do unto others what you would have done unto you."

That's the formulation of the Golden Rule. It is closely related to the greatest of all commandments for human conduct, as stated originally in the Old Testament: Love thy neighbor as thyself.

What is the overt message? What is the covert message? The overt message is easy. The covert message is that self-regard is natural and primary and that regard for others is derivative. The covert message is that concern for others must be shaped by using the only available reliable standard, namely, that of self-concern. The implication is that without the commandment, our bias is toward indulgent treatment of the self and niggardly treatment of others. Self-love is taken as the given, inevitable, primary datum of ethical life. Love for others must be commanded. Christian philosophy therefore recognizes that a large draught of self-interest, self-centeredness, and self-concern permits the persistence and survival of the individual. An altruism that fails to take account of this, that fails to grant that one's own interests are inherently part of any situation, is misled and shortsighted, a consequence of faulty perspective—and probably the root error underlying Marxism. The failure to consider individual self-interest is probably the root cause of the failure of communism to deliver as many goods and as many services for the majority of people under the same constraining economic resources as are delivered by capitalism.

Work on the following statement: "Any other person, when I entered the room, would have snapped to attention and taken their feet off the desk and stopped reading the newspaper. But, because you are one of my most productive employees, it doesn't bother me."

Pause and think. What is the overt statement? What is the covert statement? How many covert meanings do you detect? What items about the employee's behavior does the boss like? What does she dislike? Is it true that the employee's behavior does not bother the boss?

Answer: If the employee's behavior didn't matter, why bring it up? The covert message actually contradicts the overt message. Not only that, the covert message particularly describes in a kind of divisional definition all the behavior that the boss does not like. She really wants the employee to snap to attention when she enters the room. She really wants the employee to keep his feet off the desk. She really wants the employee to stop reading the newspaper in her presence. She may even want the employee not to read the paper on the job at all. If the items enumerated did not matter, then why would she have so precisely enumerated them? Further, this boss sends a covert message that if productivity should falter, the employee will be in trouble, since that is the only redeeming feature mentioned about the employee and maintaining his employment.

Question: Can you think of any advantages that this employee would gain if he decoded the hidden meanings behind what the boss said?

OK. Did you get the answers? Some of them are obvious, right? When we do what the boss wants, we are more likely to get a pay raise, more benefits, and more favorable consideration when making requests. When we meet and exceed the boss's expectations, we are more likely to get a promotion and other things that taken together tend to increase our own personal happiness and security.

But did you get the real covert messages in this boss's statement? The real messages, in my view, were two: "Respect me" and "Continue to be productive." In dealing with this kind of a boss, I would try to cater to those two things, especially respect, because that is what she said she wants. Chances are that feeding her ego with some fawning attention would confer great benefits. Worth a try anyway. Worth a try, that is, if you have the guts for it.

On the other hand, having gotten the covert message, you may decide that you don't like and don't want to work for a boss that has such trivial concerns. You may decide that that kind of bossing style with that kind of boss who has some kind of gigantic ego defect is not your cup of tea. In the which case you might decide to exit early and find a company to work for that more closely matches your needs. Either way, uncovering the covert meanings has put you a step ahead of the competition because you understand the truth, the reality situation, better than they do. Because you understand the truth better, you are better positioned to take intelligent action.

The feet-on-the-desk example above showed how detecting hidden meanings can improve your future, boost your career, enhance business success, and help achieve other goals toward personal happiness. But beyond that, detecting hidden meanings is important in two major areas: negotiating and inside information.

Stop to think about it. Every day you are bargaining. Every day you are negotiating with people about all sorts of matters. These talks and discussions, as I prefer to call them, vary from the trivial to the important and sometimes to the sublime.

Getting your granddaughter to go to bed on time, for instance, requires some understanding of your granddaughter's needs and desires. We have found that our granddaughter, Callie Suzanne Patten, doesn't want to go to bed. She will put up a fight if she is forced in that direction. But when Craig and Michelle, my son and daughter-in-law, discovered that Callie would go to bed without a fuss if they all just had a parade into the bedroom, the problem was solved. So when Craig and Michelle want Callie to go to bed, they announce the start of the parade, hum parade music and fall into line in the living room. Callie falls in between them and off they all merrily march to the bedroom. Since Callie is hardly seventeen months old, it is unlikely that she thinks in words. But that she does think cannot be doubted. She had made clear her position about going to bed, and in a certain sense, she bargained that she will go to bed if she can parade. "You give me something, and I give you something" is the net result of any negotiation, whether the negotiation is something important like getting the kid to bed or something trivial like getting two billion-dollar corporations to merge. Callie traded acquiescence for a parade. Notice that the outcome was beneficial to both parties, a win-win situation. Callie got some fun. Craig and Michelle got a hassle-free bedtime. No one knows where Callie got that deep internal desire to parade to bed. My guess is that it came from one of those Winnie the Pooh videos that she is fond of watching. Notice that the bedtime job now gets done without tears or fuss. Craig and Michelle also have learned that parading before bedtime can be fun. Having seen the ritual, I do it myself. It's fun.

Whether he is a car salesman, a labor union leader, a telemarketer, or a cold-calling broker from New York, a negotiator often covers up what he's really doing and really thinking. He wants to get the biggest possible advantage for himself and the biggest possible concession from you. The more he tells you the truth, the reality situation, the less likely he will get undeserved returns. The problem is that in order to effectively deal with you, he must appear sincere so that he can win your trust. Thus, real negotiators develop the knack of seeming to speak candidly without actually giving any information that will aid you to know the truth, the reality situation.

Fortunately, you already know that hidden meanings can be deduced and that the more the opposition talks, the more he reveals. The best way to tune into the covert messages is to listen attentively to the flag words.

Flag words give a good indication that the speaker is not speaking the entire truth. Let's go over a few flag words and phrases so that you get what I mean: *Naturally, of course, no doubt, obviously, as expected, to tell the truth, not surprisingly, as you would expect, as everyone knows*—when you hear these words or words like them, watch out. Any statement preceded by such words or phrases is suspect. These words indicate that the speaker is trying to get you to accept some questionable information as fact. The degree of certainty about any statement that follows these words is less than (sometimes far less than) he would like you to believe.

If a boat salesman says, "Of course, that is the lowest price I can offer the boat for," then you should assume that he is really willing to bargain some more. In 1999, that is exactly what I heard from the boat salesman who was trying to sell me a twenty-one-foot Chaparral inboard/outboard. Except in my real-life case, the salesman said, "Of course, $34,000 is the lowest price I can offer." If he had just said, "OK, Doc, $34K—that's it, the best we can do," I might have let him off. But knowing that numbers on a piece of paper are money, too, even though you don't see the green, I replied, "I appreciate your candor in telling me that you have to talk to someone else before you can lower the price. In that case, talk to that person. Call me tomorrow with your best price."

Notice the spin I put on the salesman's statement. I didn't argue that he could go lower. Instead, I emphasized the word *I* in his statement, construing it to mean that since he couldn't go lower, someone else could. By emphasizing that someone else could go lower, I gave him the face-saving out of consulting with someone else or appearing to consult with someone else about a price reduction.

The next day, Charlie the boat salesman called. "Boy, have I got good news for you, Doc. We'll let it go for twenty-four."

By the way, incidentally, by the by, before I forget, while we're on the subject, in passing, parenthetically—when you hear these words or terms like them, watch out. The idea is to make the statement that follows seem like a minor point, but the opposite is usually the case.

"By the way, this job involves some night work." I'll bet it does. No doubt about it. The job requires night work. The item was tossed in as a trivial matter, but it's actually important. Hearing it, you might want to know more details about how much night work, where and when, and whether more pay is involved (or less) and why. You might want to know if the job is any different at night than during the day. It usually is.

"Incidentally, this office is in a one-family residential zone, but the zoning board has always overlooked it." That's not incidental at all. That the zoning board has overlooked the violation in the past doesn't mean they will overlook it now or in the future.

"Before I forget, the renter sometimes will need to flush out the cesspool."

You bet they will. And soon. And at the renter's expense.

It is not possible because . . . or *I wish I could but I can't because . . .* when you hear these words or words like them, it means the opponent is taking some pains to tell you why he can't give you a certain special consideration. He is often also telling you exactly what he can do. When you hear these words, you can be fairly certain that he can give you everything listed after the "because," since it is highly likely that he can. Not only that, he can probably give you more. In general, the more they try to explain, the less sincere they are, and the more they can do. So don't be fooled by what I call "can't do words." People who say "can't do" frequently can do. They are just trying to dissuade you from seeking what they know they can give you, what they know you can get.

Thus, "I can't raise your salary because it would throw our budget out of whack," means "I can raise your salary. Show me why I should."

"I usually don't go to bed on the first date," means you still have a chance if you play your cards right because "usually don't" actually means "sometimes do." Otherwise stated, he is saying that he does go to bed on the first date occasionally with the implication that he does go to bed if the situation merits it or he can be persuaded. The man's statement also means that you definitely have a chance of getting him in the sack if you take him out again. Many are cold, but few are frozen.

Some hidden meanings might not be favorable to your position. They might, in fact, be downright unpleasant to contemplate. Take, for instance, "I don't want you to leave. I hope we can reach an understanding." The overt message seems clear enough. Do it his way or get out. But the covert message is worse. The covert message is that he wants you out. And he wants you out soon. Better start packing your stuff. Look for a new job or better still, retire.

"I still love you, but I am busy for the next few weeks. I'll call when I surface." Don't expect a call. She is just trying to let you down nicely. The "still" sends the covert message that there might have been some doubt about her continuing love. If she loved you so much, she should be able to call. No one is that busy that she can't call just to say I love you.

Or: "I can come tomorrow to fix your toilet, if I am able to finish another job I am working on, and if my apprentice gets over his bad cold." Here you have a fairly good indication from all those qualifying words that you won't be seeing the plumber tomorrow. Probably you won't be seeing him for a while, perhaps even several days.

Or: "Both here and hence, pursue me lasting strife, if once I be a widow, ever I be a wife!" When Hamlet asks his mother, Gertrude, "Madam, how like you this play?" Gertrude rightly observed, "The lady doth protest too much, methinks." Gertrude knows the queen in the play is overdoing it. Not only does the queen in the play want to be punished for remarrying, but also she wants the punishment to start now (here) before the event and to continue from now on (and hence), and she wants the punishment, the (lasting) strife, to last forever. That's pretty harsh punishment for a contingent event in the future that may or may not happen, and when and if it happens, may or may not be justified.

Since the play queen's curse on herself is so extreme, Gertrude reads the hidden meaning that the lady is exaggerating for effect and cannot possibly be sincere. The play queen's statement is too much. Because the statement is too much, it is likely to be an insincere exaggeration, a **supererogation.**

Incidentally, the old meaning of *protest* was vow, affirm, or state positively, not our more modern object or dissent. Current dictionaries carry both meanings. "The lady doth protest too much" means the lady vows or swears too much.

The point is that knowing the covert meanings behind what the other person says provides important clues as to how you can win the negotiation, bargain to your advantage, predict behavior, or read the other person's deep heart's core.

Knowing the hidden messages can also help you intelligently address the hidden emotional needs of others. Here's some dialogue from Leo Tolstoy's famous novel *Anna Karenina*. What hidden need is Anna expressing?

> Vronsky: The only thing I prayed for was to put an end to this situation, so as to devote my life to your happiness.
>
> Anna: Why do you tell me this? You don't think I could doubt it, do you?
>
> Vronsky: Who's that coming? They may know us![4]

What he should have said in that last line was "I love you, Anna, with my whole heart and soul. I don't care who knows. And I don't care who's coming." And then he should have kissed her passionately. Because Vronsky had not read Anna's hidden anxiety, he missed his cue. Vronsky had not understood Anna's need, her anxiety really, to be reassured about his love for her. He didn't understand why his statement, whose overt meaning is quite clear, had caused Anna to react adversely. He didn't realize that she had detected a possible hidden meaning in what he said.

Anna had assumed Vronsky's devotion to her was an unquestionable given. When Vronsky tried to reassure her on the issue, she read from his statement the hidden meaning that he did not or had not assumed the devotion was as unquestionable as she had. That understanding of Vronsky's position, so different from hers, fed Anna's anxiety. Hence, her reaction.

On the same page, Tolstoy explains the reason for Vronsky's insensitivity: Vronsky was worrying about the duel he would have to fight with Anna's husband. During that duel, honor would dictate that Vronsky would have to fire into the air and wait for Karenin to shoot back. If Karenin did shoot back, Vronsky might die. The thought of death had focused Vronsky's mind away from Anna and caused him to temporarily lose his usual sensitivity. The prospect of death focuses the mind. Vronsky's mind was temporarily focused on the possibility of his death and temporarily focused away from his love for Anna.

Covert messages can signal danger.

Rocks and shoals ahead. Decoding hidden meanings can help you avoid trouble. Besides flag words, pay attention to broadcast definitions that are wrong. And especially pay attention to duplicitous behavior, for it often indicates deception. Investors who had paid attention to those two things might have avoided losing money in Enron. Let's consider broadcast definition first and then go on to duplicitous behavior. Detection of either one or both gives evidence of falsehood and therefore can focus us in the opposite direction, away from falsehood and toward truth.

Remember we defined *evidence* as any sign leading toward the perception of truth. The broadcast definition that people use is a form of evidence that reflects individual thinking about an issue. When the broadcast definition is wrong, we have evidence that we are being led away from the truth toward error.

The January 28, 2002, edition of the *New York Times* (p. C2) reported the following statement from Dr. John Mendelsohn, president of the University of Texas M. D. Anderson Cancer Center in Houston: "Dr. Mendelsohn said he had been careful to avoid any conflict of interest with ImClone, a biotechnology company. 'I give a lot of speeches and I always state that I am on the board of ImClone and I own stock in the company. I always say this.'"

What is the overt message? The overt message is that Dr. Mendelsohn wants us to believe that he is, and that he has always been, honest and above board with the public. The reason that he cites, the reason that he feels should convince us of his honesty, is that in his many speeches, he always mentions that he is on the board of directors of the company that makes the cancer drug C-225 and that he owns stock in that company. Later in this book, we will learn that mere assertions not supported by evidence are unreasonable. Enlightenment philosophy requires that we believe only that which has been proven by relevant and adequate evidence. We are not supposed to believe anything that is merely asserted. Therefore, since Dr. Mendelsohn's assertion is not supported by evidence, we need not believe it. That is one consideration. Another is the hidden meanings in his statement.

The doctor flags his statement for close examination by repeating the word *always*. Why say *always* twice? Once is enough. Or rather, once should be enough. Because he repeated *always*, he sent a signal to the alert listener that perhaps we might do well to question him on this issue. Because he repeated *always*, he has raised a doubt about his own truthfulness. If he himself believed what he said fully and without question or reservation, why would he need to apply such emphasis? The man doth protest too much, methinks.

By the way, what about *always* were we supposed to remember? Both here and hence, pursue us lasting strife, if once told, we ever fail to remember that *always* always means always.

So, if we are able to show that Dr. Mendelsohn did not mention his connection to the company ImClone in one of his many speeches, then we could prove his assertion wrong. But that is beside the point. What we want to examine here is the covert message that the doctor's statement makes. What is it?

The covert message is that he doesn't know the definition of *conflict of interest*. He is confusing a *conflict of interest* with *disclosure of conflict of interest*. Furthermore, he thinks that the disclosure of a conflict of interest excuses the conflict and (and this is worse) he wishes to confuse the public by confusing the definition. Dr. Mendelsohn is trying to confuse the issues and flummox us. If you can't convince them with evidence, baffle them with bullshit.

Not convinced? Reread the doctor's statement.

He says he has been careful to avoid any conflict of interest in his relationship with the company ImClone. Yet he admits he owns stock and he is a director. His care to avoid *any* conflict of interest was not of sufficient magnitude to prevent what he was so careful to try to prevent. In fact, he admits he has a conflict of interest and not just one conflict but two: he's on the board of directors of ImClone and he's a big shareholder.

Thus, the man contradicts himself. If he were careful to avoid any conflict of interest, how come he has two such conflicts? Two **contradictions** cannot be simultaneously true. One must be false. Two contrary assertions can't be simultaneously true. One must be false or both must be false. Conclusion: the doctor is confused, or he is lying.

The definition of *conflict of interest* is that a person in a fiduciary position, that is, a position of trust, has a conflict of interest if he has a personal interest in the outcome of his decisions or actions related to his fiduciary position. This is not the definition the doctor uses or wishes us to use in the evaluation of his conduct.

Once again, reread the doctor's statement. See what I mean? Not only does he tell us that he has a conflict of interest, he tells us that he has two of them. He tells us what those conflicts are. Furthermore, he tells us that he uses an erroneous definition of *conflict of interest* to excuse his conflicts. Changing the definition, in my opinion, is more offensive than the actual conflicts. And using the changed definition to excuse the conflict is even more egregious. The change in definition smacks of Newspeak and shades of *1984*, George Orwell's famous book.

> *Principle:* When the broadcast definition is wrong, a fraud is being perpetrated on language, and, chances are, a fraud is also being perpetrated on you.

From which follows:

> *Lesson:* When the definition you hear does not match the definition you know, watch out. Chances are that someone, usually the person who has misstated the definition, is up to no good.

With that lesson in mind, would you trust Dr. Mendelsohn's statement about the value of C-225, ImClone's anticancer agent, which Dr. Mendelsohn helped develop and test? Would you trust him or his statements about Enron profits? Yes, Dr. Mendelsohn is on the Enron board of directors, too. We'll examine his directorship in more detail soon.

This book is about clear thinking and how to tell when they are handing you bull. It is not a book about psychology or psychiatry, but it wouldn't hurt at this juncture to give you some further insight into the full implications of Dr. Mendelsohn's statement. These implications are based on what I learned in my psychiatry training at Columbia and my experience in dealing with patients during a medical career that spanned over thirty years.

Defensive statements flag conflicts that require further examination.

Dr. Mendelsohn's statement is defensive. As such, it suggests he is using the unconscious mental mechanism of denial and displacement to conceal a concern that he himself has on some level, perhaps unconsciously, about a more important and more serious conflict of interest in another realm. The disclosure of a conflict of interest in giving a speech is, after all, a relatively trivial matter. Because it is trivial, the question arises: Is that disclosure designed to focus attention on it and away from something else that might be of much greater import? In other words, is the doctor's defensive statement a form of misdirection? Is it a kind of magic trick to throw us off the track and conceal the real? Psychiatrists are trained to reason darkly. I can't help it.

Dr. Mendelsohn was the developer and at one time the principal investigator of the drug C-225, now known as Erbitux, the drug once touted as miraculous and now at the center of a scandal over stock trades by executives, board members, and friends of executives (like Martha Stewart) of ImClone, the company paying for the testing of the drug. Dr. Mendelsohn was at the time of this writing the president of the University of Texas M. D. Andersen Cancer Center, an institution that tested the drug on 195 patients *without* informing them that its president, Dr. John Mendelsohn, had a gigantic financial interest in the medication and in the results of the study.

On June 30, 2002, a center official (according to the *Houston Chronicle*, July 1, 2002, p. 1) began telling patients in November 2001 about the financial conflict of interest. That was one month before the Food and Drug Administration refused to consider the drug, calling its study—that designed and conducted by Dr. Mendelsohn and others—too flawed to tell if it benefits patients. That was only one month before ImClone tanked.

So Dr. Mendelsohn might have been careful to tell audiences (which mainly consisted of medical doctors) about his conflict of interest, but he failed to tell the patients about a much more important conflict of interest: He was experimenting on them and yet had a personal financial interest in the outcome of the experiment.

Thus, the conclusion that he might have been diverting attention from a real disclosure issue to one that was minor appears justified. His was a diversionary argument to conceal the real issues. All this discovery of truth, mind you, followed from a careful analysis of his original statement. That is the beauty of dissecting hidden meanings. That is why such dissection can be so helpful.

ImClone's collapse cost investors and pension funds millions, left hopeful cancer patients in limbo, and brought a congressional investigation into charges of fraud and insider trading, the last of which has been directed against lifestyle maven Martha Stewart, a former girlfriend of ImClone's CEO Dr. Samuel Waksal, arrested by the FBI and subsequently convicted of securities fraud.

Marcia Angell, a Harvard lecturer and former editor of the *New England Journal of Medicine*, said that "disclosure is the bare minimum—involves the possibility that financial interests could put pressure on researchers to produce favorable results and to play down harmful outcomes."[5] Dr. Mendolsohn knows this or should have known this. His e-mails to the faculty certainly focus on conflict-of-interest issues. His e-mails don't yet focus on the more important ethical issue of carrying a conflict despite its disclosure. Not only was the conflict not disclosed, the conflict of interest was also continued throughout the testing of the drug, a drug the testing of which the FDA subsequently said failed to meet minimal scientific standards.

Hindsight is 20/20.

Because the causal conjunctions that determine events are contingent, we are more often in a position to explain something that has happened than in a position to predict (in its entirety) what would or will happen. ImClone is a case in point. What happened is worse than anyone predicted. But you know what? I predict the ImClone story will be even more damnable. Perhaps the rest of the ImClone story will be even more damnable than the rest of the Enron story, which has recently revealed that Enron admits frauds.

We now know from the 217-page report from the Enron Corporation's board that executives intentionally manipulated the company's profits, inflated them by almost $1 billion in the year before Enron's collapse. They did this through byzantine dealings with a byzantine group of partnerships. As oversight broke down, the Enron report says, a culture emerged of self-dealing and self-enrichment at the expense of the energy company's 64,000 shareholders. The report harshly criticizes of Enron's accountants at Arthur Andersen and the company's lawyers, saying they signed off on flawed and improper decisions every step of the way.

An Arthur Andersen executive testified before Congress about shredding accounting documents at Enron. He said, "This policy toward document disposal reflects sound audit practice."[6] On questioning the official, Congress learned that by "sound audit practice" the witness meant "financially healthy." Obviously, Arthur Andersen has twisted the definition of financially healthy and uses the term *sound audit practice* in an idiosyncratic way. Arthur Andersen's broadcast definition is obviously wrong. That fact exposes fraud on our language and raises serious questions about Arthur Andersen's accounting integrity.

Subsequently, Arthur Andersen was convicted of obstruction of justice, and its license to do public accounting has been rescinded. Reality crashed down on Andersen's head. Hard. The company is defunct.

Prescience is impossible, but intelligent analysis is not impossible.

It was impossible for the public to know the details of all these things before Enron collapsed. But it was possible to suspect something by analysis of content and actions. In 1999, when someone asked me if I would invest in Enron, my reply was that Warren Buffet, Peter Lynch, and I all say, "Never invest in what you don't understand." Since I didn't understand Enron's business, I wouldn't invest in it. If you had had a chance to practice intelligent analysis on what Ken Lay (Enron's CEO), Mendelsohn, and the likes of CFO Andrew Fastow said and did, you wouldn't have invested in Enron either. You especially would not have invested in Enron if you knew about their conflicts of interest and their duplicitous behavior.

Conflicts of interest are unethical because it is almost impossible to prevent our love of power, wealth, and possessions from interfering with our judgment. Judges have to retire from the bench (recuse themselves) if a case comes before them in which their friends, business associates, or relations are involved, and countless precautions are taken in civil and criminal trials to eradicate personal prejudice.

There is a story about a Texan explaining to a man from Louisiana about communism: "If your neighbor has two houses, he has to give one to you." The proposal met with immediate acceptance. "If he has two cars, he has to give you one." Again happy agreement. "If he has two boats, he has to give—" That brought a stern interruption. "No way, José. You know I have two boats."

Knowledge of a conflict of interest can help you uncover a hidden meaning and therefore lead you to a better understanding of the truth. The tip off that you are witnessing a conflict of interest comes from analysis of duplicitous behavior.

Most cases of duplicity occur in situations of conflict of interest. Usually the person who has a fiduciary responsibility says one thing but does the opposite. For instance, at the time that Dr. Mendelsohn was talking about ImClone's positive outlook for the future, according to the *New York Times*, he exercised options on 90,226 ImClone shares, sold those shares, and received $6.3 million. Subsequently, the Food and Drug Administration refused to consider licensing C-225 and ImClone's stock went south. Bristol-Myers Squibb, the company that bought those shares from Dr. Mendelsohn, paid him $70 per share. Imclone shares were selling for $16.49 on Friday, January 26, 2002, when I checked them. On June 28, 2002, the shares traded at $8.02, and the headline for the stock said that Congress was investigating conflict of interest in ImClone directors, including Dr. Mendelsohn.

> *Principle:* When there is a conflict between what a person says and what he does, what he does is more likely to point to the truth. In other words, actions speak louder than words. The evidence of action is more powerful than the evidence of words. For this reason, the Latin motto of the Royal Society of London, one of the world's great scientific institutions, is *Nullius in Verba* (Take no one's word for it).

From which follows:

> *Lesson:* When people in authority say one thing and do other, watch out. Uncover the hidden meaning of their contradictory action. By analysis of duplicity, predict what trouble's coming. And as always, act accordingly. Furthermore, consider the possibility that duplicitous behavior is evidence of bad character.

From which follows:

> *Lesson:* Listen to what people say, but also check what they do. If what they say and what they do don't match up, consider what they do as stronger evidence of the truth. Any duplicitous behavior is evidence for fraud, hypocrisy, insincerely, or stupidity—one, all, or any com-

bination of those four things. Try to profit by using evidence of duplicity to evaluate character. Once that character analysis is done, act accordingly by predicting future trouble.

Duplicitous character usually runs true to form. That's reasonable and probable. Always bet on the reasonable and probable because they are what usually happens.

If you discover, after you get home, that the one pound of chuck chop that you bought from the corner butcher actually weighs 0.8 pounds, you can bet that the same butcher will have his same thumb on the same scale again next time you attempt to buy the same thing from him.

If Dr. Mendelsohn was on the inside of ImClone when the public and the employees were getting screwed, would it have been possible (from that fact) to predict his behavior as a director of Enron?

Make predictions based on character analysis.

Knowing what you do about Dr. Mendelsohn's public statements and the evidence derived therefrom of his character, can you predict how he functioned as a director of Enron?

Go on. Take a guess. Pause now to formulate clearly your guess about Dr. Mendelsohn's behavior as an Enron director.

Answer: As a member of the Enron board of directors, Dr. Mendelsohn was active in many of the board's most controversial decisions—the approval in June and October 1999 of the partnerships with the company's chief financial officer at the time, Andrew S. Fastow. Dr. Mendelsohn also figured in the Enron board's decision to suspend Enron's own code of ethics so Mr. Fastow could serve as the general partner of the partnerships that led to Enron's implosion. Dr. Mendelsohn was also a member of the Enron audit committee that dealt with Arthur Anderson's highly questionable audits of Enron.

See how a short analysis of this man's statement suggested that ImClone and Enron might be headed for the shoals? See how knowledge of hidden meanings might have helped you not invest in Enron?

Not convinced? Need further examples?

Ken Lay, former Enron CEO, touted Enron stock to his employees and to the general public at the same time that he was selling his Enron shares. In fact, employees were led on at the very end while executives were selling like crazy. Was that duplicitous? You bet.

Aristotelian logic: Two contradictory things cannot be simultaneously true. Therefore, one or the other must be false. Either Enron stock was good, the way Ken Lay said, in which case buying the stock would be good. Or the stock was bad, in which case selling the stock would have been the thing to do. The truth, we now know, was that if you knew what Ken Lay knew about Enron, you would have been selling your stock too, just the way he did.

Yes, Ken Lay spoke with forked tongue. Ken Lay advised one thing while he was doing the opposite, which led to his own personal profit and helped him. But it also led to losses and harmed the public.

Although this was a breach of fiduciary duty, Ken Lay's behavior was, on a psychological level, understandable. He was on the take. So were the accountants, on the take. So were the other Enron officers, the Enron board, the attorneys who advised the corporation, the politicians who supported legislation favorable to the company, on the take. They were all, in one way or another, on the take. Their loyalty to the company was bought.

Their actions were understandable—but not excusable. In fact, their actions were forms of self-preservation. Human nature dictates that we take care of ourselves. It's normal human nature that Ken Lay didn't have the same concern for his employees or Enron shareholders that he had for himself. Give his character, as shown by his actions, to expect him to do otherwise is to expect the impossible. (From someone else, Mother Teresa, for example, we might expect more, but from Ken Lay, no.)

The same instinct that protected Ken Lay encourages a tigress at bay to fight until she drops. Ken Lay's was a basic instinct to attempt to keep his own fortune intact. Self-preservation, the law of the jungle, is so basic an urge that it exerts a profound influence on behavior. It can even cause unprofessional conduct, breach of fiduciary duty, and criminal acts. Whenever there are conflicting interests where a party has a personal stake in outcomes, watch out.

The indicated action to prevent future Enrons is institutional controls to prevent conflicts of interest, fraud, double dealing, and so on. Here we are more concerned with what we as individuals should do or should have done to prevent personal investment losses. What investment action would have been reasonable if stockholders knew at the time of Ken Lay's duplicitous behavior?

Confidence in an investment rests on the belief that directors and managers will be truthful. When you catch the CEO in a lie, watch out. If you own stock, and you catch an officer of your company in duplicitous behavior, you have to wonder about his integrity. If you know a manager is dishonest, sell the stock. If you don't know whether a manager is honest, you should act as if he were not. That means you have to discount the price that you will pay for the stock to adjust for the increased risk and uncertainty.

Pause now and exercise your power of analysis on the following statement made in October 2001 by John J. Legere, CEO of Global Crossing, Inc.: "Bankruptcy is not a possibility at all."

Tell why the statement is likely to be wrong. Tell what action should be taken when such statements are heard. Even if your answer may differ from mine, consider your answer correct if you got the gist.

The gist, the essence of the statement, is a denial of the possible. Since most things are possible, to say that they are not possible is an uphill fight and would require proof of the assertion. Furthermore, the addition of the "at all" at the end of the statement means that the possibility of bankruptcy is completely denied. By the addition of the "at all," the man doth protest too much—he shows us that his statement has to be false because bankruptcy can hardly ever be completely impossible. And for Global Crossing at that time when revenues were failing, bankruptcy could not be completely impossible. Bankruptcy had to be possible, even if only a little possible.

If John J. Legere's statement is false, then the contrary must be true: It must have been possible that Global Crossing could go bankrupt. Since the Legere statement is false and the opposite true, the statement must alert vigilant, ready-to-act investors, those who are thinking, to the possibility of bankruptcy. Those alert and thinking people sold Global Crossing stock that day. Those alert and sophisticated investors sold their stock right after Mr. Legere's statement.

Why? Why should they sell when the obvious, overt meaning of Legere's statement is that bankruptcy is not possible at all?

Simple. Intelligent investors ignored the overt message and read the deeper covert message. The covert message said that the man was denying the possible and therefore lying. A man who lies cannot be trusted. Furthermore, if everything is so peachy, then why is he cheerleading? Wall Street traditionally regards such cheerleading with distrust, reasoning darkly that if top officials, especially the CEO, give the market advice and reassurance, things are worse, much worse than they appear.

Subsequently the stock price of Global Crossing went into a steep decline from two dollars a share to one cent a share.

Global Crossing filed for bankruptcy protection under chapter 11 on January 28, 2002. Yes, Global Crossing crossed over to the dark side and went bankrupt just four months after the CEO (Legere) said that it was not possible that Global Crossing could go bankrupt.

History, the unimaginative jade, repeated herself. Another major American corporation like Enron went bankrupt after its CEO said that bankruptcy was not possible, not possible at all.

I guess Legere didn't know what he was talking about. But you—you could have known by analysis that bankruptcy was possible *three months* before bankruptcy actually occurred. You could have had time to investigate. You could have had time to sell the stock before it headed south.

Next lesson. What does the false statement say about Legere? Any reflection on his character? From your analysis of his character, can you predict the truth or falsity of his next statement? "I am taking a 30 percent cut in pay as part of my wider effort to conserve capital at Global Crossing."[7]

Sounds pretty good. Doesn't it? The man is willing to make a great personal sacrifice to help conserve and preserve shareholder value. That's nice. Isn't it? It tends to indicate that Legere feels the pain that the stockholders have. He wants to do his bit to help. That's great. Or is it?

Would it interest you to know (according to the *New York Times*, April 8, 2002, p. C5) that Legere told Global Crossing stockholders that he was taking a 30 percent pay cut from his $1.1 million at Global Crossing as part of his wider effort to conserve capital at the same time that he accepted a $3.5 million signing bonus from Global Crossing and the forgiveness of a $10 million loan from Global Crossing?

The salary reduction was not the whole story. Legere didn't tell the whole truth, just part of the truth that he wanted us to hear. He told only the part that made him look good. He excluded the part that made him look bad. Partial selection of the evidence is an error in thinking because it can lead to a false conclusion. By looking at only one bit of evidence, the salary reduction, we might have concluded Legere was a nice guy. But looking at the full evidence tells us that he wasn't.

The omission was a deliberate deception. In fact, Legere received a $3.5 million signing bonus and was forgiven a $10 million loan from Asia Global Crossing (another company owed mainly by Global). Asia Global Crossing also paid the taxes that Legere would have owed the United States Treasury from the transaction. Thus, Legere saved the shareholders $1.1 million times 30 percent, or $330,000, by taking a cut in salary. But he cost the shareholders $13.5 million plus $3.6 million in taxes paid for him. The net cost, therefore, to the company and to the owners of the company, the shareholders, was $16.77 million. The ratio of bad to good, as far as shareholders are concerned, is fifty-one to one, for that was the ratio of the amount of money Legere saved the company versus the amount of money he took. The ratio of good to bad as far as Legere's personal stake was concerned was the same, fifty-one to one. Which end of the stick would you prefer to be holding? The shareholders' or his?

Selling stock on the basis of information not available as to the general public, as Ken Lay did, is insider trading, which can be unethical because it may take unfair advantage of others. Under certain circumstances, insider trading is illegal. It is definitely illegal (except for sales of the stock back to the company that issued it) if it has not been reported to the Security Exchange Commission within ten days after the month in which the sale took place.

Wouldn't it be nice to know inside information without having to look it up in the SEC report? That report tells what insider did what. Public information like that is good. Sunshine is a great disinfectant. But the key information is lacking. Sure, we want to know who did what and when. But we also want to know why. Why did the insiders sell? How can we get that kind of inside information—information that is not reported?

Answer: Content analysis. Content analysis gets you insights about the inside information. Without much work you can deduce the why. Here's how.

Inside information can sometimes be deduced by the analysis of the content of a series of statements. CIA and other government agencies do this to try to deduce the hidden or inside meaning of what has been publicly stated in communiqués from other governments. The technique, called content analysis, reveals hidden meanings by looking at the frequency and use of words and expressions.

"Joan went to the dance last night with me. She is so cool and so cute. She has a nice car too, a Jag XJ. And her father said he will take us to the Titans game next week."

If your son is always talking about girls, you can bet girls are on his mind. If he is always talking about one girl, Joan, you can bet she's the one, his heartthrob.

When Nikita Khrushchev said (while pounding on the lectern with his shoe), "We will bury you," you can bet that his intentions were not peaceful. You can also surmise that he had doubts that Russia could win a war with the United States, else why would he talk that way—so belligerently? If he knew he could win easily, why would he try to scare and intimidate us? So you can bet that he had grave doubts that Russia would win a war against the United States. He was bluffing just as so many people who talk that way are bluffing. Later on, many years later, we learned Khrushchev really was bluffing. The great mighty Russian military machine was falling apart under communism, just like the rest of the USSR was falling apart.

When people tell you that the tax situation in your city is basically that the city government needs more money, you can bet that basically they haven't taken the trouble to do a basically detailed analysis to see if basically that was basically the case. You can bet that because if they had done such a detailed study, they would have stated the conclusion directly without using the hedge word "basically."

In his State of the Union message in February 1973, President Nixon said, "The basic state of our Union is sound, and full of promise." The use of the defensive modifier *basic* may have reflected (just before the Watergate scandal took hold) that the apparent, or surface, state of the nation (that is, the side opposite the basic underlying condition) was not as sound or full of promise. There is an old song, "Call me at six on the dot. Little things mean a lot." In this case, I believe that the president's use of the qualifier *basic* meant a great deal. Subsequent events proved that supposition correct.

> *Principle:* In the case of words, little words can mean a lot, especially little hedge words.

From which follows:

> *Lesson:* Pay attention to the little words that tend to modify larger statements. Those little words can reveal the hidden meaning at the core.

Examine the following statements taken from the stockholders meeting of a prominent software company:

"Our new line will go a long way in getting back our competitive position vis-à-vis Dreamweaver."

"The lay offs have streamlined our staff and cut costs dramatically. We hope to retire another 600 employees by the end of the year, positioning ourselves again for profit."

"When the economy turns around, particularly when it turns around in Japan, we fully anticipate getting back to our previous performance levels."

"7.0 will replace our other products that are being discontinued."

"The difficulty with the dot coms will hopefully be over soon and they will once again become our foremost customers."

Any of the above statements when taken alone means little. But when taken together at the same stockholders meeting in 2000, the hidden meanings are clear. The theme is trouble.

This company, Adobe, is struggling against Macromedia's product Dreamweaver. The company has had so little demand for its software that it had to lay off workers. Adobe is not currently making a profit. Unless the general economic climate improves in Japan, things won't get better. Version 7.0 is not a new product but merely an upgrade that will replace the existing PhotoShop programs. Unless the general economic climate improves among the dot-coms, things won't improve for the company.

See what I mean? These hidden meanings raise the question: What to do? What do you think? What would you do? I would sell. Wouldn't you? In fact, I did sell. I sold all of my 20,000 shares at $93 a share. Last I checked, Adobe shares were selling for $16.

Here's another practical example from a robbery that happened at my apartment in the East Village of New York City in 1969. See if you can detect from content analysis whether the criminal intends to return to my place: My wife, daughter, and son and I got into the elevator. Before the door shut, a man with a knife jumped in, grabbed my daughter, held the knife across her throat, and demanded money. I gave him my wallet. "Only eight dollars!" he shouted. "All I got," I said. The robber made a disgusted face, threw my daughter down, and escaped.

Two days later, a telephone caller told me, "Don't worry, Doc, I found your wallet in the trash in the subway. All your stuff, credit cards and your driver's license, are [sic] here. Nothing is missing."

I told the caller there was a twenty-dollar reward for the safe return of the stuff. He liked the idea of a reward. We made an appointment for him to deliver the next day at 6 PM.

Meanwhile, I went down to Centre Street (police headquarters) and told the two detectives on my case that I was sure that the next day at about 6 PM the perpetrator of the crime would be at my apartment. At that point, dear reader, the detectives asked the same question that I ask you: Doc, how do you know the robber will return?

What part of the conversation tips you off about the identity of the caller? How does content analysis prove that the caller was the robber?

Answer: The caller said that all the credit cards were in his possession; nothing was missing. How would he know that for sure, if he had simply found the wallet? The only way he would know that all the cards and the driver's license were intact would be if he himself were the criminal. Someone who had found the wallet could not reasonably know whether something was missing.

There is no other reasonable conclusion. Content analysis proves that the caller was connected closely to the crime. Content analysis proves that the caller was so closely connected to the crime that he himself was most likely to be the criminal. If that were true, then he himself would return to collect the reward.

I explained content analysis to the Dick Tracys.

Detective one scratched his head, leaned back in his swivel chair, took a long, deep drag on his Camel cigarette and announced, "Geezus, Doc, you're too logical. They never come back. It's just some kid that found the wallet."

After much discussion, both detectives promised to be at my apartment at 5:30 PM so that they could capture the criminal.

Yes, they promised. But those of you who have dealt with New York City detectives know what that promise was worth. My hopes were not high that the detectives would show. But I was pretty sure the guy who held me up would show. I armed myself with a big kitchen knife and waited.

At 6:12 PM the bell rang. I opened to find a kid about thirteen years old. The kid handed me a small packet of credit cards wrapped with a rubber band. "Where's the wallet?" I asked.

The kid shrugged his shoulders. "Search me. I'm just the messenger."

"The wallet was cowhide—worth about twenty bucks. I want it back."

"I don't know nothing, mister. Like I said, I'm just the messenger."

"You didn't find the wallet. Who did?"

The kid said nothing, but he did glance down the hall toward the elevator, where what to my wondering eyes should appear but the guy who held me up.

"Call the cops," I shouted to Ethel, my wife. And I chased the guy down the hall. The robber had put a wedge in the elevator door and was easily able to get in and close the door before I got there.

By the time I had run down twenty-three flights of stairs, the robber was dashing into the adjacent housing project. The cops arrived soon thereafter and commiserated, but they refused to pursue the guy into that housing project. "Too dangerous," they said.

Here is another example of the benefits of content analysis. Consider the following quotations from the State of the Union messages of presidents Harry S. Truman and Dwight D. Eisenhower. How does content analysis reveal differences in the management style and inner psychic state of each of these fine men?

Harry Truman: "I am happy to report to the 81st Congress, the one after that 80th Republican do-nothing Congress, that the State of the Union is good." The following year Truman said that the state of the union "continued to be good."

Dwight Eisenhower: "The State of the Union continues to vindicate the wisdom of the principles on which the Republic is founded."

Answer: Truman's statement is simple and direct. It is peppered with a slur against the previous Republican Congress that Truman feels did nothing. Indirectly, Truman is asking for action to improve the state of the union even though he has told us that the state of the union is "good." You may not agree with what Truman said, but at least you know where he stands.

Eisenhower's statement is abstract, so abstract that we have trouble determining from it whether the state of the union is good, bad, ugly, or none of the above. The use of words like *wisdom* and *vindicate* suggests that Eisenhower (or more likely his speechwriter) does not form clear, concrete thoughts and has difficulty communicating simply and directly. *Vindicate* also has a connotation that suggests the union had been accused of something or was on the defensive. Also, if clear thinking is a part of wisdom, then the statement, since it is not clear, implies its opposite. The Eisenhower statement suggests there is room in the state of the union for clear thinking and by extrapolation, more wisdom. It's hard to agree or disagree with what Eisenhower said because we don't know where he stands or what he means.

Every statement has overt and covert meanings. Learn to decode the overt and covert meanings to learn the truth and the reality underlying the puff, misrepresentation, lies, publicity, distortion, slant and spin, perversion, dishonesty, tricks, pretense, cheating, fraud, duplicity, and deceit so common in modern everyday life. Convert this knowledge to your advantage and, when possible, to the advantage of those around you. In the process, enjoy your newfound power brought to you by clear thinking.

REVIEW

Time spent in review is never wasted. Review cements the memory and augments understanding. D. O. Hebb, the great neurophysiologist, said, "Neurons that fire together, wire together."[8] So let's get to it. Let's do some firing and some wiring:

EXERCISES

1. Reread all the main points in this chapter. When you have done so, give yourself a check here ___.
2. Reread all the main points in this chapter aloud. When done, give yourself a check here ___. Rereading aloud fixes the memory better than silent rereading. Rereading on separate days fixes the memory better than rereading twice the same day. The more you reread, the more you will fix the memory. But don't overdo it. Four times should be quite enough. You don't want to acquire the reputation of being a harmless drudge.
3. Consider the following advertisement: "Put a tiger in your tank." Can you define the idea? What is the overt message? Is there a covert message? Give yourself two checks if you think you know. Give yourself one check if you don't know but did think about the question for more than a minute ___. Explain the message behind slice-of-life commercials, the products hurtling out of darkness, the coded items and the endless repetitions, like chants, like mantras. (Hint: The message is about something the advertisers want you to do so that they can get something you have. What do you have that they want? Another hint: What you have and what they want starts with an M and rhymes with *honey*.)
4. Explain why the media overflow with sacred formulas and stupid ideas. Explain how we can remember to respond innocently and get past our irritation, wariness and disgust. Give

yourself up to five checks in proportion to your understanding
_____.

5. Explain in your own words why words are important. Give yourself a check if your answer sounds intelligent ____. Explain why
little words can have big meanings. Give an example of a little
word that has a big impact.

Check your answers to the questions above by rereading the appropriate sections of the text. If you got most of them correct, stop here and
reward yourself in some way with a simple pleasure that will also serve
to fix the memories. Rewards for work well done help the brain function effectively. Then relax and have some fun as you coast through
chapter 3, which covers the common error in thinking called post hoc.

NOTES

1. Aristotle, *Politics* 3.15–16.
2. Anthony S. Fauci et al., eds., *Harrison's Principles of Internal Medicine*,
14th ed. (New York: McGraw-Hill Health Professions Divisions, 1998).
3. Ibid., p. 1874.
4. Leo Tolstoy, *Anna Karenina* (New York: New American Library, 1961), p.
323.
5. *Houston Chronicle*, July 1, 2002.
6. The quotation is from the *New York Times* report of the testimony before
Congress and is obtainable from the National Archives, http://www.archives
.gov/.
7. *New York Times*, April 8, 2002, p. C5.
8. Quoted in Eric R. Kandel, James H. Schwartz, and Thomas M. Jessell,
eds., *Principles of Neural Science*, 4th ed. (New York: McGraw-Hill Health Professions Division, 2000), p. 1260.

chapter 3

Post Hoc,
Ergo Propter Hoc

The aim of this chapter is to give you a much-deserved rest by covering a simpler and easier to understand common error in thinking known by its Latin title as *post hoc, ergo propter hoc,* called here henceforth *post hoc, propter hoc.*

Post hoc, propter hoc means "after this, on account of this." The Latin phrase exactly describes the error in thinking that assigns cause on the basis of association in time. Because one event follows another, the two events are not necessarily connected as cause and effect. To assume that they are leads us away from the understanding of reality and toward error and is therefore unreasonable, an error in thinking.

Post hoc, propter hoc is the first of many fallacies that we will encounter in our pursuit of truth. A **fallacy** is a mistaken idea or opinion, an error in reasoning or defect in argument, especially one that appears to be reasonable. For economy of expression, and because some people have trouble remembering the word *propter,* the post hoc, propter hoc error is often abbreviated as simply "post hoc."

A common error in thinking is the assumption that because one thing follows another the second thing must relate to the first as a consequence. That is, the first event caused the second. Whether the first event caused the second cannot be determined from mere association in time. The cause-and-effect association must, instead, be proven by other evidence.

The rooster crows and the sun rises. The crow of the rooster did not cause the sun to rise. Yet both events were associated in time. A primitive mind might assume the two were connected as cause and effect. A really primitive mind might assume that the rooster made the sun rise. How do we know that the rooster doesn't cause the sun to rise?

When I was a boy, we had a chicken coop in our backyard. Every day the rooster crowed and the sun rose. That happened every day until we killed the rooster. Despite the rooster's terminal absence, the sun continued to rise. Because event two, the sunrise, now occurred without event one, the rooster crow, we know for sure that the effect (the sunrise) does not need a rooster. Something else must be playing a role in the sunrise. The rooster was not necessary for the sun to rise.

When two conditions occur side by side, especially when they occur side by side repeatedly, it is tempting to conclude that the one explains the other. Don't believe it. There may, of course, be a necessary connection between the two things, but before the relation of cause and effect is established, it must be shown that if the effect did not follow the cause, some accepted general principle would be violated. An even more powerful proof would be to find the effect occurring independently of the supposed cause, as shown in the case of the rooster.

It turns out that the rooster crows not because the sun is about to rise but because in the morning, the rooster wants to mate. His desire to mate makes him call the hens to action. His crow only indirectly relates to the sun rising as a simultaneous but noncausal event. When the rooster is eliminated from the loop, the sun continues to rise as it always has and always will until 2.5 billion years from now, when scientists tell us that the sun will become a red giant and burn out the Earth.

George Bernard Shaw was a vegetarian. He was also a great playwright. Will abstaining from meat make you a great playwright?

No way!

The two things are independent and not codependent variables. Don't believe me? Try eating vegetables for a year. See if it makes any difference in your playwriting ability.

> *Principle:* Two things connected in time may not be connected as cause and effect.

From which follows:

> *Lesson:* Because one event followed another, or events are associated with each other in time, never assume that the two are causally connected.

It rains, and the streets get wet. Then it stops raining, and the streets get dry. And when the streets are dry, it rains again. Do dry streets cause it to rain? Do wet streets stop the rain? Primitive thinking might conclude that dry streets cause it to rain because, dang it, every time the streets are dry, sooner or later, it will rain.

Those two examples, the rooster and the dry streets, were selected because they show simply how two events can be linked in the mind but not associated as cause and effect. To connect them as cause and effect would lead us away from an understanding of more complex truth: how the Earth rotates or what changes in temperature and dew point produce rain, and so forth. Anything that dulls our understanding of the true nature of reality is an error in thinking and, to the extent that it is an error, may hurt us in some way.

When Ethel and I were coming back from Delos to the Greek island of Mykonos, our ship ran into a great storm. The Greek sea captain assured us that we would be OK. He knew he would arrive safe and sound because he had prayed to the Virgin Mary.

"How do we know for sure that she will help us?" I asked.

"Didn't you see all those little churches on Mykonos? Whenever there is a serious storm at sea, the captains promise the Virgin that they will build a church to her."

"But where are the churches built by the sea captains who prayed but didn't make it back alive?" I asked.

The captain could not answer. He understood that his reasoning was defective. The captain's reasoning was seriously defective. Why?

Because someone prayed and then survived doesn't mean that he survived because he prayed. The mere fact that one event follows another does not mean the two are connected as cause and effect. To assume that praying and safe arrival are related is to commit the error of post hoc, propter hoc. Furthermore, because those who prayed and did not survive wouldn't construct churches, only those who survived would construct churches. Therefore, there would be a partial selection of evidence so that the number of churches on Mykonos would multiply, proving that people had prayed and survived. But that would not prove that they had survived because they had prayed.

What we need to know is what would happen if we took a group of similarly endangered sea captains and had one half randomly selected to pray and the other half randomly selected not to pray. If the ones who prayed survived and the ones who did not pray did not survive, then we might be able to conclude that prayer worked.

Until such a study is done, we might be better off and much safer if we followed the standard procedures for safety at sea: Batten down the hatches. Head into the wind and quarter into the waves. Slow to the minimal speed to maintain steering way, put on life jackets, lower the life boats, call for assistance, and so forth. These reality-based techniques, which have been proven effective by numerous studies, are more likely to foster survival than prayer.

Candidates for a sea captain's license or a master's certificate would flunk the required Coast Guard examination if, when asked about what should be done during an emergency at sea, they said, "Pray to the Virgin Mary."

Religious mania is frequently associated with post hoc errors.

The ancient Mayans believed that their great god Chaac controlled the rain. The Mayans recognized how dependent on rain the corn crop was. Repeated observations showed when there was little rain, there was little corn. When there was no rain, there was no corn.

What's the solution? How can we get rain when it doesn't rain? That's the question.

The real solution was to pump water from underground. That solution was beyond Mayan capabilities at the time. They were too busy thinking about something else, a fake solution that didn't work. The Mayan fake solution was called human sacrifice. Eventually, they did stumble on a solution that worked for them. The real solution was to move elsewhere, where it does rain. That is what the Mayans did to finally solve the rain problem. But until they arrived at that solution, the priests experimented with human sacrifice. Whenever a drought took hold, volunteers were drowned in the cenotes at Uxmal and Chichén Itzá and elsewhere throughout the Mayan kingdom. Besides humans, many valuable objects were thrown into the cenote. The idea was to appease Chaac and to get Chaac to have his maidens, those of the heavens, pour water down on those beneath using their special water jars.

We know this was the motivation behind the sacrifices because the hieroglyphics written in stone left by the priests as well as the sacred Mayan books tell us it was. The evidence recovered from the cenotes, including human skeletons adorned with gems, confirms the sacrifices.

So what happened?

After some sacrifices, it rained. Conclusion: Sacrifice worked. Action indicated: When it doesn't rain, kill people.

All this sounds pretty stupid. But the point is that it happened. A whole civilization went haywire because it assumed that when one event follows another, the two must be related as cause and effect. There was no rain, so they threw people into the cenote. Eventually, it rained. Therefore, the Mayans induced the general principle: For drought, kill people.

Once the erroneous general principle had been accepted, there was no stopping the Mayan theocracy from finding lots of other reasons to sacrifice people for lots of other gods and goddesses and any special purpose that they could think of. In fact, a reasonable theory of the destruction of Mayan civilization is based on the decimation of the population by the need for sacrificial victims. We know that toward the end of the Mayan classical period, wars were organized mainly to obtain humans for sacrifice. Think about all those young men and women killed for post hoc, propter hoc. Think about them and weep.

In 1692, the Salem witch trials were judicial proceedings and therefore were recorded verbatim. Read those over if you have a chance. See how many errors of post hoc, propter hoc you can find.

Because a farmer's cart lost a wheel three miles down the road after passing the home of some eccentric old woman, the court assumed the woman was a witch. The court assumed that she had somehow made the cart lose its wheel. Since she was three miles away when she did this, she had to have used witching powers to remove the wheel. If she used witching powers, she must be a witch. Therefore, the court sentenced her to death. She and eighteen other "witches" were hanged.

The story is fascinating. It all started in May 1692 with accusations by a few young girls (who believed they were possessed by the devil) against the older women in the community. Special court was convened; trials quickly grew into mass hysteria implicating even Governor William Phip's wife. Fortunately, Increase Mather and his son Cotton were influential in ending the witchcraft trials at Salem in 1692. Both men believed in witches, but they were convinced that the trial evidence was unreliable. Both men disliked the post hoc, propter hoc evidence, especially when it assumed the form of a specter, an imaginary being resembling the accused. Under the conditions of these trials, the accused was responsible not only for events that happened beyond her control (like the loss of the cart wheel) but also for acts committed by her specter, over which she had no control whatsoever. Modern psychiatry now recognizes the specter as a hallucination of the witness, which, incidentally, it was.

Public opinion first stopped then condemned the trials. The legislature adopted a resolution for repentance (December 17, 1696), including a fast day on which one of the three judges, Samuel Sewell, admitted his mistakes, mistakes mainly in appraisal of evidence. The jailed women were released. Reparations were paid to them and their families. The correction of the errors came too late for the "witches" who were hanged. They were beyond compensation. They were beyond the beyond. They were dead.

If you can't read the original proceeding of the Salem witch trials, take a look at Arthur Miller's play *The Crucible*, which is based on the transcript of the trials. Take a look and weep. Weep for all the innocent people sacrificed to the post hoc, propter hoc error in thinking.

Doctors and politicians sometimes benefit from and are sometimes excoriated by post hoc errors in thinking.

Doctors as well as politicians find the fallacy of post hoc, propter hoc flattering to their reputations. Doctors make a diagnosis, prescribe a course of treatment, and the patient's symptoms disappear. The mere fact that some medicine was taken and a cure ensued proves nothing except that one thing followed the other. The medicine might easily have been utterly useless and the recovery due to natural forces. Most illnesses recover by themselves. If they did not, the human race wouldn't be here. History teaches us that in many cases not only were highly regarded medical treatments ineffective, but also they were downright harmful. Mercury and arsenic salts, for instance, not only did not work, they also poisoned the person who took them. Abraham Lincoln thought the little blue pills he took were making him sicker, so he stopped them. They were mercury salts. We now know that they were poisonous and of no therapeutic value for Lincoln's depression. In fact, they made Lincoln feel lousy. Lucky he stopped them. Otherwise we might have had a presidential suicide.

George Washington died of quinsy (abscess of the throat). His demise was probably helped along by the repeated bleedings he received as a treatment. Bleeding was considered excellent medical care in those days. The doctors who did it were considered orthodox mainstream healers. Those who did not do bleeding were considered marginal at best. Now we know that a severe throat infection like quinsy not only would not be helped by bleeding but also would be made worse.

Bleeding might have actually hurt Washington's resistance to the bacterium that causes the disease. At the present time, the medical profession looks down on bleeding as a treatment for infection. Which would you rather have for your sore throat—blood letting or antibiotics?

There was a time when the British Medical Society opposed vaccination for smallpox. The medical establishment was wrong on that issue, too. And not too long ago, Ignaz Semmelweis, a Hungarian physician, lost his hospital privileges by suggesting that it was the doctors who were responsible for puerperal sepsis (childbed fever) because they didn't wash their hands! The medical establishment was wrong on the hand-washing issue, too.

The lesson is clear: Watch out for medical claims. Unless supported by reams and reams of data, such claims might be bogus. Even the so-called standard of care, accepted treatments, operations, and procedures might be questionable and possibly harmful.

Of course, post hoc, propter hoc works both ways. The fallacy could increase the doctor's reputation by ascribing cures to him that he did not effectuate. On the other hand, the fallacy could offend the doctor's reputation by ascribing misadventures to him that he had no part in doing.

Recently, doctors have had a terrible time with the post hoc fallacy in malpractice suits. A doctor gives a medicine, and the patient dies. Doesn't that raise the presumption that the medicine caused the death?

Of course not.

It might seem to raise that presumption in the popular mind. But it raises no such presumption to those of us who know how to think correctly. Unfortunately, it does raise that presumption in the minds of some (unscrupulous) plaintiff attorneys. That should not surprise us. Attorneys as a group are people who like to twist the truth and make things seem real that are not. They are advocates. Bending the truth is part of their business.

Just as a treatment can't be assumed to have helped a person recover who recovered, so also a treatment can't be assumed to have hurt a person who did not recover. Whether the treatment helped or harmed must be established by other evidence than the mere fact that one event followed another.

And don't forget, there was a reason the patient got the medicine. That reason may have had more to do with the poor outcome than the treatment.

All people treated for cancer die. Most people treated for cancer die of their cancer. It's a pity, but it's a fact: The cause of the death in patients who have cancer is most often the cancer, not the treatment. Most so-called medical misadventures or medical malpractice were merely events preceding a problem. Disease, old age, accident, bad luck, and misfortune provide a more convincing explanation of the death of a patient than do more remote contingencies of willful misconduct of medical personnel.

By the same token, a politician who wishes to gain the credit for some measure his party has inaugurated must show that the improvements that he maintains have followed its introduction would not have taken place anyway. About receiving credit and taking blame politicians can be duplicitous. They always seem to claim the credit and pass the blame. So if a period of prosperity occurs during their administration, they say they caused it. On the other hand, they are often very ready to point out that economic depressions that occur during their tenure are due to the adverse balance of world trade, supply side economics, high interest rates set by the Federal Reserve Board, fuel cost gouging by the Saudis—any scapegoat they can think of—anything else they can reasonably claim to have had no connection whatever with their own policy or administration.

History is full of post hoc errors.

Historians fall into the same error. The prosperity of America in the twentieth century is frequently ascribed to free trade or the firm establishment of capitalism (not specifically defined). Prosperity did follow free trade and did certainly seem to follow capitalism. Prosperity did certainly not follow capitalism's opposite, communism. But in a larger sense, the connection remains unproved. We already know that there are no simple answers to complex questions. So we already know that it would be highly unlikely that the prosperity of the whole nation would or could depend on just one or two things.

More likely, multiple complex factors played a role, including the productivity of immigrant people who came here with the drive to succeed, the railroads and excellent roads, the great navy and army that, by victories in the great wars, made the imperial market for American goods, the remarkable inventiveness of the American inventors, and so forth.

My point is that the fallacy of post hoc, propter hoc often coincides with the mistake of historians who overgeneralize from selected instances of public policy or a small number of selected items or events that present only a partial picture of what really happened. Capitalism may have been the cause, or one of the causes, of prosperity, but this is not proved by showing that prosperity followed capitalism. That one followed the other could have been mere coincidence.

Unless we have other evidence to demonstrate the necessary connection existing between capitalism and prosperity, we are bound *not* to believe the connection causal.

A man walks under a ladder. Two years later he dies. Does this prove that walking under the ladder is unlucky? Provided we ignore the fact that he died by crashing his boat while drunk. Provided we forget that he had walked under a ladder numerous times before without dying. And provided we never consider the extraordinary improbability of the alleged cause of death (how could the ladder have anything to do with a boat crash?), it is possible to believe such nonsense.

All superstitions are nonsense.

Yes, that's a platitude: Superstitions by definition are unfounded and are, therefore, all nonsense. They are stupid, too. Because they are stupid, we have a right to call them stupidstitions. But why are they bad?

Superstitions are bad because they work to divert our minds from reality. They waste our time considering something fake when we should be concerned with what is real. Refusing to walk under a ladder probably had its origin in the perceived danger that objects might fall on your head while you were there under the ladder. That is a real danger, but that's not what we are talking about here. Here we are talking about the superstition that walking under a ladder has some kind of remote effect on your life and luck. That a ladder could exert an adverse remote effect on you or your destiny is complete and utter bunk.

Fear of Friday the thirteenth makes no sense either. Nor does carrying a rabbit's foot for luck. No doubt some people carrying a rabbit's foot will get lucky. But it won't have anything to do with the foot. Tying tin cans to the car of newlyweds probably originated in the notion that noise would frighten away evil spirits. The same may be said of New Year's fireworks and noisemakers. Avoidance of black cats has a religious origin. During the Middle Ages, it was believed that witches could turn themselves into black cats. Thus, when such a cat was seen, it was considered to be a witch in disguise.

Principle: Superstitions are bunk.

From which follows:

Lesson: Superstitions? Forget them. They are a waste of time.

Closely related to superstition is the belief in miracles. Belief in miracles is common enough and is sometimes based on the post hoc, propter hoc fallacy. A miracle can be (merely) something considered good or remarkable that accidentally happened at the right time, in the right place, to the right person.

Some miracles sound plausible enough until examined under the cold light of reason. Usually, a simple natural phenomenon will explain the so-called miracle.

I remember reading Saint Teresa's autobiography wherein she was ascending the staircase with a lighted candle in her hand. A cold blast of air, a cat's paw, came along and blew the candle out. But within seconds the candle relit again. Saint Teresa knew that the dimming of the light was the work of the devil, who she felt was trying to prevent her from reaching her room to pray. The devil blew out the candle. But by a miracle, Jesus restarted the flame.

More likely the devil had nothing to do the candle's apparent extinction; nor did Jesus light it up again. The wind just seemed to blow out the candle. The candle just seemed to come on again. The same has happened to me many times without the special intervention of the devil or of Jesus. Perhaps the same thing has happened to you.

By the way, where does a flame go when it goes out?

Alice wonders about that in her adventure in wonderland. Where, exactly, does it go? Do we know? The pre-Socratics enjoyed that problem. But as far as I know they did not come up with a satisfactory answer. To say that the flame goes nowhere seems to beg the question but actually doesn't. The flame that goes out doesn't go anywhere. Our thoughts on the matter are simply being preconditioned (channeled) in the wrong direction by the words of the metaphor that describe the extinction of the flame. Some language, as the case here, comes to us with implied commitments, commitments so deeply ingrained that it is easy to overlook them or be fooled by them. Overlooking implied elements in language may lead to a simple-minded or (as in this case) a wrong view of nature. The problem of the flame is one of those pseudo-problems that arise, as Ludwig Wittgenstein observed, when language goes on holiday. If we had just said, "the flame became extinct" or "ceases" or "ceased," there would be no further discussion or conclusion, for put this way, the question doesn't get off the ground. So when you are asked next, "Where does a flame go when it goes out?" reply that the flame goes nowhere. It joins the null set, the class of non-existing things that includes secular churches, square circles, four-sided triangles, and whales that fly.

The real test for the flame problem and the other problems of that ilk is to ask whether the disagreement would be resolved by changing the terminology. For instance, no one could reasonably oppose the above resolution of the flame pseudoproblem by objecting that expressions like "the flame ceased" leave out relevant facts captured by "the flame went out." With the case of the flame, there is no substantive fact under dispute, as became clear when the linguistic confusion was pointed out. On the other hand, a problem that cannot be resolved by changing its language or the angle in which it is viewed is not a purely semantic difficulty and must be resolved by examination of relevant and adequate evidence.

Because a person goes to some shrine and leaves his crutches there does not mean that a miracle has taken place. As a physician, I have cured many patients with placebos. I have actually gotten them out of a wheelchair after years of so-called paralysis. The problem was in the secret workings of the human unconscious mind and the will to remain disabled. Once that will is broken by a belief in the placebo, or the faith in the physician or the Virgin Mary or Saint Anne or whomever, the disability disappears.

Such patients have real illnesses. But their illnesses are psychological in origin, not physical. Their illnesses are conversion reactions in which unwanted psychic material is converted to a physical symptom. Many conversion reactions are cured by strong suggestion. Nothing supernatural is involved. To assume that something supernatural is involved leads us away from the truth. Anything that leads us away from truth and toward error is an error in thinking.

> *Principle:* Although some miracles are based on post hoc errors, other miracles are based on other forms of defective reasoning or misperceptions.

A great many miraculous claims have nothing to do with the post hoc fallacy, owing instead to a rich variety of other causes, such as the misinterpretation of photographic effects, the misunderstanding of natural phenomena, the imaginative identification of religious imagery in random patterns in nature, "mass hallucination" or delusion (as discussed in the chapter on groupthink that follows), outright fraud, hoaxes, confabulation of memory, and so on.

Principle: Miracles are bunk.

From which follows:

Lesson: Miracles? Forget them. The belief in them is a waste of time.

OK. Now that we know about post hoc, propter hoc, let's work out on the following. Let's test our powers. Examine the statement from the United States Coast Guard collision regulations (also known as 72 Colregs): "If a collision has occurred, there must have been a risk of collision. Since there was a risk of collision, the parties involved were required to take appropriate action to avoid the risk. Since they did not take sufficient appropriate action, they are responsible for the collision."

Question: Are the collision regulations reasonable? Why or why not? Pause and think about this. Write down your answer so that you can have something definite to compare with the sample answer I give below. Cast your answer into two parts. In the first part, state whether the Colreg is reasonable or not. In the second part, explain how or why you arrived at your conclusion. Your explanation may differ from mine. Consider it correct as long as it makes sense.

Answer: Part 1—The regulation is unreasonable.

Answer: Part 2—The regulation is unreasonable because (among other errors) it is based on the post hoc, propter hoc fallacy.

Give yourself checks if you got the answers right. Give yourself two checks each if you had a good reason for your answers.

Discussion: In dissecting statements like this, stand back and take an overall view of what the net effect of the language is. Sometimes words, especially highfalutin words expressed by a governmental authority, tend to intimidate us into not thinking. Under such conditions, it is best to step back and analyze the effect. The net effect of this Colreg is to claim that for every collision, there is a cause, and for every collision that cause is an error in judgment. Essentially the Colreg asserts that every collision is due to failure to take appropriate action. This is the medical malpractice fallacy in disguise as a government regulation. It is as if the government asserts that if a patient dies after surgery, the doctor must be at fault because he did not take appropriate action to prevent the death. The government can decree that, but it cannot make it so. Even governments are bound by reality, which is revealed by the operation of the laws of logic, reason, and clear thinking.

There are as many reasons to die after operation as there are people who do so. Infection, old age, and disease cause more postoperative deaths than all the physicians in the world put together. Some postoperative deaths are mere accidents. Others are due, we now know, to psychopathic nurses putting potassium in the intravenous fluids and so forth. One-size statements just can't, just don't, fit all. They never will. The world is not that way. The world is not that simple.

Two things linked in time (surgery and death, risk of collision and collision, or errors in judgment and collision) do not imply cause and effect. To claim that they do is an error in thinking. Some people have trouble seeing this clearly. If you do, then consider other approaches to the problem.

If A (accident) happened, then cause of A was E (error in judgment). That can't be true, for if it were, then every accident would imply an error in judgment ($A \supset E$ and $E \supset A$). But we know there are many Es without As and probably some As without Es. Therefore, since accidents happen without errors in judgment and errors in judgment happen without accidents, the two (accidents and errors in judgment) can't strictly relate to each other as cause and effect. They certainly can't be cause and effect at all times under all conditions.

How about this. Ask yourself: Are these regulations simplistic? If they are, shoot them down. Simplistic thinking has no place in a complex situation. Remember simple things in a complex world are likely to be wrong. The regulation is simple because it assumes all collisions have to be due to the human error of failing to take appropriate action. That is impossible. Some collisions might be due to human error. Even most collisions might be due to human error. But all? No way.

How do we prove statements that have the word *all* in them are wrong? Find the exception.

All we have to do is find one exception, and the generalization is proved wrong. Can you think of an instance where a collision could occur without there being an error in human judgment or a failure to take appropriate action?

When the last hurricane rolled through Clear Lake, hundreds of boats collided and sank. Most of those boats were not under control. Most of those boats had been avulsed (torn off) their moorings and were under way, not making way. In other words, the boats were not under command and were drifting about tossed by storm and sea. Most of the owners, operators, and pilots of those boats were not around. They had been ordered out of the area by the Coast Guard in a general evacuation. Even if the owners were around, even if they had violated the orders of the Coast Guard, it would have been unlikely that anything substantive could have been done against the enormous forces of nature engendered by the hurricane. More than anything else, it was those natural forces that caused the multiple collisions.

Whose judgment therefore was defective in causing the hurricane-induced collisions? Realistically, probably no one's.

Therefore, the generalization implied by the regulation that all collisions must have involved risk of collision for which inadequate measures were taken is proven wrong. In other words, the Colreg is an overgeneralization, a simplistic overgeneralization of a complex situation. We have proven that it is an overgeneralization by showing one exception. In fact, there are many other exceptions because life is a lot more complicated than people imagine. Just as there are as many causes for postoperative death as there are people who die postoperatively, there are as many causes of collisions as there are collisions.

Here's the key point: It is important to study each and every collision to try to understand the causes of that event. That way real progress can be made in preventing mishaps in the future. Maybe better lighting or compulsory use of radar, fog horns, and such is the solution. To assume that an error in judgment is the sole cause of collisions blinds us from seeing the true complexity of the problem and prevents us from dealing effectively with the reality situation so that we can arrive at a successful solution that might actually work to prevent a similar collision in the future.

Another way to approach a statement like the Colreg is to take it apart and examine the individual pieces. If one part of the chain of reasoning can be shown to be defective, then the whole **sorites**, the concatenation of premises and reasons, that led to the conclusion will have been proven fallacious.

Item: If a collision has occurred, there must have been a risk of collision.

Complete baloney.

This is the classical error of post hoc, propter hoc presented in its native, unadorned, naked self. It is an overgeneralization and hence wrong. It is simplistic. It is a mere assertion and as such would require load on load of data to substantiate itself. Furthermore, the statement is a tautology, an error in thinking because it merely restates an assertion rather than proving it. Morphine induces sleep because of its somniferous properties. That statement is a tautology because the word *somniferous* means sleep inducing. What is being said is that morphine produces sleep because it produces sleep. The statement leads nowhere. It certainly doesn't enlighten us about why morphine works.

If a collision occurred, there must have been a risk of collision is a tautology because it is saying the same thing twice. Any occurrence of anything implies that it can occur because it did occur. So saying a collision was associated with a risk of collision isn't saying much. In fact, it is a circular argument. A similar and equally intelligent statement would be that in boating accidents where there is a fatality, someone dies. The Cheshire Cat told Alice that everyone around there was crazy. "But I'm here," said Alice. "And I'm not crazy." Replied the cat, "You must be, because you're here" (pp. 72–73). The Cheshire Cat has made an unsubstantiated statement and then made a conclusion based on that assertion. Then he used a circular form of reasoning to restate the assertion. The Coast Guard regulations are just as circular as the arguments of the Cheshire Cat but with an important difference: The cat is just an amusing fiction. The Coast Guard regulations have the force of law.

If the Colregs are reasonable, I could, in the same way, say that if a collision occurred, a boat must have been involved. Lighthouses don't collide with each other, but boats collide with each other or with something else. That's what these regulations are about, aren't they: collisions at sea. So why not pass from the silly to the absurd? Why not claim that since all collisions involve boats, the boat must be at fault, for if there were no boats, there would be no collisions. From which follows that the solution to all collisions is to prevent boats from entering the water. No boating, no collision.

Get it?

Conclusion: Since the first premise of the Colreg statement is wrong, the entire statement is **unsound**, that is, defective.

In like manner, we could take each of the other statements of the Colreg apart. But we won't. Instead, I want to move on to another important error in thinking, something that you will see every day and night (if your eyes and mind are open)—the subject of the next chapter, false analogy.

EXERCISES

1. By now you know the drill: Reread all the main points in this chapter aloud. When you have done so, give yourself a check here ___.
2. Explain why post hoc, propter hoc is an error in thinking. Check your answer by reading the definition on page 129. Give yourself a check if you got it right. If you did not get it right, forget it. Pass on to the next chapter. Cudgel your brains no more about it. When you are asked this question next say, "I know it is wrong to say a thing caused a something else because the two things are linked together in time. Patten told me so in his little book of practical clear thinking."

Now give yourself a rest somewhere nice before you go on to the next chapter, which discusses the error known as false analogy.

chapter 4

False Analogy

This chapter covers a common error in thinking known as false analogy. Analogy forms much of our thinking because once two items are linked in the human consciousness, each tends to recall the other. Because this is the basic psychological mechanism of human thought, we are sometimes led astray by it. This is because the associations the brain makes are not necessarily reasonable or related to the reality situation. Because our brains naturally connect two things together, we tend to assume that the items resemble each other in certain ways, and we may erroneously conclude that further similarities exist when they don't.

Comparison of one item with another by analogy should never be used as the sole support of a theory or judgment. It can be used to illustrate a fact already established, or it can help establish a train of thought or working hypothesis. It can do no more than this and should be forced no further.

False analogies are errors in thinking because they lead away from the truth and toward error.

Arguments by analogy are often easy to spot but hard to contradict unless you think about them. We have already gone over the reasons that the domino theory had to be wrong. But now we know why it was wrong: It was a false analogy. It compared countries to metastable dominos ready to topple over and was wrong because countries are not dominos, are not lined up on end, don't tip over if one of them tips, don't fall anyplace because they have no place to fall, and so forth. Even dominos don't behave like dominos unless they are properly spaced less than an inch apart and then given the proper push by the kid playing with them. Another way to expose the domino theory as a false analogy is to follow it to where it leads, assume the theory correct, and then question whether the result is really all that bad.

I know from my thirty years of gardening that one plant that flourishes in one soil may wilt in another. My lettuce grows great in spring and wilts in summer. My corn won't grow well in spring but grows great in summer. Is it possible that forms of government can't be easily transplanted?

Get it? What's my analogy?

I am comparing plants to countries. Is that reasonable? If not, then how about more direct reasoning. How about this. Our form of economic organization might not be ideal for Vietnam. What's good for us might be bad for them. Could the export of our capitalism to Vietnam occur without risk? Measures agreeable in one set of circumstances may only be aggravating in another. Besides, who are we to decide what form of government the people of another nation need? Aren't those other people in a better position to decide about where their future happiness might lie? Doesn't our Declaration of Independence explain the necessity for a people to control their own destiny through their own government? Isn't it hypocritical for us to claim the principle of self-government for ourselves but to deny it for others?

See what I mean?

A little thinking and a whole political theory that contributed to the United States's involvement in Vietnam is easily exposed and refuted. Correct clear thinking could have and should have kept us out of Vietnam. Clear thinking should have and could have kept our boys and girls safe at home—and alive.

Implied in the domino theory is that a particular action is just one, usually the first, in a series of steps that will lead inevitably to some specific, usually undesirable, consequence. President Johnson claimed that if Vietnam became communist, Cambodia would follow. Then Laos would fall, then all of southeast Asia, and then India. And then (I'm not making this up, for I have a tape recording of one of his speeches) the world would become communist.

President Johnson's application of the domino theory to American politics had disastrous consequences. His error included not only the false analogy (countries are not dominos) but also the assumption, without evidence, that every element in the chain of predicted events would occur.

For each event in any series of events, an independent argument (supported by relevant and adequate evidence) must be presented. In no case should one assume that one event will automatically lead to or cause another event or series of events without making a separate inquiry into the causal factors that might be involved in each.

Cambodia is a different country from Vietnam. People do things differently there. Since Cambodia is a different country, why would it be safe to assume that it would follow Vietnam into communism?

As stated, it turned out that after Vietnam won the war, even Vietnam didn't go communist. Not entirely. The Vietnamese preferred a mixed economy, as do most of the countries of the world. Vietnam is now a trading partner of the United States. Subsequent to United States involvement in Vietnam, the Vietnamese fought other wars to keep out foreigners including the Chinese communists.

How about this contemporary example? "If we permit gay and lesbian marriages, next there will be some who want group marriages, and soon no one will even bother to get married." Recognize the domino theory applied to homosexual marriage? Note that neither the causal connection between gay marriages and group marriages nor between group marriage and the demise of regular marriage was proven. Sufficient evidence is not provided to support these claims. Therefore, the conclusion is not supported and does not follow. In fact, just the opposite could be argued—gay and lesbian marriages would promote, not stifle, regular marriage. In the absence of evidence one way or the other, we just don't know.

"Once you start smoking cigarettes, you'll smoke weed. Once you smoke weed, you'll start using cocaine and all the hard stuff. After that, it's all downhill either to jail or to the cemetery." Recognize the domino theory as applied to tobacco cigarettes?

How about this? "History proves that people whose name has six letters and ends in *er* are evil aggressors. Kruger (staunch defender of the Transvaal), Hitler, and Kaiser, for example. Let's stop the next aggressor before he gets started." Intuitively, we know that can't be right. Six letters to a name and ending in *er* can't have anything to do with aggression. But the facts are there.

What about the facts?

The people listed were military leaders. But that had nothing to do with their names. The situation, their rise to power, and the social and economic forces that led to their aggressive leadership were much more important than their names. In fact, their names had little or nothing to do with what they did. The names were arbitrary appellations. "What's in a name? That which we call a rose by any other name would smell as sweet" (Shakespeare's *Romeo and Juliet* 2.2.1–2).

The fact that these men, who were political leaders in war time, all shared names that had six letters and that their names ended in *er* was a mere coincidence. Expressed as an argument, the analogy says that because aggression is associated with the property name of six letters that ends in *er*, the next guy with a six-letter name ending in *er* must have the same aggressive tendencies.

Using symbols, this would go something like, if X has a and b, and Y has a and b, then Y must also have property c that belongs to X. That's not true, of course. Whether Y has c depends on the situation, facts, evidence, and reasons, not on the mere extension of the (possibly false) analogy.

Even more sophisticated historical analogies often break down because history doesn't repeat itself. Never exactly. Turn to the past as a possible guide and to discover lessons about human nature, which doesn't change much. But don't apply the past situation to the present. Chances are the differences between the past event and the present far exceed the similarities. Indeed, history is filled with misapplications of lessons learned from history.

World War I was not World War II.

Because the trenches were so effective in blocking German advances in World War I, this didn't mean that the Maginot Line would work as well in World War II. There were many deceptive similarities between 1914, when World War I started, and 1940, when World War II began: The fighting started in the low countries; the Germans were fighting France and England again; the economic problems were the same. Yet the situation had changed. In World War II, the Germans had invented a new form of warfare. They called that new form of warfare *Blitzkrieg*, which made all the difference. Any French argument that failed to take into consideration this new form of warfare suffered from the disastrous defect of pushing a historical analogy too far into a wrong conclusion. Because French thinking was not based in correct reasoning, the French suffered and suffered greatly.

The official name for the French error in thinking is the fallacy of the continuum. The French based their actions on the false idea that the situation in World War I had not significantly changed in World War II. That is, they thought that there was a continuum from one period of time to the other. Thus, they made an analogy comparing the one time with the other, assuming that the two times were the same or similar. Actually, the analogy did not hold. Times had changed, and so had the situation. Those who were not prepared to change would function at a disadvantage and suffer. And they did.

Recently, I got an e-mail from Norma Rubin, professor of anatomy and neurosciences at the University of Texas Medical Branch, in which she said, among other things, that the Jews were entitled to the lands that are now the state of Israel because the Jews held the ancient kingdom of Solomon in 1020 BCE.

Norma failed to mention that Solomon had many foreign wives whom he allowed to set up altars to the gods they worshipped. To maintain his luxurious court, Solomon taxed his subjects heavily. And as his character weakened, so did his hold on the people and the lands. Under his son Rehoboam, who succeeded him, Solomon's empire was lost, his kingdom divided.

But facts of history aside, the idea that the Jews own Israel because Solomon controlled it in 1020 BCE is simply wrong because it presupposes that because something existed in the past, it should continue to exist in the present. It ignores the fact that times have changed. Things are different now. Israel today is not the same country that it was under Solomon. Therefore, any analogy that assumes it is the same is false.

Furthermore, such arguments can be shown absurd because if they were true, then Israel belongs to Italy, since the Romans ruled Palestine as a province. Or the American Indians own America because they were here first.

In standard form, Norma's argument, the fallacy of the continuum, might look like this:

Since X was X,
X should still be X.

Pretty circular, right? It's also an argument that negates and prevents progress. And don't forget after three thousand years, X is never the same. After three thousand years have elapsed, X is always different. After three thousand years, X is always X plus three thousand years times $\Delta X \Delta T$ (the change in X with the change in T, time).

The ancient name of this fallacy is the *fallacy of the beard*. Such a name originated in the ancient debate about "How many hairs would one have to have in order to have a beard?"

We are reluctant, because it appears arbitrary, to state an exact number of hairs needed to make a beard. Obviously, there is a difference between having a beard and not having a beard. Some cutoff point has to be established. Or does it? Why not admit that this is a fuzzy set, a concept that might depend on relative relationships and not on absolute numbers? Lots of concepts that we deal with are fuzzy like this. When is a person tall or short? Fat or thin? We all have a general idea of what is meant by such terms. But why not confess that some people might not be exactly tall or short; they could be neither.

The same pertains to grades. The difference between a sixty-four and a sixty-five is one point. So, in a sense, there is little difference between a student who has an average of sixty-four in algebra and a student who has a sixty-five. But for practical purposes, there has to be a cutoff point between those who pass and those who don't. The scale of grades is a continuum, but the breaking point between pass and fail is not. Basically, sixty-four is not the same as sixty-five. Because it is not the same, the analogy breaks down and the kid with the sixty-four fails and the kid with the sixty-five doesn't.

Actually, most teachers know that this is a fuzzy set. Teachers will not fail a student who has an average of sixty-four. Usually, they will raise that student's average to a passing grade and will not apply the fail grade to anyone with an average of sixty or better.

The same applies to credit card debt. A salesman may persuade the customer to buy a new TV because it will add only fifty more dollars to the customer's current monthly payment of $215. That sounds innocent enough. The salesman's argument is that small changes in payments have a negligible effect. Such reasoning, if it leads one to a purchase, need occur only a few times before the customer will be in financial difficulty with the credit card limit. There also will be a point (the cutoff in the continuum) when the customer's required monthly payment exceeds the available money and credit, and the customer will have no more money and no more credit and consequently cannot pay.

The classic false argument based on the fallacy of the continuum is that it is impossible to walk from here to there because one would first walk half the distance, then walk half of the remaining distance, then half the remaining, and so forth, never reaching the destination. Such false arguments are easily refutable by getting up and walking there. The physical act of transit is strong evidence contradicting the false argument.

"Did you hear the news that's going round? Pat O'Grady is running for the Senate. I knew that dodo in sixth grade. No way am I going to vote for him."

If O'Grady is running for Senate, he is now an adult over age thirty-five. To assume that O'Grady is the same person he was in the sixth grade is to make the error of continuum. It is making a false analogy that O'Grady today is the same person that O'Grady was in the sixth grade. As kids grow up, they change, often maturing and acquiring wisdom and knowledge. O'Grady could have changed, too. He might be much better. Or he might be much worse than he was in the sixth grade. A more reasonable way to decide about voting for O'Grady would be to evaluate O'Grady's present status and study his positions on the issues and his qualifications for office.

Many continuum false arguments relate to diet or withdrawal from drugs, alcohol, or tobacco. What person who is on a diet or who is trying to cut down on smoking has not been deceived by the argument that one little doughnut or one more cigarette surely can't make any real difference?

The less the better and the more the better are both bad continuum arguments.

If too much cholesterol is bad for you, it does not mean that no cholesterol is good for you. Cholesterol is a natural body chemical needed in the construction of cell walls and many essential hormones. Too much cholesterol is bad, but too little is bad, too. What is needed is just the right amount.

Vitamin A is good for you, and without it you will get sick. But too much vitamin A is toxic. Way too much vitamin A is fatal. Too little vitamin A is bad, but too much is bad, too. What is needed is just the right amount. Some salt or pepper might improve the taste of a food, but too much or too little might not.

Closely related to less-the-better and more-the-better fallacies is the *tyranny of numbers and size.*

Big numbers may not lead to the truth and can lead to big errors.

Large numbers tend to impress people more than small numbers do. Add this to the fact that most Americans don't understand statistics, percentages, and fractions; it is usually more persuasive to quote the large number rather than the percentage. Such large numbers might obscure the truth and mislead the naive. For example, in the 2000 presidential election, the winner, George W. Bush, got fewer votes than did the loser, Al Gore, because of the operation of the electoral college and the US Supreme Court. Therefore, the winner's total votes are often quoted (in the millions) to obscure the fact that more than half the voters voted against the winner. Conversely, just as large numbers may be unreasonably impressive, so small numbers tend to be overlooked. For example, in discussing international politics, Saddam Hussein pointed out that America has only two parties, whereas Iraq has one. He implied that this was an insignificant difference because it was a difference of only one.

Big people are not necessarily right. A tall person is not necessarily right and a short person is not necessarily wrong. Yet size makes a difference in how we view people. This is unreasonable. J. Edgar Hoover stood on a raised platform, kings sit on thrones, judges sit on a bench—all to exploit the unreasonable assumption that height makes right. For the same reason, you can't buy a small egg. The smallest eggs that are sold in American stores are called medium.

Many government programs are sold to the public by false analogy.

Still not convinced about false analogies? Consider some analogies that are truly absurd:

"This 72-billion-dollar farm subsidy program generates food. Food is like money. You can't have too much of it," said a legislator from a farm state. My apologies. I am sorry I don't know this legislator's name, but that is what he said on NPR one afternoon as I walked into the kitchen.

Whether the $72 billion farm program generates food should be proven, not just asserted. Since the program actually pays farmers not to grow food, it is hard to imagine how the program would create food. Mere assertions are errors because they tend to lead us away from the truth and toward falsehood.

What about the analogy? Is food really like money?

You can eat food, but only psychotics eat money. Food spoils. Money does not spoil. And why can't you have too much food? Wasn't the farm program created to stabilize the production of food so that there wouldn't be too much food around to lower prices paid to farmers? You can certainly eat too much food, and if you do eat too much, you get fat.

Politicians say the dumbest things. This statement is just another example of how dumb some politicians can sound.

Scientists can and do say dumb things, too, many of which are predicated on false analogies. Consider this from Desmond Morris, the famous zoologist who wrote *The Naked Ape* and *The Human Zoo*: "Behind the façade of modern city life there is the same old naked ape. Only the names have changed: for 'hunting' read 'working,' for 'home-base' read 'house,' for 'pairbond' read 'marriage,' for 'mate' read 'wife' and so on" (*The Naked Ape*, [London: Corgi, 1968], p. 74).

The idea of this analogy is that if we evolved from apes, then we must really remain apes. The analogy is false. Hunting and working are two different things. Can you think of some differences? Most modern houses look quite different from the caves of our very ancient ancestors. Can you name five differences? In fact, to say we evolved from apes implies that we are now different from apes, not the same. By the way, civilized people are not apes. And because modern humans wear clothes, modern humans are certainly not naked apes.

Language analogies are often wrong because language depends on custom, not on reasonable or reasoned relationship, for its proper and established use.

Because *mice* is the plural of *mouse*, *hice* must be the plural of *house*. Because *slough* rhymes with *cow*, *ought* should rhyme with *cow*, too.

Obviously, false. The trouble is that the words are similar in only some respects, but they differ in others. Words with *ough* are spelled alike, have that same combination of the four letters, but that does not mean they are pronounced alike. That these words have *ough* is related to their history. Although the words look similar, their origin is quite different. Their pronunciation is quite different, too. *Mouse* and *house* share four letters, but the plural of *house* is *houses*, not *hice*. *Ought* rhymes with *caught* and not with *cow*.

Recently, I attended a neuroscience lecture at Rice University. The lecturer demonstrated a case of a Canadian surgeon who had Tourette's syndrome. The surgeon has a mass of tics and shouts and barks and curse words throughout his waking life, except when he is in the operating room, where he never has any abnormal involuntary movements, nor does he make any abnormal vocalizations there. The lecturer claimed that this surgeon had some kind of brain disease that accounted for his abnormal behavior, but the lecturer could not account for the complete remission of signs and symptoms of the disease during operations.

My explanation was that the surgeon didn't do those things in the operating room because if he did, he knew they would jerk his license and he would lose a significant source of income. My explanation was rejected out of hand. The lecturer, who had no idea that I was a board-certified neurologist on the full-time academic staff of the local medical school, implied that my understanding of this complex brain disease was simple and unschooled. The lecturer implied that I was unsympathetic and possibly biased against this poor, sick patient, the surgeon.

When people attack me personally and not my argument, I know that I hit a sensitive nerve and that I am on the right track. Arguments that attack the person and not that person's argument are called **argumentum ad hominem**, which is Latin meaning "argument about the man."

Argumentum ad hominem, like argumentum ad verecundiam, is a diversion, totally irrelevant to the rational consideration of the issue. Whether I am simple or unschooled has nothing to do with whether I am right or wrong. About a particular issue, a simple and unschooled person can be right or he can be wrong, just as an intelligent and educated person could be right or wrong about a particular issue. Calling me names or subjecting me to abuse is totally irrelevant. In the same way, whether I am sympathetic, unsympathetic, or even biased toward the surgeon does not demolish my argument. Prejudiced, unsympathetic people can be right, and impartial people are sometimes wrong. Calling me names is just another attempt to distract attention from the real point at issue, which was the weakness of the lecturer's argument.

There is a maxim in trial law that relates to this: "No case: Abuse the plaintiff's witnesses." That might work in front of a gullible jury, but it should not work in front of us.

The next day, a reporter from the *Houston Chronicle* called:

"Are you the person who questioned the integrity of the Canadian surgeon who has been struggling against Tourette's syndrome for years?"

"Yes, I am."

"Don't you know that people afflicted with this disease are able to suppress their tics and vocalizations for a while?"

"Of that, I have no doubt. The surgeon is a case in point. My question questioned the reason the symptoms stopped in the operating room, not the fact that they stopped there. I suggested one reason they stopped in the operating room was that if they didn't, the licensing board would pull his license. The selective milieu of the cessation of symptoms raises the possibility that there is no disease whatever and that the surgeon's behavior is under voluntary control. The selective milieu of the cessation of symptoms proves that the symptoms are at least in part under voluntary control."

"After the lecture, all that was all explained very simply," said the reporter. "There is a physiologic build up of tics and foul language which can be held in temporarily. Eventually, it all must come out. It's like having a full bladder. You can hold it for a while, but eventually you have to empty the bladder. The urine has to come out, the way the foul language and the tics have to come out."

Pause here and try to refute the reporter's argument. In what way is the reporter's argument a false analogy? The bladder analogy was offered to explain the surgeon's signs and symptoms. How do we know that that cannot possibly be true? Think about this for a while. List your answers on a piece of paper so that you can compare them with mine.

Before we start with my answers, let's strike down the reporter's statement for the usual reasons. What's the evidence that holding urine and holding behavior are equivalent? That idea is too simple. That idea is an unsubstantiated assertion for which no evidence is offered. That idea assumes facts not in evidence. Such facts must be put into evidence and examined for their credibility. Furthermore, where does that thinking lead? Couldn't we excuse any abnormal behavior, even criminal behavior, on the same basis? If so, where would society be? Where would it all end? Someone has to decide what is reasonable and correct behavior.

After you have struck down the lecture's assertion on general grounds, concentrate on the false analogy. Tell why it is an analogy. Tell why it is false. Prove it false. Prove that even if it were not false, it still wouldn't excuse the surgeon's postoperative behavior.

Here's how I would approach the problem:

It's an analogy because the surgeon's tics and other symptoms are compared to a full bladder that must be emptied sometime.

OK. It is an analogy. Next question: Is it true? Is it false?

Who knows?

I don't know. You don't know. We don't know. The reporter doesn't know. All we have to go on is the assertion of the lecturer. Chances are the lecturer doesn't know, either, because it sounds like the lecturer just made up the bladder analogy to try to explain the evidence that the surgeon could at least for a time control himself. But the lecturer is the one who is on the spot. Under the circumstances, how much can we trust his assertion?

When such a thing is asserted, we must have proof that it is true, that it really does reflect the real situation. When confronted with such comparisons, such analogies, we can test their truthfulness by thinking of ways in which the comparison breaks down. In this case, the analogy encourages us to think about urine and a full bladder. Let's do that.

If my bladder is full, I empty it. The surgeon does the same with his bladder. But I empty my bladder in the bathroom, not any old place around the office and the home. And I empty my bladder at specific times, not any old time when I feel like emptying it.

When the surgeon comes out of the operating room, he is, according to the analogy, obliged to spew his barks and foul language anywhere and with anyone around who happens to be in that location. He is permitted to do so any old time he feels he has to. Why can't he save the bad vocalizations for a soundproof room or the bathroom, if need be? Why can't he get it over with in the three minutes it takes the normal person to pee?

No sensible person would let this surgeon pee in public. Why let him shout obscenities in public? Thus, the analogy breaks down. Even if the bad behavior were a physiological necessity (a case in point not yet established by evidence), it still would not be excusable. Bad behavior is not excused by physiologic necessity. Since even if the analogy were reasonable, it doesn't work, the premise of the analogy must be wrong.

If you don't get those points, here's something easier to grasp: If Tourette's and a full bladder are both physiologic necessities, why can't the surgeon empty his Tourette waste under the same societal controls that he empties his bladder wastes? Well, you might say, perhaps he can't control his tics the way he can control his bladder.

Right! That's my point. It wasn't I who put forth the bladder analogy. It was the lecturer. If the bladder analogy is breaking down, it is the lecturer's problem, not mine. Perhaps the surgeon can't control his Tourette's the way he can control his bladder? Yes, perhaps he can't. But the evidence is that he can. He can control his bladder and his tics in the operating room. He doesn't pee there, and he doesn't curse there.

Man and machine analogies are often false.

My car and I both can be found in Clear Lake, Texas. Because my car and I share that common property, that doesn't necessarily mean we share other properties. In fact, some properties we don't share at all. My car needs gasoline to go. Gasoline for the car is a fuel. If I drank it, I would die.

On the other hand, it would be reasonable to say that just as my Lincoln's engine will stop when it runs out of fuel, that is, when it is starved, I also will stop if I don't eat. Provided the analogy is pressed no further, the comparison holds. Cars and humans need fuel. The fuel for the car is gas; the fuel for humans is food. Both cars and humans need a source of energy to keep going. It both instances, function stops if an energy source is not supplied.

It would not be reasonable, though, to assert that just as an engine that has been stopped for months can restart when given fuel, a corpse can be revived after death by being fed. Pause here and think why that is so. Think how a machine and a dead body differ. Yep, the analogy breaks down because a machine is not dead when it stops. In fact, the machine was never alive in the first place. If the machine were dead, it could not be restarted, death being irreversible.

Insofar as my car and my body are similar, what is true of one is true of the other. Insofar as my car and my body are different, what is true of one is not true of the other.

So watch out for machine analogies. The machines are often compared to life, to health, to the human body, and to all sorts of things for which there is no real connection. The differences between machines and anything else on this planet are far more numerous, more important, and more striking than their resemblances. What applies to machines often does not apply to anything but machines.

The government is not a ship, and the president is not a sea captain.

One such machine analogy that bugs me lots, and should bug you, is comparing government to a ship. Consider the following fragment of a poem. Try to decide what the analogy is and how it relates to the real world, if at all.

O Captain! my Captain! our fearful trip is done,
The ship has weather'd every rack, the prize we sought is won.
The port is near, the bells I hear, the people all exulting,
While follow eyes the steady keel, the vessel grim and daring;
   But O heart! heart! heart!
     O the bleeding drops of red,
      Where on the deck my Captain lies,
       Fallen cold and dead.
    (Walt Whitman, "O Captain, My Captain," 1–8)

Discussion: Poetry is one thing. Exact thought is another. Poetry aims to express feelings and emotion. When it achieves that aim, it is wonderful. The above lines from Walt Whitman's book *Leaves of Grass* are such good poetry that many school children are required to memorize the poem. In grade school, I memorized it. Perhaps you did, too.

The poem expresses Walt Whitman's feelings about the assassination of President Lincoln. Whitman loved Lincoln and felt that Lincoln's death was a great loss to the nation. But, in a larger sense, Whitman compares Lincoln to a licensed sea captain, which Lincoln wasn't. Whitman compares the government of the United States to a ship, that of state, one might say, the proverbial ship of state. What's wrong with that?

As poetry, nothing is wrong with that. But as fact, it just ain't true. It is a false analogy. It leads us away from the real to the fake. It obscures the reality and concentrates our attention on the bogus.

The poem's breezy line of thinking, though sincere and genuine, lacks clearness of vision that is imperative for truth. This is a flaw inherent in the poetic mind, and we may do well to tend to it, considering all that the poetic mind has done for us. But when the concept gets exploited for political purposes, we must pause and protest.

President Nixon often told the press that he was the skipper steering the ship of state. He told the media that they and the public need not know about his secret plan for ending the war in Vietnam because he, as captain of the ship, knew where we were going and why. The implication was that we should just shut up—just acquiesce and obey his orders—that we should not question his judgment. We should just trust him. We should obey him as if he were our captain.

But should we? Should we obey a president as if he were a licensed sea captain? Is the analogy false? Does it lead to behavior that has adverse consequences?

Nixon was pretty good at secret plans, as we subsequently learned. In 1969, he had authorized the secret bombing of Cambodia, which continued for four years. The total number of bombs dropped there was 539,129 (information obtained through the Freedom of Information Act). Almost half those bombs fell in the last six months. Much of the ancient irrigation system of Cambodia was destroyed. A lot of the rice-growing areas fell to ruins. Hundreds of thousands of people were killed. What was the point of doing that? What's my point in telling you about it?

I use this to illustrate the possible consequences of secret government action. I use it to show that blindly obeying a president as if he were a licensed sea captain can be wrong. Nixon's secret plan to end the Vietnam War, it turned out, was simply to get the hell out of there. What secret plan was in the erased tapes? We'll probably never know. But you can bet it was nothing too nice, else why would Nixon erase the tapes?

The point is that considering the president a captain and the government some sort of ship is wrong. It is a false analogy that can lead to serious, and sometimes dire, consequences.

Why is it a false analogy? Think of several reasons why the captain–ship of state analogy just doesn't work. Write these down in outline form so you can check your answers against mine.

By now, you should have started your objections with the statements that the comparison of government to a ship assumes facts not (yet put) in evidence. It is a mere assertion that would require piles and piles of evidence for us to believe it. It is also too simple, so simple it has to be wrong. Running a country is more complicated than commanding a ship. The reverse is true, too: Commanding a ship is a lot simpler and more direct than running a country as vast as the United States. The false analogy breaks down because government is not a ship; it does not float; and it doesn't transport its people someplace on the high seas. In addition, a ship doesn't do a lot of things a government does. It doesn't tax people; it doesn't go to war; and so forth. If the government is not a ship, then it doesn't really matter whether a president is a captain. If he were a captain, it would not relate to his office as president because the government is not a ship. The truth is that a president and a captain are two different positions of power. A president's power is checked by Congress, the Supreme Court, and, to a limited extent, by the press and by public opinion. On the high seas, the captain is master of the ship and in full command. His word is law. He is not checked by anyone. He is, of course, checked by natural forces such as wind and weather, as are we all.

In fact, the main reason elected officials want to be considered captains is so that they can co-opt the absolute powers of command that captains enjoy at sea. That's what Nixon wanted. That's what he got. That's what he got for a time until reality caught up with him and his abuses of power were uncovered. These abuses were so egregious that Nixon had to resign his office. Nixon became the first president to resign the presidency.

Since Lincoln was a reasonable man, he would have thought "O Captain! My Captain," flattering but a little odd. He probably would have said wryly, "My license covers the practice of law, not seamanship. Besides, I have been on a boat only once and got terribly sick."

Principle: What applies to ships, cars, planes, and other machines often applies only to machines.

From which follows:

Lesson: Watch out for machine analogies. They are likely to be deceptive. Many of them are wrong.

Now that we know to watch out for machine analogies, let's work out on a common analogy that I have heard repeatedly:

Classic false analogy: The brain is a computer. Or (expressed slightly differently) the brain is like a computer.

Think about it. The brain is a computer. Is that analogy true? Is that analogy helpful? Does it lead us to a better understanding of the reality situation, the truth? Does it help us better understand the brain? Does it help us better understand computers? What, if any, good is it to compare a brain to a computer and vice versa?

Aside from the usual objections (unproved assertion, assumption of facts not in evidence, overgeneralization, and simplistic thinking), how can we break down this argument?

Don't pause to think about this. You have done too much thinking in this chapter already. Give yourself a rest. Just glance over my exposition.

The brain is not a computer, and it is not like a computer. The brain is part of a living organism. The computer is not. The brain uses glucose and oxygen for its metabolism. The computer uses electricity to work. When deprived of glucose or oxygen for more than four minutes, the brain dies and can't be restarted. When deprived of electrons even for months, the computer will restart if you turn it on again. No irreversible damage occurred when the computer was shut off. A brain is made of 100 billion nerve cells called neurons. A computer is made of silicon chips. The brain is over 90 percent water. The computer has practically no water at all. Deprived of its aqueous environment, the brain will stop functioning. Put in a water environment, the computer will short out and become completely functionless, probably forever. Finally, the brain can think. Computers so far cannot think. Conclusion: The brain and the computer are two different things.

Is the analogy helpful?

Another way of attacking a false analogy is thinking about where the analogy leads. In a practical sense, can we learn anything about how computers work by studying the brain? What is the consequence? Where does this analogy lead? Does considering the brain a computer help us in any way, shape, or form? Can the analogy tell us how computers work?

Highly unlikely.

To learn about how computers work, we would do much better studying computers per se and not the brain. To learn about computers, we should go to computer school and not to medical school. How about the reverse? Can we learn anything about the brain by studying computers?

Highly unlikely.

To learn about how the brain works, we would do much better by studying the brain per se and not computers. To learn about the brain, we should go to medical school and not to computer school. Recent spectacular advances in neuroscience are based on just that, the detailed and relentless study of the brain, its structure and function. No advance in neuroscience arose from the study of computers.

> *Principle:* The brain is not a computer, nor is it like a computer.

From which follows:

> *Lesson:* Use your computer for the purpose for which it was intended. Use your brain for thinking.

The brain-computer analogy is so bad it is considered in neuroscience circles a **conceit**. A conceit is a fanciful, witty notion that is often a striking but strained and arbitrary metaphor. A conceit is a false analogy gone further awry.

Throughout history, conceits have derailed our understanding of the brain. The usual idea was to compare the brain to the highest technological achievement of the age. Thus, the ancient Greeks, who had just learned hydraulics, considered the brain a hydraulic machine. The fluid-filled ventricles at the center of the brain were thought to contract, thus sending fluid through the nerves, causing the nerves to expand slightly and making the muscles contract. Even Descartes, the great mathematician, thought this was the way nerves worked.

Descartes could have proven himself wrong if he had taken the trouble to dissect the optic nerves of just one animal. Optic nerves have no fluid-filled cavities. In fact, no normal nerve has a fluid-filled cavity. If nerves have no cavities, they can't work by contraction or expansion of what is not there. Thus, the hydraulic analogy is refuted.

When mechanical clocks were the rage in Germany, the brain was considered a form of mechanical clock. When the telegraph was prominent, the brain was likened to that device. When I was a boy, I learned in grade school that the brain was like a telephone operator with multiple switches on a switchboard deep inside my head. For a long time, I went around thinking there was some kind of telephone operator inside my skull. That image had to be revised when the adding machines came into prominence. My mental image of my brain then became an adding machine. You can imagine how I felt when I learned in medical school that the eye was not a camera, that lungs were not air-filled balloons, that the kidney doesn't make urine (anymore than a steel mill makes slag), and that the brain was not anything but itself.

Sing along to the tune of Oscar Hammerstein's "There Is Nothing Like a Dame":

> There is nothing like a brain
> Nothing in the world
> There is nothing you can name
> That is anything like a brain.
> There is nothing that talks like a brain
> Walks like a brain
> Thinks like a brain
> There is nothing you can name
> That is anything like a brain.

All those ideas about the brain—the hydraulics, the clocks, the telephone, the adding machine—were all conceits, analogies so bad they were egregious, remarkably bad. They led mankind away from the truth toward error.

And what is worse, all those ideas about the brain were wrong. They were errors in thinking. They delayed human progress and understanding. And by way of lesson, note that the original ground for accepting those arguments was scanty. Nevertheless, such arguments caught on and were held with conviction by the majority of people, scholars included, sometimes for centuries. In the case of hydraulics, the erroneous conviction held sway for over 1,500 years. Isn't that puzzling?

Isn't that stupid? How the devil can we explain the ready acceptance and retention of such drivel, poppycock, and nonsense?

Most people will accept such arguments by analogy as these because they don't question the alleged similarity between the things compared. Moreover, many analogies have no intellectual force whatsoever and depend for effectiveness upon stimulating the imagination into the wishful thinking that something is understood when, in fact, it is not understood at all. Secretly we want to deceive ourselves into thinking that we know more about something than we really do. Secretly we want to think that comparing the computer to the brain was not a bad idea. The brain? Oh, sure, I know about it. I know all about it. It's simple. Really. It's really, really very simple: The brain is just a computer. I use my computer every day. Since I know about computers, I must know about the brain. See how smart I am!

What's wrong? Such a comparison has adverse consequences. It is better to admit ignorance than labor under false perceptions of knowledge. At least you know that you don't know and cannot be misled by all those things you think that you know that are wrong.

In the political arena, false analogies and conceits emerge in abbreviated form as slogans. These slogans short-circuit serious discussing of the topic they announce. In many cases, the slogans are self-contradictions that mean nothing or contradict themselves: "genuine facsimile," meaning (I guess) a highly realistic imitation; "nonviolent force," meaning (I guess) force accompanied by the rhetoric of nonviolence; "white nigger," meaning a white person sympatric to blacks. Other terms are not quite slogans but euphemisms designed to obscure meaning rather than promote it: "social extraction," meaning, when used by the CIA, a form of murder justified by political considerations; "terminate with extreme prejudice," meaning kill by official order; "Symbolic speech," meaning an act other than speaking that is justified on the grounds that it is symbolic of speech and therefore protected by the First Amendment. Flag burning and cross burning are two such acts said by proponents to be "symbolic speech."

Consider the slogan "war on drugs." You have heard that before. It represents a policy of the US government. Work on it now. Tell what it means. Tell why it leads us away from truth toward error. Jot down the main points of your thinking. Compare your analysis with mine. By now, your attack on stupid government slogans and programs like this one should sound pretty sophisticated. You should be able to tick off all the big errors in thinking that the slogan implies. You should be able to break down the false analogy without difficulty.

Item: Simple and simplistic.

The drug problem is complex and complicated. There cannot be a simple solution to it. That is just impossible. If the problem were that simple, it would have been solved long ago by previous administrations in the previous wars on drugs. Don't get me wrong. I want the drug problem solved. I wish that making war on drugs would solve the problem—forever. The reality is that it won't. That is just wishful thinking, which gets us nowhere. I have a better chance of flying to the moon by flapping my arms than the government has of solving the drug problem with a war on drugs.

Item: Assumes facts not in evidence.

The announcement of a war on drugs implies that the issues involved have been thoroughly discussed and understood and that the people, Congress, and the president back this kind of drastic action to achieve goals that have been almost universally recognized as important. Such is not the case. Meaningful discussion of the pros and cons of drug interdiction has not and does not take place. Such discussion, if it did occur, would have to consider the pros and cons of legalization; the cost (time, energy, money) of further enforcement procedures; alternative ways of dealing with drug addiction including medical treatments; the history of previous failures of similar wars on drugs; the causes of addiction; the individual drugs and their properties; and so forth. Such an analysis would be long and complicated and, if undertaken for the proper degree of scholarship, confusing. To those who want a quick and easy solution to the drug problem, the process needed to actually solve the drug problem would be tedious.

Item: Overgeneralization.

Obviously, we are not about to make war on all drugs. Some drugs are good for us. Painkillers are needed for those in pain, antibiotics for those who have infections, insulin for diabetics, and so forth. In other words, medical uses must be excepted. Yet the statement does not say that. Since we are not about to make war on drugs, the type and quantity of the "enemy" drugs should be specified. Even better would be to mention the specific drugs, the quantities that would be interdicted, the reasons for the interdiction of that particular agent, and the cost-benefit analysis that shows that the interdiction is worth the effort. Other exceptions should be specified also. For example, American Indians may use peyote and other hallucinogens in their religious ceremonies. Recreational use of marijuana in Alaska and some counties of Nevada is legal. Medical use of marijuana is legal in thirteen states, including California.

Item: Unsupported assertion.

The implied assertion that a war on drugs is justified or even needed must be proven by evidence. We just can't be presented with a multi-billion-dollar program without piles of evidence that it is needed and is likely to be effective. In general, a nation makes war when its very survival is at stake. Is that the case here? If so, prove it. It is not sufficient merely to assert that the drug situation is so severe that it parallels the situation requiring a war. It is not sufficient merely to state the cases are parallel; they must be *shown* to be parallel. In fact, multiple important differences exist.

Item: Vague definitions.

Putting aside for the moment the misuse of the word *war*, the word *drugs* in this context is not adequately defined. Probably what is meant is illegal drugs, but even among these there is a variety of illegal drugs, some more powerful than others. Some, like LSD, are not addicting. Some, like cocaine, are less addicting than tobacco cigarettes. Yes, a survey of the fifty top physician experts on drug addiction lists tobacco as more addicting than cocaine. And I know why: It is. How much sense does it make to interdict a drug when a more addicting drug like it (in the dopamine-releasing family) is legal?

Some drugs, like marijuana, are relatively harmless. Two government committees have in fact reported that marijuana is relatively harmless, as did the LaGuardia commission as did the American Medical Association.

Yes, the American Medical Association testified before Congress that there was no medical evidence that marijuana was harmful. The American Medical Association lobbied against any federal laws restricting the use of marijuana. The Harrison Narcotic Act of 1914 was passed specifically exempting marijuana as a nod to the American Medical Association. In 1937, the penalties for opium, heroin, and related drugs were applied to unauthorized handling of marijuana. Subsequently, all physicians had their marijuana licenses revoked, mine included. Thus, marijuana was no longer available even for medicinal purposes. What is the consequence of lumping marijuana with heroin?

Arresting people for possession of marijuana might jam the court system to the hilt. It does in some jurisdictions. Because of the jams,

England has effectively legalized marijuana by proclaiming there will be no further enforcement against users.

Currently, for that reason, among others, marijuana laws are not enforced in Houston nor are they enforced in Galveston. If the marijuana laws were enforced in Houston, 90 percent of a certain segment of the population would be behind bars.

Frankly, I don't care if someone smokes a joint. Do you? Even if you did care, how much do you care? How many of your personal dollars are you willing to spend on the cost of arresting, arraigning, prosecuting, trying, sentencing, and jailing someone who got caught smoking marijuana?

Item: Diversionary thinking.

Is it possible that the idea of the war on drugs was constructed to divert our thinking from another issue or to push us in a certain direction (i.e., toward more societal control of individual lives) rather than simply a method to control drugs? If that is true, then to the extent that it is true, the war on drugs is irrelevant for all attempts to divert attention from real issues are irrelevant.

One is reminded of the "WAR" in the famous novel *1984* by George Orwell. According to the Goldstein handbook, the "WAR" is not real. Not only is the "WAR" not real, but it will never end because it is an instrument of power, an excuse, whereby the rulers can inflict their control on the masses. The "WAR" in *1984* conveniently diverts attention from the wretched poverty and servility that the citizens of Oceania have to endure. By giving the citizens a fake enemy and a fake war for them to worry about and hate, the power elite divert attention from the real issues: loss of freedom and loss of human dignity. To Big Brother and his minions, power is not a means; it is an end. And power means the capacity to inflict unlimited pain and suffering on another human being. It is the power, as Simone Weil tells us, to transform a living person into a corpse, that is to say, into a thing.[1]

My point is not to debate the drug question but to point out the kind of thinking involved in this slogan. Such thinking can result in some pretty bad consequences. All this is confounded by the fact that most of us use drugs every day. My morning coffee has a drug called caffeine. Tea has the same drug, and so does Coca-Cola. Caffeine works by binding to the adenosine receptor, thus preventing the destruction of multiple neurotransmitters. The net effect of caffeine is to stimulate the brain. As a drug, caffeine works quite well. That is why we use it. By the same reasoning, in a very real sense my morning coffee mug is a drug delivery device. Tobacco and alcohol are also drugs. Their sale is controlled and their use restricted to adults. Last night at Tony's restaurant, there were lots of adults using alcohol—but they were not abusing alcohol. There's a difference. Could someone use currently illegal drugs and not abuse them? Why or why not?

Also at Tony's, I saw some men at the bar who seemed to be enjoying cigars, and a young lady, God forbid, was smoking a cigarette.

So what?

That's the point. So what. Why couldn't similar programs for controlled legalization and use work for at least some of the drugs that we are told we need to make war on? England has a program where any physician can use his judgment to support a drug addict, even by giving that addict heroin. The program has been in place for years. It's not ideal, but it has cut drug-related crime. Could such a program work in the United States? Why or why not?

Item: False analogy.

The slogan compares drugs to an enemy nation and states that we will make war on it. Drugs are not a nation. Drugs will put up no fight. The war, if there is to be one, I imagine will be against someone, a person or persons unknown.

Who?

The slogan doesn't say. If we are going to war, shouldn't we know who we are going to fight? Could it be addicts? Most of them are unarmed and will not be in military uniform. If the war is against addicts, it might not be justified because many addicts are just sick people seeking in the temporary oblivion of some drugs a surcease from sorrow. Is the war against dealers? Many of them will be unarmed and not in uniform. If the war is against dealers, what dealers? The kids who do the running on the street barely scrape by with a living. Yet they are the dealers facing the most danger, mainly from other dealers. But they also face the danger of arrest and possible harm from the police. Are the kids, the runners, who are mainly black boys, the target? And speaking of police, how do they fit in here? How about corrupt police? Are corrupt police the enemy? Drugs cannot exist in Harlem without police protection. So are the police the target of this new war on drugs? How about corrupt politicians in this country and others? Do we get them, too? And by the way, how is the war to be fought? Machine guns? Antitank weapons? Ground troops? The H-bomb?

The devil is in the details. In a democracy, to be truly informed, we must know the details to know if the ideas and the program are reasonable or not. If people were not so resistant to careful thinking, they would realize how often the analogies like this one that encourage them to accept propositions could equally well be used to establish opposite conclusions. From which follows: How about peace on drugs?

Item: Broadcast definition wrong.

The word *war* is misused in the slogan. It is probably misused because of the emotional effects of the word, which are exactly what we are trying to prevent by clear thinking. When emotions get in the way of thought, watch out.

A war is an open armed conflict between countries or between factions within the same country. If the war on drugs were a real war, then Congress would have had to declare it. Since Congress did not declare a war and no military action against another nation is specified, we must conclude that the war on drugs is not real. If it is not a real war, then it must be fake.

Have you noticed that there are too many fake things in modern America? Do we need another fake thing? Do we need a fake war? Do we need a fake war on drugs?

Isn't it high time to stop the war metaphor? Isn't it high time we started thinking about the drug problem intelligently?

Item: **Begging the question.**

We will discuss this error in thinking in chapter 7. Begging the question is a subdivision of the error known as partial selection of the evidence. In brief, the war on drugs implies that we will win the war. No sane person or nation should declare war unless it has a reasonable chance of success. Previous wars on drugs have not been successful. In fact, previous wars on drugs have been failures. How those wars differed from the new one just proposed should be specified so that we can decide if the chance of this war having a different outcome is better, the same, or worse than those in the past.

Along these lines, it would be interesting to review the nation's experience with other drug interdiction programs that have failed. Prohibition, for instance, resulted in more, not less, alcohol consumption; introduced women to drinking in speakeasies; led to gang crime of gigantic proportions; and even worse, put on the market alcoholic beverages that were contaminated with wood alcohol, a substance highly toxic to the human visual system.

Eventually, the great national experiment was deemed a failure, and the prohibition (18th) amendment to the Constitution was repealed. Adult Americans can now freely imbibe the contents of bottles. Interestingly, after the repeal of prohibition, the crime wave engendered by the prohibition disappeared. The reason the crime wave disappeared is that the illegal market for the product disappeared. There was no way in either price or quality for illegal alcohol to effectively compete with legal alcohol.

That result raises an interesting question: What would happen if all currently illegal drugs were legalized? Would the crime associated with drug trafficking also disappear? Who knows? But it is something to think about before we assume that the newest and most costly war on drugs will work.

Consider the following thirty-second TV spots.

The first spot, called "I Helped," shows a series of young people saying things like, "I helped murder families in Colombia"; "I helped a bomber get a fake passport"; "I helped blow up buildings." The spot ends with the tag line: "Drug money supports terror. If you buy drugs, you might, too." The second spot, called "AK-47," follows the style of MasterCard's "priceless" advertisements by McCann-Erickson Worldwide Advertising in New York. Images of rental cars with trunks full of automatic weapons, a safe house, and a man buying box cutters—poignant images for American viewers after September 11—are flashed on the screen followed by: "Where do terrorists get their money? If you buy drugs, some of it might come from you."

The spots were first aired during Super Bowl XXXVI at a cost of $1.9 million each, paid by (your) tax dollars. Variations of the "I Helped" advertisement appeared in more than three hundred newspapers.

Critics, including some parents, say that the advertisements' negative-niche strategy is unlikely to be effective. Jane Marcus, a mother of two and a member of the PTA in Palo Alto, California, said, "The argument is fallacious to begin with and plays on people's fears—the two aren't connected," she said of the link between terror and drug abuse. Good for you, Jane. Ethan A. Nadelmann, executive director of the Drug Policy Alliance, which favors a strategy based more on treatment, said: "This is a shameless exploitation of the war on terror. The government is trying to bolster a failing war on drugs by linking it to the war on terrorism." Good for you, Ethan.

That's what they say. What about you? What do you say? Do you say no to drugs? Do you say no to the war on drugs? Do you say no to irrational slogans in general? Let's review without comment some war slogans of the past:

"Save the tomb of Christ from the Heathen!"
"Down with Popery!"
"Liberty or Death!"
"Cotton, Slavery, and States Rights!"
"Libertad O Muerte, Vive Puerto Rico Libre!"
"War to end all war!"
"Remember the Maine!"
"Fifty-four forty or fight!"

Each of the above slogans is now a permanent part of the irretrievable past. They influenced thousands to go to war. They collectively must bear partial responsibility for hundreds of thousands—some of them, millions—of deaths.

Principle: Slogans can obscure thinking.

From which follows:

Lesson: Slogans are suspect. Watch out for them. Watch out for slogans that are repeated over and over again. They are usually dead wrong. Slogans that are repeated imply that the opposite of the slogan's implications is closer to the truth. Repeated slogans are a form of cheerleading, which should make us reason darkly about why such cheers are being foisted on us.

Anyone out there remember this slogan from a previous chapter? "We are the master race!" Who's we? The Third Reich, of course.

Is the word *are* in the above slogan a predicative or an existential? Are the Germans really a race? If the Germans are a race, are they really the master race? Is it that simple? What's the evidence? If the Germans are the master race, how do they explain their defeat in World War I? What conclusion would follow from the idea that the Germans are the master race? (Hint: If there is a master race, then there must be a slave race. In fact, Hitler used this lie as the rationalization to justify aggression against and subjugation of others.)

William L. Shirer's best-selling classic about the Nazi era and World War II, *The Rise and Fall of the Third Reich*, tells how Hitler had the idea of establishing a Ministry of Propaganda (subsequently expanded to Popular Enlightenment and Propaganda). Hitler appointed Joseph Goebbels minister of popular enlightenment and propaganda. Hitler directed Goebbels to make up slogans that, though stupid and untrue, would through repetition eventually would be believed. All radio stations and newspapers were brought under Goebbels's control. To be an editor in the Third Reich, one had to be, in the first place, politically and racially "clean." The Reich press law of October 4, 1933, which made journalism a "public vocation" regulated by the state, stipulated that all editors must possess German citizenship, be of Aryan descent, and not be married to a Jew. From this it was inevitable that a deadly conformity would come over the Germany's press. Big lies became the news du jour. A few mad leaders with a talent for verbal demagoguery, mass manipulation, and deception led the world toward a tragic destiny.

Even when, without warning, the German boat U-30 sank the British liner *Athenia*, killing 112 people, including 28 Americans, Hitler personally ordered (Nuremberg documents show) a radio broadcast and newspaper article that said that Churchill, the first lord admiral of the British navy, sank the *Athenia* by placing a time bomb in the ship's hold! Churchill did that to make Germany look bad!

After you finish reading this book, it will be an interesting experience for you to work out on the history of Nazi Germany as detailed in Shirer's scholarly work. As you do so, you might pay attention to the multiple errors in thinking that allowed Hitler to gain power. Pay attention to Hilter's war on drugs, then his war on drug addicts and the reasons for it. That war was followed by war on private ownership of guns. Pay attention to Hilter's arguments against private possession of weapons. We hear the same and similar antigun arguments today. After that, work out what was behind Hitler's castration of child pornographers. And then, consider the Hitlerian target "the degenerate homosexuals." The gypsies were next, followed by the communists, socialists, artists, writers, and, of course, the Jews. In each case, the attack on the segment of the German population seemed to make sense. It seemed to make sense unless you thought about it for a few minutes. After you thought about what Hitler did and why he did it, it still made sense but with a darker significance. See if you don't agree that a little thinking would easily have disclosed the grim plan that Hitler and the Nazis had in mind. As Bunsby says in Dickens's *Dombey and Son*, "The bearings of this observation lays in the application on it."[2]

REVIEW

By now you know the drill. Review the chapter as you did the previous ones. On the other hand, if you feel you don't need a review, pass on to the next chapter. If you are not sure whether you need the drill, answer the twelve questions below. If you get 70 percent correct or better, you're OK. If you get less than 70 percent, better reread all the italicized sections not only in this chapter but in all the previous chapters.

1. Consider the statement: "Logic is like a fine-edged sword; the more you use it, the sharper it gets." Which of the following is truest?
    A. The statement is correct.
    B. The statement is a false analogy.
    C. The statement is a false analogy because a fine-edged sword becomes blunt when used, whereas the use of logic does tend to improve performance.
    D. Logic is an exact science, so sword analogies do not apply to it.
2. Consider the statement: "Coke is it."
    A. The statement is vague.
    B. Both *Coke* and *it* remain undefined.
    C. The statement is an advertising slogan designed to have the widest possible application to sell, despite its lack of intelligent reference to reason or evidence, Coca-Cola to the widest possible audience. Cynical advertising men have made the statement vague on purpose.
    D. A, B, and C are true.
3. After the September 11 attacks, President Bush announced, "Those who did this were cowards." Considering the dictionary definition of *coward*, "someone who out of fear fails to act," what can be said of the president's statement?
    A. The statement is not true.
    B. The statement is an example of broadcast definition wrong.
    C. The president should have said that the terrorists were das-

tards, because the word *dastard*, a sneaky evildoer, is much closer to what the terrorists really were.

    D. A, B, and C are correct.

4. Consider the statement: "The brain is a computer."

    A. No way, José.

    B. The statement is true because both the brain and a computer can add numbers.

    C. The statement is true because learning about the brain teaches us about computers.

    D. The statement is true because the brain and computers are made of similar materials and work in the same way in the same environment.

5. Consider the statement: "History repeats itself."

    A. Historical analogies are exceedingly common and frequently fallacious.

    B. History seldom repeats itself exactly, despite the maxim to the contrary, because present and historical situations are seldom exactly the same.

    C. The statement contains no grounds beyond mere assertion for the suggestion that history repeats itself.

    D. A, B, and C are true.

6. A cold-calling broker from New York tells you that the investment tip he is about to give you is perfect. He says that if you follow his tip, you cannot possibly lose. What can you conclude from the man's statement?

    A. He is lying. Nothing is perfect. The future performance of an investment can never be predicted with absolute confidence.

    B. He might be on to something.

    C. It's a long shot but worth sending him some money to see what happens.

    D. A, B, and C are correct.

7. The war on drugs

    A. begs the question by assuming the war on drugs is a good thing.

    B. begs the question by assuming the war on drugs can be won.

    C. begs the question by assuming the drug problem is solvable and that the solution, or part of the solution, is a war on drugs.

    D. A, B, and C are correct.

8. Consider the statement: "Another politician sent to prison. It shows that politicians can never be trusted."
   A. The statement is a generalization.
   B. The statement is true.
   C. The statement is founded on complete and adequate evidence that supports it entirely.
   D. The conduct of a few members of a group is a good indication of the conduct of the group in general.

9. Consider the statement made by a reporter for PBS: "Everyone in this little town of 20,000 people knows that the al-Qaida are now fighting to the death on the hillside just nineteen kilometers from here."
   A. The statement can't be entirely true unless everyone in the town was interviewed and agreed that al-Qaida was fighting to the death on the hillside nineteen kilometers from where the reporter was standing.
   B. The statement is an example of exaggeration by the reporter.
   C. The statement can be proven wrong by finding one person in the village who does not agree with the statement.
   D. A, B, and C are correct.

10. Consider these headlines that were taken from the *Washington Post*, December 23, 1988: "Drexel Settlement Is Taken in Stride by Wall Street"; "Drexel Case Likely to Have Serious Impact on Wall Street."
   A. One or both headlines must be wrong because two opposite things cannot be simultaneously true. If both are wrong, they are contraries. If one is wrong and the other is right, they are either contradictions or contraries.
   B. The headlines are a fine example of fine journalism using a technique called "doublethink" in which contrary ideas are held to be true as discussed in the novel *1984*.
   C. The headlines taken together are a self-contradiction in which their conjunction has a truth value of zero.
   D. A and C are correct.

11. Consider the following:

WAR IS PEACE

FREEDOM IS SLAVERY

IGNORANCE IS STRENGTH

    A. The three statements are slogans.

    B. The three statements are bizarre contradictions *and* examples of "doublethink."

    C. The statements are the leaden motto of Ingsoc, the government of Oceania in the novel *1984*.

    D. A, B, and C are correct.

12. "These are the best sultanas," says the grocer, who then adds in one breath: "How can you expect the best sultanas at that price?"

    A. The two statements contradict each other because statement two implies that statement one is not true.

    B. We can't figure out whether the statements are true without knowing what sultanas are.

    C. The grocer's statements may reflect a flaw common to the business mind.

    D. A and C are correct.

Answers:

    1. C is correct because it is the answer that is the most true. D is wrong because logic is not an exact science. Who said it was? Whether logic is a science depends on the definitions of *science* and *logic*. Under ordinary definitions of those words, logic is neither a science nor is it exact. In fact, in the introduction I did not call logic a science. I called logic an art. Logic is an art in the sense that it is an immediate, personal, creative, and imaginative craft requiring adroitness and cunning for successful performance.

    2. D

    3. D

    4. A

    5. D

    6. A

    7. D

    8. A

    9. D

    10. D

    11. D

    12. D

NOTES

1. Quoted in Eric Fromm, afterword to *Nineteen Eighty-Four* by George Orwell (New York: Penguin Putnam, 1950), p. 263.

2. Bunsby in *Dombey and Son* quotes Marcus Tullius Cicero, "Paradox 3," in *Familiar Quotations* by John Bartlett, 13th ed. (Boston: Little, Brown, 1955), p. 34, column a.

chapter 5

Partial Selection of the Evidence

This chapter covers a common error in thinking known as *partial selection of the evidence*, which leads away from the truth and toward blunder. To arrive at the truth, we must consider all the evidence, not just part of it. If we exclude reasonable evidence from consideration, our view of reality dims and the chance of error increases.

In a way, partial selection of evidence is the root error in false analogy, overgeneralization, and simplification. Those errors extract elements from an argument while ignoring other elements that are just as important. Hence, the partial selection. Partial selection is also the root error in a particularly pernicious form of error known as prejudice.

Prejudice damages not only the victim, the person who is prejudiced against, but also the perpetrator, the person being prejudiced. At times, prejudice heads us to a form of self-serving bias called **special pleading** wherein we adopt arguments favorable to ourselves while neglecting those favorable to our opponents.

Any opinion based on inadequate evidence, incomplete evidence, or erroneous evidence is, to that extent, a partial selection and therefore unreasonable. Thus, evaluating evidence becomes key, but it is quadruplely difficult: (1) We must include in our considerations all the relevant available evidence. (2) We must decide whether that evidence is adequate and sufficient—that is, whether we have enough evidence to reach a reasonable conclusion and whether the evidence justifies the conclusion. (3) We must decide whether all the evidence is reasonable. (4) If not all the evidence is reasonable, we must decide which part of the evidence is reasonable and which part is not.

Sifting evidence to make sure it is true is not an easy task, especially in modern times, when deliberate efforts have been made to deceive us. Aside from overt fraud, the irrational feature that interferes with our correct evaluation of evidence, aside from mental laziness and stupidity, is our emotions. Emotional factors derail our thinking because fundamentally we are not entirely rational beings.

A delusion is a false belief not part of a religious system that is not amenable to logical persuasion. One of the most remarkable delusions that most of us hold is that we are purely rational by nature. Multiple lines of evidence point to a rather large role for emotion in the human scheme of things. (That, perhaps, is why we need a little book like this one to teach us how to be more rational.)

Some psychologists even say that the majority of our species are governed by brute passion, greed, and prejudice. Our most confident judgments and received opinions owe more to instinct than to serious thinking. In fact, reason, like virtue, is something of which we are capable, but it requires effort, often great effort, to achieve.

We are under the delusion that we are purely rational because it is more comfortable for our bruised egos to believe that idea than to accept the reverse. We tend to operate in a way that protects our egos. We do this unconsciously through the operation of our unconscious mind.

Yes, unconscious mind. Considerable psychological and psychiatric evidence indicates that our mental lives consist of two parts: the conscious part, with thoughts and feelings of which we are immediately aware, and the unconscious part, which shelters our primitive instincts, our automatic responses, our emotional drives (like the drives toward sex and food), as well as our memories not at present in the consciousness, including some important memories that are not immediately recallable because they are, for emotional reasons, suppressed.

When someone tried to kiss my wife at a party, I was furious. Momentarily, I wanted to kill the guy. That that thought crossed my mind need not surprise us. Five thousand years of civilization could scarcely abolish instincts based on two hundred thousand years of savagery. Instead of hitting the guy, my drink "accidentally" spilled on his crotch. He had to leave the room to wash up. Thus, discretion prevailed. My drive to kill a rival man became suppressed. But it mutated, changed into a different form, and surfaced again in (thin) disguise as a milder form of aggression directed (significantly) at the anatomical area with which my unconscious mind was most concerned.

Mental mechanisms conceal emotional truths.

Was my reaction entirely irrational? Probably not. Substantial work shows that emotions can have (at times) epistemic content. The instinctive distrust of strangers, for example, puts us on guard against a clever con man. Sensing danger to my domestic tranquility and happiness, my behavior appears more understandable.

The mental mechanisms by which our conscious mind conceals the unconscious emotional truths from us are well known to psychiatrists. They include things like suppression, repression, projection, isolation of affect, derealization, depersonalization, displacement, déjà vu, and so forth. They are more germane to a psychiatry textbook than they are to a handbook on thinking. But knowing them will help you understand your emotional life better and lead to emotional truth. These mental mechanisms, though not directly related to thinking or logic, are important enough for you to look them up in a textbook of psychiatry. One of them, rationalization, the assertion of a false reason for our opinions or action, is discussed more fully later in this chapter. At present, our task is to try to understand the fact that unconscious drives do interfere with clear thinking.

Having worked with the mentally ill as a physician, I know that lunatics are quite human. Their delusions, hallucinations, and abnormal thought processes have counterparts in everyday thinking. Only a matter of degree and certain qualitative differences separate a psychotic patient who thinks he is Bill Gates, the billionaire, and the normal daydreamer who imagines what he would do with Gates's money if he had it. Imagining that you will win the Texas lottery is only one step removed from daydreaming that you are rich. No one plays the lottery without wishing to win. No one plays the lottery without thinking how to use the money.

Consider the following patient. She is a woman, thirty-two, dressed in sloppy army fatigues. When asked if she wanted to tell me anything, she said, "I am really very beautiful. But I am disguised as something ugly."

"Why are you disguised?" I asked.

"Because I came to Earth in a spaceship and found that the people here like to kill the beautiful. Why is that, doctor?"

"Why is what?"

"Why do Earth people like to kill the beautiful?"

"What I think is not important. What do you think about that?" I asked.

"Don't give me that psychiatry shit!"

This woman was dressed for battle, so I expected a fight. Notice she knows that she is not beautiful but wants to live with the false idea that she is beautiful. To make that idea fit with the contrary evidence seen in the mirror, she has constructed an elaborate fantasy that she came to this planet in a spaceship. The elaboration of the fantasy is that she discovered on arrival here that Earth people kill the beautiful. Her ego finds this false idea more consoling than facing the truth and doing something constructive to improve her looks. Notice when she invited me into her fantasy, I could not support it. To support or agree with a delusion would have been unprofessional. Instead, I asked her for *her* opinion. She had seen enough psychiatrists to know that that was a ploy. She replied in anger. Her mind cannot endure the idea that she is wrong on this important issue. To maintain her inner harmony, she must attack others who threaten her delusional system. In fact, she was in the hospital for acting out her anger by stabbing another woman (who was beautiful).

Is there much difference between this patient and a woman who wants to be told that she is beautiful even though she knows in her heart of hearts that she isn't? Is there much difference between this patient and a woman who reacts in anger when her doctor advises her that she is too fat and needs to lose fifteen pounds? Is there a difference between this woman and a small boy who is unlikely to become an astronaut, pretending that he is flying a spaceship to Mars? Is there much difference when we go to a play or film or read a novel and use those things to (in part) fulfill in our imagination what we cannot enjoy in reality?

> *Principle:* Deep-seated emotional needs may prevent perception of the truth.

From which follows:

> *Lesson:* Whenever the response exceeds the stimulus or weird, unjustified, and unjustifiable reasons are given, look for emotional factors at work.

Yep, it's really too bad that the human mind works that way. But that is the reality—we like to delude ourselves into thinking that we are important or famous or that we know more than we do or that we will be rich someday. What's wrong with that?

Such delusions prevent reality-based actions that might actually improve the situation by leading to a correction.

The human mind cannot usually endure conflict and is prepared to go to any length in the pursuit of a certain false harmony. The policy is appeasement. In the process of repelling thoughts and ideas that threaten to disturb its composure, the mind is most recklessly irrational. Scientists know this and try to prevent it by conscious action.

Emotional factors tend to make us select evidence we like and neglect evidence we don't like. Such an emotionally based partial selection clouds our view of reality and is an error in thinking.

Darwin kept a notebook in which he recorded objections to the theory of evolution. He found that if he did not write down the objections as soon as they occurred to him, he would forget them and remember only the ideas and facts that supported the theory. In other words, he knew that his mind, that of a great scientist, had trouble resisting the pull of an idea in which he had so much vested personal interest. Objections to his theory created mental disharmony. His mind protected itself by tending to forget the disturbing ideas, to partially select the ideas favorable to evolution, and to reject or forget ideas unfavorable to his theory.

Later on, Darwin's notebook came in handy when Darwin was attacked on all sides for his book *The Origin of Species*. He was ready for the objections because he had already thought of most of them himself.

Our need to have our egos flattered makes us vulnerable to the flattery of con men, sycophants, and all sorts of hangers-on. Entertainers and some newspaper and magazine editors prey upon the same human (irrational) need to think well of ourselves, to think that we know more than we actually do.

Theme parks do the same. This was explained to me by Mr. L, a man who worked for Disney. Mr. L was responsible for constructing the rides at Disney World and Disneyland. I had hired Mr. L as a consultant to advise me about constructing a theme park in Clear Lake, Texas. My theme park was to be called Ancient World of Texas. The idea was to make exact replicas of ancient sites such as the tombs of the nobles in Egypt or the arranged rocks at Stonehenge in England. I wanted the public to come to the theme park and to learn about ancient civilizations. Mr. L told me the idea was a good one except that the rides would have to show the public what they thought they already knew. No new information could be provided, nor could old theories or received standard information be changed. In short, whatever the public knew or thought it knew is what would be shown. The net effect of the ride and the exhibits, Mr. L explained, had to confirm in people's minds that they knew all there really was to know. The ride had to show them that their knowledge was complete. The goal was to gratify the public's inflated ego. The goal was not to instruct anyone in anything.

Of course, I objected. "This can't be true," I said.

Mr. L assured me it was true and backed his statements with data that showed that rides that presented the banal and humdrum were commercially successful. Rides that presented real information failed. Thus, the only way my theme park would succeed would be by pandering to the mental habits of the visitors by oversimplifying what is inherently complex, by appealing to emotion and prejudice, and by partial selection of historical evidence to give a false picture of the way things were. Mr. L assured me that that was the theme park reality situation, that millions of people had been exposed to rides that encouraged every sort of crooked thinking—rides that set an example of which the owners of the rides should be ashamed—and that the other people he had worked with knew perfectly well what they were doing and cynically defended their greedy corruption of the masses.

"In that case, the project is not worth doing," I said.

I paid Mr. L his well-earned fee of $18,000. Mr. L was right. By clueing me into the reality situation, he saved me three million dollars, the amount of money that I was going to invest in Ancient World of Texas.

Principle: The public gets the rides it deserves.

From which follows:

Lesson: When you hear someone cite a theme park ride, or worse, TV (even the Discovery Channel), as the source of information, the only reasonable response is to cringe.

Rationalization—assertion of false reasons—is a common error in thinking.

Another way of avoiding conflict and thereby protecting the ego is to find or even invent reasons for behaving and believing as we do. That is called the mental mechanism of rationalization. In psychology, rationalization superficially gives a rational or plausible explanation or excuse for our acts, beliefs, and desires, usually without being aware of our real motives.

Rationalization is common because people like to adduce arguments to support their views. But most of those arguments are not really reasons. They are the views themselves masquerading as the cause of the view. Indeed, much of our so-called reasoning consists in rationalization, an attempt to justify what we already believe. Most times the rationalization follows the opinion, belief, or behavior we wish to justify. Sometimes the rationalization is invented not to justify ourselves or our opinions but to cover a personal inadequacy.

The fox couldn't reach the grapes, so the fox decided that he did not want those grapes. He did not want the grapes because he decided that the grapes were sour. Since the grapes were not sour, the conclusion that they were is contrary to fact and therefore wrong.

In effect, the fox is avoiding collision with the idea that some defect in himself, some lack of cleverness, some lack of ability, or some lack of height is the real reason behind his failure to get the grapes. Rather than face his own inability, the fox invents a consoling lie—that he does not want the grapes. But the lie is too blatant. He knows he wants the grapes, so he has to come up with a better reason. To conceal the lie from himself, the fox must elaborate or transform the lie into something more consciously acceptable. The usual elaboration of a lie is a fantasy or a rationalization. The fox rationalized (offered a false reason for not wanting the grapes). That rationalization was that the grapes were not desirable because they were sour.

Sour grapes is a rationalization that people use when they don't get what they want. Thus, sour grapes is often the excuse (rationalization) for lost or unrequited love. The irrational thinking might go something like this: She is beautiful, but she doesn't want me. Therefore, I can't have her. Because I can't have her, she is not worthy of my love. Because she is not worthy of my love, I don't want her. The rationale may also elaborate to include things like she has bad breath or she is a bad dancer, or any number of other items that, though off the point, may or may not be true. More serious elaborations might actually flip the emotion: I don't love her. I hate her. Or she doesn't love me. Therefore, I don't love her. Not only do I not love her, I hate her.

Or, even more silly, a trivial defect is partially selected and overemphasized: She is beautiful. But her beauty has a flaw. Her hands are not beautiful. Therefore, I can't love her. In fact, I hate her ugly hands. Because I hate her ugly hands, I hate her.

Thus, through an interconnecting chain of bad thinking, love can become hate. And then, in some extreme cases, hate might lead to violent behavior.

Sound weird? Impossible? You bet. It's weird. But it's not impossible. Such a sequence of false and inverted connections underlies many crimes of passion.

Partial application of ethical principles is a partial selection and wrong.

Rationalizations are often used to justify the partial or misapplication of ethical principles. Contact between opposing sets of ideas can rarely be avoided. When contact happens, rationalization comes to the rescue, and intrapsychic discord is averted. By isolation of areas of endeavor, the full significance of what is being done is concealed and the relation between opposing ideas is distorted.

For example, some people who go to church every Sunday have no qualms about cheating on their income tax returns. The arguments for cheating on income tax are too familiar to require comment: "The government would misuse the money anyway"; "My family and I need the money more than Uncle Sam does"; "Everyone is doing it"; "Cheating the government and cheating an individual are not the same"; "Taxes are so unfair that it is justifiable to evade them"; "A government that has revenue of a trillion dollars a year is not going to miss my mite." And so forth.

Pause here and try to think about the excuses you yourself have used to cheat on your income tax. I say try to think about these things because it is awfully hard to actually think about them at all. Because we like to think well of ourselves, we cannot bear to realize that we are cheats. Incidentally, how did I know that you cheat on your income tax?

Another common cause of mental conflict is the frustration of our instincts and desires. We want a new car, but we can't afford one. We would like to steal some money from a bank, but we know that is wrong.

Principle: Frustration of instincts and desires is the commonest cause of mental conflict.

From which follows:

Lesson: Fantasy is not the way to handle frustration. Satisfy your instincts and desires (when possible) more directly—with reality.

Collisions of behavior and ethics can be (irrationally) avoided by keeping the two systems apart. Thus, an honorable man in private life, a churchgoer like Ken Lay, CEO of Enron, can lie and cheat in business, provided he never lets the two spheres of activity come together in his conscious mind. The psychotic do this same thing easily. They keep their delusions in separate airtight compartments so that never the twain shall meet. The supposedly beautiful woman, my patient, dressed in sloppy army fatigues, walks the wards unperturbed by the incongruity involved. By the same token, Christians who pledged to love their neighbors have often put those neighbors to the sword.

Sometimes the rationalizations are concealed so much that we need to do some spadework to uncover them. Analysis of context and a high degree of suspicion are often all that is required.

If I receive a bad review for this book, I might reasonably maintain that the critic has read the work with buried resentment and profound jealousy. After all, reviewers have no creative bones in their body. That is why instead of being authors they become critics. We should have none of them. What they say is prejudiced, unreasonable, and sometimes utter bunk.

If the next day, I receive a favorable review and praise the reviewer to the skies, then we know that my first opinion was likely a rationalization. The unfavorable review hurt my pride. The disagreeable things said about my book threatened to conflict with my self-esteem. My unconscious mind sought ways of restoring harmony. The point is that I didn't dislike the critic for the reasons stated. Those reasons were produced because I disliked what the critic said about my book. If I knew my reasons were fake, then I would be guilty of hypocrisy, but if I was not aware of the true (unconscious) source of my reasons, then I was merely irrational.

The trouble with emotional reactions to this sort of criticism, and for that matter, any criticism, is that the comforts of self-delusion don't last. Stubborn reality tends to crash down on the fake. As that movie *Bedazzled* with Elizabeth Hurley proves, wishful thinking doesn't work. And we suffer the consequences.

Paying no attention to the critics means that I preclude constructive improvement of my writing for my next book. Since critics help sell books, it is to my economic advantage to exit my fool's paradise and stand in the harsh light of reality, however bright and painful that light may be.

Herd instinct and groupthink often involve partial selections.

Nearly everybody finds it difficult to maintain ideas that differ radically from those generally accepted. The few people who dare to maintain novel principles have not only to resist the persecution that nonconformity usually provokes but also to fight against the innate tendency to conform to the herd. Consider the following blurb sent from a New York firm trying to get my investment business:

> With the memories of the turmoil sparked by Long-Term Capital Management fading, everyone from fund managers to high-end investors is giving hedge funds a closer look.
>
> Long the glamour child of the investment community, more and more folks are eyeing these unregulated, unadvertised instruments as just the investment vehicles to smooth out the market's often-erratic ride. Assets in hedge funds have mushroomed since '95.

Christina Wise of *Investors' Business Daily* is the author of that piece of junk.

Analysis: My memory of Long-Term Capital's failure has not faded, so the first sentence doesn't apply to me. In fact, I remember LTCM quite well. Long-Term Capital Management's assets fell to less than $800 million from $1.25 trillion. There was more than turmoil in LTCM—there were losses. Its losses totaled $4.6 billion. Of course, LTCM, near collapse, had to be bailed out with the help of Alan Greenspan. LTCM was all the more riveting to outsiders for the size of the stakes, magnified by the huge amount of leverage (borrowed money) that the fund was using, and for the reputations of the two principal players, the economists Robert C. Merton and Myron S. Scholes, whose work on option pricing won the Nobel Prize for economics in 1997. These supposed masters of the universe stumbled, brought low not so much by their own theories as by global events that no theory could foresee.

To continue with the analysis of this inane article from *Investors' Business Daily*, how could everyone, from fund managers to high-end investors, be giving hedge funds a closer look? That statement can't be true. A few people might be giving the funds a look. Even *many* people might be giving a look. But everyone? No way. I am somebody, and I am not looking. In fact, I am looking the opposite way.

Wait a second. I *am* giving them a look. Because I am discussing them in this book, I am inadvertently giving them another look. But, if I am giving another look, it is certainly not the look that Wise means. In my look, I am cocking a malicious eye because I see plenty of stupidities in the blurb and in unregulated hedge funds, hedge funds that have undone so many.

And what if it were true? Yeah. What if it were true that everyone is looking more closely at hedge funds? So what? Should I do something merely because other people are doing it? Obviously, the statement is an appeal to the herd instinct. The writer wants us to think that because everyone is looking closely at the hedge funds, we should, too. We should get on the bandwagon. The trouble with following the herd is that it often doesn't know where it is going. It might be going over a cliff. You might go over with it, like all those little lemmings you have heard of.

Notice that the first paragraph doesn't mention how or why people are looking closely at the hedge funds. The looks might not be all that favorable. Multiple investigations have taken place about LTCM, and multiple criticisms have been voiced against the hedge funds precisely because they are "unregulated."

Not incidentally, the reason hedge funds are unadvertised is that they are forbidden to advertise. Furthermore, they are restricted by law to investors with more than $1 million in liquid assets or with yearly incomes of more than $200,000.

Notice the emotive language of the second paragraph. Have hedge funds been "a glamour child" of the investment industry? Not to my knowledge. Glamour child? More like a black sheep of the family, I would say. Or for those millionaires who lost their shirts in LTCM, the wolf at the door.

Notice that paragraph two contradicts paragraph one. In paragraph two, we are told that more and more folks are eyeing the hedge funds. More and more? I thought everyone was already doing it? This is of course another appeal to the herd instinct. The unsupported assertion is that since more and more folks are doing it, we should do it, too.

In the world of investments, you are neither right nor wrong because the crowd disagrees with you. You are right because your data and reasoning are right. Similarly, in the world of securities, courage becomes the supreme virtue after adequate knowledge and a tested judgment are at hand.

The desire to conform like this to the opinion or behavior of the crowd is unreasonable because it encourages us to accept the supposed opinions and views of others without evidence. Views prevalent in the community—any community, large or small, whether they are held by fund directors or high-end investors or just folks—are not necessarily true or false. All views, whether held by an individual or by a group, must be subject to further thought and analysis of evidence. Anything that tends to emphasize the difference from the herd's received opinion(s), or form a herd within a herd, is nearly always not reasonably disagreeable in and of itself. But people are only too inclined to regard the differences as bad and therefore label those differences with pejorative terms like, *wicked, bad form, below standard, undesirable,* and the like. How many times have you heard that Mexicans are lazy or irresponsible reproducers or that Ebonics is not good English?

When we find ourselves entertaining an opinion without adequately examining the evidence for it, it is a good indication that that opinion is not entirely rational. In fact, the opinion is probably founded on inadequate or partially selected evidence or some other defect in thinking.

Why is the herd instinct so deeply ingrained into the structure of our thinking? No one knows. But the theory is that for hundreds of thousands of years, the survival of our primitive ancestors depended on fairly complete cooperation in hunting and defense. Five or ten thousand years of civilization has done little to reduce the power of the ancient tribal imperative. It is part of our human inheritance, so to speak. One example of an advantage conferred by social habits in the struggle for survival is shown by a pack of wolves killing a bear. When the pack acts as one, it acts with strength, that of many. To cook a mammoth or to get everyone in the tribe to sleep together in the same cave required an organization of group behavior. Individuals had to be sensitive to the group's behavior; they had to possess the herd instinct. What's wrong with that?

Insofar as group behavior is right, there is nothing wrong with following along. But when the group is wrong, trouble lies ahead. One need only watch the old films of the Nazi rallies at Nuremberg to know how wrong group behavior can get. Too much gregariousness, too much social organization and control, can lead to disaster.

Tradition is a form of herd instinct wherein much evidence is neglected.
Blindly following tradition is irrational because it prevents us from

understanding the reasons for the tradition and therefore limits our freedom to do something differently. There may have been a reason at some time in the remote past for the strict prohibition of eating pork that is set by the Muslim and the Jewish religions. Such reasons may or may not still abide. Traditions, like everything else, must be continually updated in view of the cold light of reason, else human progress will remain limited.

Jains have such severe prohibitions on eating that many of them become malnourished. Skyclad Jains feel that eating any sort of meat is an aggression and therefore prohibited. For similar reasons, Jains are prohibited from engaging in agriculture. Thus, the scope of what Jains can do and what they may eat narrows. This Skyclad Jain fear of doing violence is extrapolated to vegetables: Jain ascetics will not eat any vegetable for fear of damaging the plant. They eat only those things thrown off the plants as detritus: leaves and fruits that fall from the branches. Further extrapolation of this dietary restriction to its natural conclusion results in Jain monks not wearing clothing, for clothes are a form of violence to something. Those ascetics who have achieved *kevalin* (absolute knowledge) do not eat at all. Most of them continue to live for about two months before achieving ultimate karma reduction on the ultimate weight reduction diet. Thus, even these superreligious people cannot avoid the consequences that naturally fall on those who follow the ultimate diet: eating nothing at all. The consequence of eating nothing at all is death. And that is what happens to all those who achieve *kevalin*.

Fear of being alone is a form of herd instinct.

Gregarious animals, even when living alone, persist in behaving as if they were part of a group. This is why a dog may eat hurriedly and "wolf" down food, although there is no reason to fear that the food may be snatched away. In man, the main item evidencing persistence of herd gregariousness is the fear of physical or emotional or mental solitude. Such fears underlie the need to talk even when there is nothing to say. Such fears underlie the need for contact with others even though we may have better things to do. Such fears underlie our species' remarkable susceptibility to leadership and our remarkable interest in celebrity. The fear of not being "in the loop," "in the know," "in the swim," "in the groove," "hip," "in fashion," or approved by the group in some matter, shape, or form has the adverse effect on our rational thinking that is nearly always damaging. This is because it encourages us to accept without reason or evidence whatever the herd dictates. This effect would be less damaging if majorities were right more often. The founding fathers of America were well aware of herd instinct, and that is why they were so much against having a state religion and so much in favor of free speech (one of the reasons, anyway). Along these lines, the free flow of correct information is absolutely necessary for considered judgment, and that is why the government should not be permitted to lie to the public or restrict the flow of information, the public should have free access to information, and state secrecy should be eliminated.

Misfits, oddballs, eccentrics, and others who don't fit in are probably engineered by evolution into the human species to aid the majority in correcting erroneous thinking or to protect the species from extinction by overdoing conformity to some kooky idea.

A good case could be made for the truth of the above statement. Most great advances in science and government have been made by people of genius, eccentric figures who refuse to accept what their contemporaries thought was obvious and self-evident. Because these individuals frighten the herd by their strangeness, many of the world's greatest benefactors have been persecuted or put to death. Look at Jesus. Look at Socrates. Look at Joan of Arc, who rid France of English domination. Look at Darwin. Look at Galileo. Look at the homosexuals whose contribution to art, drama, literature, fashion design, food preparation, and such has been enormous.

Custom is a form of herd instinct. As such, it is neither right nor wrong—just culturally relative.

Thus, American women who wear rings in their ears regard it as barbaric for African women to wear bones in their noses. Which is right? Rings in ears? Bones in nose? Both? Neither? Clearly, what women wear is a cultural social thing and is not right or wrong. To claim that wearing bones in the nose is wrong is to select evidence from one part of the world while neglecting evidence from another. This is therefore an error in thinking that, for no good reason, selects one custom as correct and selects the other as incorrect. Apply the same thinking to tattoos. Good? Bad? Who really cares? Tattoos are OK for those who want them and not OK for those who don't.

Resistance to anything that threatens mental harmony accounts for our dislike of change. When William Willett proposed setting the clocks back or forward according to the seasons to preserve daylight, he was roundly rebuked for all sorts of phony reasons. Arguments were put for-

ward that manipulating the clock was blasphemous, lunatic, or imprac-
tical. The plan was really opposed initially because it was a change,
something different.

In 1846, Boston dentist William Morton first introduced ether to
pull a tooth. Up to that time, people just had to suffer during surgery,
which was performed only in extreme emergencies. Anesthesia offered
the advantage that the operation could be performed more leisurely,
under better controlled circumstances, and without the patient feeling
pain. Such great advantages, you would think, would have led to the
rapid employment of the newly discovered agents that cause complete or
partial loss of pain. But (not surprisingly) anesthesia met with stern
opposition. The arguments advanced against it included that it was
unnatural and blasphemous. If God had intended that mankind not
suffer pain, he would not have created pain for mankind to suffer. Use of
anesthesia during childbirth was considered particularly problematic
because the Bible said that women should bring forth children in pain.
Actually, that problem was more easily solved than first imagined. The
book of Genesis did not prescribe pain in childbirth, only sorrow. Therefore, measures to prevent pain might actually be allowed by the Bible:
"Unto the woman he said, 'I will greatly multiply thy sorrow and thy conception; in sorrow thou shalt bring forth children.'" The real reason for
the opposition was that anesthesia required a revision of accepted ideas.

> *Principle:* Opposition to the new and different is irra-
> tional because it substitutes habit for consideration of
> the evidence and to that extent is a partial selection of
> evidence and therefore wrong.

From which follows:

> *Lesson:* What's new and different is neither good nor bad,
> save that reason makes it so. Adopt new things as soon as
> they are proven safe and effective advances over the old.

Habit is frequently a partial selection.

Yes, we are creatures of habit. As creatures of habit, we dislike
change. From infancy to adulthood, many of us are taught to accept the
prevailing ideas of our age, the traditions of our class, the customs of
the country, and the opinions of the people in charge, including our

parents. In later life, we look back on the world in which we grew up as the best of all possible worlds and describe our youth with a partially selected forgetfulness as the "good old days." Most times, customs are so ingrained that we can't even think our way to something new and different. When I traveled to England with a group of American tourists, I heard complaints that the traffic was moving on the wrong side of the road and that made it hazardous for Americans to cross the street because instead of looking left initially, they should be looking right.

When my physician friend came to visit me in Paris while I was there on sabbatical, he complained bitterly that the people were speaking French instead of a language that could be better understood, namely, English.

Such people assume, without thinking, that there is no other view than that which they happen to enjoy. From their standpoint, only one facet of the truth is revealed. They don't care how different things can easily be and yet remain commodious.

Prejudice is a form of herd instinct based on partial selection of evidence.

In chapter 1 we discussed how a prejudiced person can suffer greatly. We learned about the cops who were arrested by the county judge. Thus prejudice can hurt both those who are prejudiced and the victim. A prejudiced person is unreasonable because he has based his opinion on preconceived notions without paying due attention to the evidence. Remember, the only reasonable ground for holding a belief is that the facts require us to do so. People guilty of prejudice *prejudge* the facts and hence have jumped to unwarranted conclusions.

> *Principle:* Prejudice is an error in thinking.

From which follows:

> *Lesson:* Don't hold unwarrantable opinions. Don't believe what is comfortable to believe. Don't let your thinking be influenced by feelings or the opinion of the group.

> *Principle:* All personal provincial prejudices are wrong.

My opinion that doctors should not have to pay taxes because doctors perform such important social services is obviously suspect, since I am a doctor and thus likely to have allowed irrelevant personal considerations—like my desire for a new and bigger boat—to have more weight than they deserve. A hunter who has just shot a deer might tell himself that the kill was clean and painless and that the deer didn't really mind because it didn't know what hit it. The hunter might believe this and, in fact, the hunter might be right, but the hunter is nevertheless prejudiced insofar as he reaches his conclusion not because of the facts but because he derives pleasure from a pursuit that is too cruel to contemplate objectively. Consider the following statement: "Hunting is really an act of kindness to deer. It reduces the number in the group and allows for the herd to have enough food."

Any prejudice in evidence?

What if the statement came from a hunter? What if the statement came from a farmer whose crops have been devastated by deer? What if the statement came from an environmental protection park ranger who has a PhD in wild animal management?

Law must make every effort to eliminate prejudice, else justice will suffer.

The law understands prejudice and bends over backward to avoid it. That is why juries are not permitted to know about the previous convictions of accused persons. If they did, it might be almost impossible for them to judge the present case without prejudice. That a person previously broke and entered is not proof that he committed the same crime again. (If you don't get this, stop here and think about it.)

Knowledge of a prisoner's past would color his trial. What is necessary to convict the accused is evidence, not that he did a previous crime but that he did the crime for which he is now being tried.

The rules of evidence, the constitutional protection from self-incrimination, the requirement that testimony of accomplices (especially accomplices given immunity for their testimony) be independently corroborated, and many other fine principles of law are based on the need to avoid prejudice. Where would the testimony of Monica Lewinsky be if there were not the DNA evidence on that cocktail dress? How much could we believe her testimony when she had already lied under oath and was now changing her story to (in part) get less harsh treatment from the justice department?

The law recognizes that self-interest makes people susceptible to prejudice. Persons should not vote at a board meeting of Enron, at a city council meeting, or (God help us!) in the US Senate if they have a personal financial interest in anything under consideration. Heavy penalties should attach to any such dishonorable conduct by any member of Congress sworn to represent the interest of all the people. Unfortunately, in the cold, harsh light of history, we learn that many public servants are not in their positions to serve the public but to line their own pockets.

Beware vested interests; they can cause trouble.

When Saint Paul attacked the goddess Diana at Ephesus, the center of Diana worship, he met considerable opposition from the guild that made the silver statues of the goddess. When Christ challenged the powers that be, he got into serious trouble. What happened is a good illustration of what happens when vested interests are threatened.

"Pilate then went out unto them, and said, 'What accusation bring ye against this man?' They answered and said unto him, 'If he were not a malefactor, we would not have delivered him up unto thee'" (John 18:29–30).

Note the tautology and the circular argument. The crowd is merely restating that it thinks Jesus is doing wrong or has done wrong; we can't tell which. The argument is circular because, in effect, it says, "Jesus is a criminal. If he were not a criminal, he wouldn't be accused of being a criminal." The type of malefaction, and the evidence for what Jesus did wrong, is not stated. Therefore, irrational factors are at work. The real reason that Jesus is in trouble is never stated. The chief priests wanted Jesus killed because Jesus had criticized their hypocrisy.

"Then said Pilate unto them, 'Take ye him, and judge him according to your law.' The Jews therefore said unto him, 'It is not lawful for us to put any man to death'" (John 18:31).

Notice that the crowd members are not particularly concerned with the formality of a trial or the detailed examination of Jesus' guilt or innocence. Their concern is that they don't have the real authority to put Jesus to death. That's what they want. They don't want to judge Jesus; they want to kill him. The Jewish law at the time forbade capital punishment, but it didn't forbid getting around the law by having the Romans do the dirty work. The Jews depicted here are guilty of the extreme error of selecting all evidence out of consideration and letting their emotions ride free.

Further along, Pilate asked Jesus, "What hast thou done?"

Note that Pilate is still trying to figure out the problem. Pilate is, like any good judge, interested in the evidence for the transgression. And like any good judge, Pilate is getting irritated because the crowd is just feeding him bullshit. The crowd just wants blood. But the crowd knows it doesn't have the right to crucify Christ.

"Jesus answered, . . . 'for this cause came I into the world, that I should bear witness unto the truth. Everyone that is of the truth heareth my voice.' Pilate saith unto him, 'What is truth?'" (John 18:36–38).

Jesus is now making assertions without evidence. His generalization can't be correct. It is impossible that everyone that is of the truth hears him. It is a big world out there, and Pilate knows it. Jesus' voice carries only so far and no further. And Pilate justly asks Jesus to define the word *truth* because in this context Jesus seems to be begging the question (an error wherein something is asserted as true that needs to be proven true). Jesus has assumed the point in the dispute and taken for granted the truth of something that requires proof before his argument can be accepted. Therefore, Jesus has "begged the question." The very extravagance of the emotive language frequently betrays it for what it is. Only the simplest-minded person could believe that the trial was objective. So perhaps Jesus, who appears to have been an intelligent man, realized that his was a lost cause. Perhaps Jesus was just trying to get across his core message that the truth was important. Perhaps Jesus wanted to make one final assertion for posterity, an assertion that my personal bias backs and supports: that truth is important, so important it is worth dying for.

In fact, Jesus telling the truth about current conditions among the Hebrews was the root cause of his political troubles. For it was the truth that generated the hatred of the Scribes and Pharisees. If Jesus had attempted to explain even the premise of his argument that the Scribes and Pharisees were corrupt, they would have probably stoned him then and there, particularly as the reluctance of an audience to be instructed is usually proportional to its ignorance.

The Jews in question, unlike Pilate, were not prepared to hear the arguments on the other side but preferred to shout "Crucify him, crucify him" (their slogan) repeatedly, thereby silencing opposition.

The episode illustrates what happens when cherished beliefs and long-standing traditions and entrenched powers are threatened. The crowd gets pugnacious, stops thinking, and starts shouting slogans to encourage itself.

> *Principle:* Chanting crowds are herds out of control: The stronger the crowd feels about something, the less likely it makes sense.

From which follows:

> *Lesson:* Chanting crowds mean trouble. Avoid them. Usu-
> ally, what the crowd wants is wrong. Have nothing to do
> with it.

"Pilate therefore went forth again and saith unto them, 'I find no
fault with this just man. See to it yourselves'" (John 18:38).

In effect, Pilate has told the crowd, no evidence, no case. This is
exactly the correct conclusion, the only justified conclusion at law.

Watch out for truths labeled as obvious.

Despite our knowledge that most of the great advances in science
and in ethics have been made by rejecting "obvious" truths, we cling
uncritically to habits and traditions. Remember, it was once thought
that the heart was the center of the soul, that the red blood cell was
inert, that Earth was the center of the universe, that kings were chosen
by God, and so forth.

The quest for certainty and the irrational belief that certainty exists
is an error in thinking often due to partial (and premature) selection of
evidence.

The human mind likes to keep things the same and simple. Because
the human mind seeks comfort, questions that should remain open
and undecided become prematurely settled. Skepticism that the evidence demands is discarded. Unable to bear the suspense of judgment
that reason often requires, we find it intolerable to live in a world that
doesn't entirely make sense; therefore, we construct a false image of that
world, which we consider reality even though it is fantasy.

Think of any political, moral, esthetic, ethical controversy. For instance, the Earth goes around the sun. Why did it take so long for it to
be generally accepted that the Earth revolves around the sun and that
the Earth is not the center of the universe? Take evolution. Why did the
theory of evolution (which, by the way, is a fact, not a theory) take so
long to be generally accepted? How about equal rights for women?

The more passionately something is believed, the more likely it is wrong.

The number of people who believe with passionate conviction that
they understand the problem involved must indicate that most of them
must be mistaken. Admittedly, there might be many reasons behind
passionate convictions, but one of those reasons is the need to avoid
the discomfort of uncertainty.

Principle: Few things are as simple as we would like them to be. The ability to reason decreases as emotions increase.

From which follows:

Lesson: Skepticism, though uncomfortable, is probably more useful than faith. Opinions on most subjects are seldom more than opinions. The more inflamed we become, the less able we are to think clearly.

Emotional interest often makes it much easier for us to detect prejudice in other people than it is to recognize it in ourselves. Why do you think a man who suffers from leukemia told me that his doctor never told him what his problem was? How in the world could this guy report for weekly chemotherapy and still claim ignorance of the reason for the treatments? The poor soul refused to believe he might die because to face that fact was too much for him. That he is seriously ill is too unpleasant for his ego to handle. So he denies the illness by denying that he knows about it. He explains why he doesn't know anything about his disease by blaming his physician for not telling him. Having prejudged the issue, he has forced the facts to conform to his emotional need. How easily do we see through his facade! We can see through others. But we are unlikely to realize that we deceive ourselves when our wishes for wealth or happiness or our dread of ruin and death lead us to believe propositions that, if true, would secure the objects we desire or avert the disaster we fear.

What's wrong with that? It doesn't work.

Does this sound familiar? Such wishful thinking doesn't work because it is contrary to the truth, to the reality in which we are situated, and to the reality from which we cannot escape (for long) without significant risk to life and limb.

For example, "My Enron stock has gone from thirty to six. I'll just hold it until it comes back." Did holding on to Enron work? No way, José.

What does this selection from the Gospel according to Saint Matthew mean? "And why beholdest thou the mote that is in thy brother's eye, but considerest not the beam that is in thine own eye? Or how wilt thou say to thy brother, 'Let me pull out the mote out of thine eye,' and behold, a beam is in thine own eye. Thou hypocrite, first cast out the beam out of thine own eye; and then shalt thou see clearly to cast out the mote out of thy brother's eye."

Yep, it is easy to see the defects in others, in what they believe and what they don't believe, but to recognize the same process at work in ourselves would be to discard personal prejudice.

Color prejudice is a partial selection and therefore unreasonable and wrong.

Judging anyone from a single trait or quality partially selects the evidence and therefore is unreasonable. "The Irish are drunks." "The Hispanics lazy." "The Jews control the media." Sweeping statements like those are bound to be wrong and, even if they were not wrong, they would require load on load of evidence to support them before we should accept them as true.

Among the common errors of judging we find the color problem. There is no reason (apart from some very special considerations related to the increased sensitivity of white skin to sunlight and the decreased sensitivity of black skin to the same) to judge anyone merely on the basis of skin color anymore than it would make sense to judge, say, a presidential candidate on the basis of eye color or hair color. Color, any color of any body part, is just not relevant to the office of president.

Color prejudice has caused lots of trouble. It may have played a role in the war that killed more Americans than any other war ever fought by the United States, the Civil War. Color prejudice certainly plays a role in the social upheavals that plagued the United States in the sixties. Of interest, the writers of the Declaration of Independence said that "We hold these truths to be self-evident, that all men are created equal." Yet slavery continued in the United States for eighty-seven years. How come? The founding fathers were smart men. They must have spotted the contradiction right away.

Yes and no.

In a sense, they knew about the problem, but few subjects are more promising for the study of how the human mind refuses to get around prejudice than the color problem. Millions of Negroes were kept in slavery while their masters proclaimed the principles of liberty and equality for all men. This contradiction between ideal and practice naturally troubled sensitive consciences. Opponents of slavery pointed out that the Declaration of Independence said that all men, not just a few and not just the whites, were created equal. How would the slave owners get around this irrefutable point? Think for a second. If you were a slave owner, how could you rationalize owning slaves and yet still subscribe to the idea that all men were created equal?

Answer: Slave owners discovered that the phrase "all men" excluded Negroes because Negroes were, properly speaking (according to slave owners), not humans. Rather, Negroes were considered (by slave owners) a kind of subhuman species. In some cases, it was proclaimed (irrationally) that Negroes were intellectually and morally inferior to whites and completely uneducable. In other cases, it was proclaimed, (irrationally) that Negroes were children, even though they might grow old, and therefore Negroes required someone to take care of them. And by extrapolation, if Negroes were children, it was in their best interest to remain under the control of the masters, who were parental substitutes.

Despite these ingenious arguments, a few obstinate eccentrics continued to challenge this racial theory. These challenges brought forth further arguments. When it was found that on the average, the Negro brain was forty cubic centimeters smaller than the average white brain, these measurements were alleged to establish the black man's inferiority. Any problems with that reasoning?

Besides the argument's simplicity, the argument is based on the assumption that brain power and brain size are directly related. They are not. Alphonse Daudet, the French writer, had a brain that at autopsy weighed only half normal, about 750 grams. The weight of Albert Einstein's brain was about 150 grams below average. Once the argument of brain size had served racist purposes, it would never have done to investigate the question more closely. Polynesians, Kaffirs, and Eskimos all have larger brains on average than European whites.

To use an argument when it supports our preconceptions and reject it in another context when it fails to do so is known as special pleading. Watch out for special pleading, for it is an exceedingly common error in thinking. It usually arises in discussions in which the person advancing the argument claims some special exemption or special benefit for himself while denying that exemption or benefit to others.

My argument that doctors should be tax exempt would be highly suspicious in light of the fact that I am a doctor and would benefit financially from tax exemption. Viewed in this cold light, the special pleading for tax exemption seems entirely self-serving and silly, yet our tax laws are riddled with all sorts of special exemptions (often known as loopholes) just as self-serving and silly. These special exemptions apply to individuals and corporations for political reasons, often in return for contributions to political campaigns.

The trouble is that so many of these special exemptions are hidden from the public. For instance, did you know that certain legislators receive payments from the government over and above their salaries that are in lieu of expenses? They need not account for these payments, which are not taxed on the theory (a rationale) that the funds were expended as legitimate expenses of office. In reality, the payments represent tax-exempt pay for public office holders, particularly those in Congress. The people in power have a deep affection for these payments in lieu of expenses and affectionately call them *Lulus*—payments in lieu of expenses, often those that were not spent for government business.

The argument that such payments are needed to attract qualified people to government or to permit the proper execution of the duties of office are arguments that, if not supported by relevant and adequate evidence, smack of special pleading.

One of the major offenders in this area of crooked thinking is the United States Government. The government has constructed sets of special exceptions to what is otherwise the general law of the land. Thus, federal employees (including the members of the Senate and House of Representatives) do not pay Social Security taxes. They are excused from participation in the program because they have their own plans. Yet if I wished to be excluded from the Social Security system because I have another pension plan, force of law would prevent me. And if I insisted on not paying Social Security taxes, I would be sent to jail. Government office buildings are exempt from regulations that control the safety of nongovernment buildings. VA hospitals, among the least safe in the nation, are exempt from multiple rules that govern all other hospitals except the Indian Service, which, incidentally, is also run by an agency of the federal government, the Public Health Service. Until recently, the House and Senate was exempt from OSHA rules. Now they are only partially exempt. And so forth.

Consider the following from page 1 of the *New York Times*, March 30, 2002: "The Pentagon is seeking an exemption to laws that protect endangered species and their habitats, saying that they interfere with training and weapons development." Pause and think. Any evidence of special pleading? How would you counter this argument?

Answer: This is a special pleading because the Pentagon is applying principles, rules, and criteria to others while failing to or refusing to apply them to itself. The Pentagon's self-serving and silly argument that it should be exempt from environment protection laws is highly suspicious in light of the fact that the Pentagon would benefit from the exemption and would be excused from past offenses in which it was out of compliance.

How would you argue against such exemptions?

"The equal administration of justice is the firmest pillar of good government" is the motto engraved on the Second District Supreme Court building in New York City. If that is true and the government believes it, then special exception to laws would be a violation of equal administration. Hence, exemptions are wrong.

The Pentagon has not provided relevant and sufficient evidence (in number, kind, and weight) for the need for the exception. Some people, myself included, would argue that the weapons programs, since they are so destructive to wildlife habitats, should not only not be exempt, they also should come under special scrutiny to make sure they conform to environment protection rules.

This book is not concerned with arming you to attack fallacies. It is designed to help you reach the truth by reasoning things out. This book is not designed to help you attack the unclear thinking of others or win arguments. But special pleading by the government is so widespread and egregious that I will give you some tips on what to do to effectively counter arguments like this one.

The most effective attack against special pleading is to accuse your opponent of applying a double standard, playing favorites, or being inconsistent. Each of these charges is commonly understood outside academic circles and has strong negative connotations, with which even the Pentagon will not wish to be associated.

Another effective attack is to ask why such a special exemption is justified and then attack the reasons point by point, showing their absurdity.

Sometimes, to help clarify the thinking on the issue, it helps to reduce the request for exemption to what is called *standard form*, that is, the form of a syllogism:

> Premise one: Environmental protection laws should in general be applied uniformly.

> Premise two: But because the work of weapons development is so important, and not like the work of any industry in the degree of importance, the Pentagon should be a special exemption to the environment rules.

Conclusion: Therefore, environmental protection should not be applied to the Pentagon.

The Pentagon must agree with premise one because it is stated in the Constitution under the equal protection clause. Most people, including those in the Pentagon, would agree that premise two contradicts premise one, and therefore the conclusion that rests upon premise two must be wrong.

The rich often advance arguments why they should be taxed less than the poor. The rich feel that they need the money to create jobs and to advance other important societal goals. CEOs believe they need a large salary because of the particular importance of the work they do, because their savings increase the wealth of the nation, and because their expenditures maintain full employment. Sometimes the argument is even more silly: that the money given to advance the prosperity of the rich will trickle down to others and will eventually reach the poor. Otherwise stated: Give money to the rich, and everyone benefits. Yet while advocating high salaries and benefits for themselves, many CEOs would argue that the wages they pay others should be kept low to advance the company's bottom line, to protect stockholder value, to prevent inflation, and so forth.

Couldn't the argument be reversed and remain equally cogent? Give money to the poor, and everyone benefits. Pay high wages and more money in circulation will boost the general prosperity?

How would you counter the following argument: "Money to the poor? No way. The poor will just spend it on beer and betting on horse races." Besides the usual objections, the mutual inconsistency of propositions like this statement can be brought out by changing the context of the application. Have the rich person who propounded this absurdity admit the underlying assumption of his argument. Think for a moment and try to discover what is the assumption underlying the above argument.

Got it? Great. Proceed to the next paragraph. Don't get it? Then reread the statement. Doesn't it imply that the poor should not be permitted to spend their money they way they wish? If that is true, then wouldn't it be consistent to consider that the rich should not be permitted to spend their money the way they wish?

Yep, that's the way to nail a special pleader. Force them to apply their general assumption to the particular case that hits closer to home. In this instance, the real question is, "Are the poor entitled to spend their money the way they wish, even if they are spending it on beer and horse racing? If the poor are not entitled to spend their money on such things, then how come the rich are entitled to spend their money on expensive French wines, foreign travel, yachts, private jets, luxury meals at the Four Seasons, diamonds and pearls, and so on?" If the general principle is that no one can spend their money on frivolous pastimes, then the general principle should apply to rich and poor alike. Otherwise, the principle is not generally applicable and therefore fallacious.

Of course, the rich person who dislikes the poor spending money on beer will have strong objections to anyone preventing them from spending money on wine.

> *Principle:* Bad arguments are easy to detect when they involve money, personal interest, and power.

From which follows:

> *Lesson:* If there are vested interests in a person's argument, watch out. Most likely, the argument is wrong. Expose the interest and counter the argument by eliminating the interest for that person. After the vested interest is exposed and eliminated, most bad arguments will disappear.

How would you approach this argument if it were offered by an oil company executive? "We should drill for oil in the Arctic wildlife refuge. That will assure our energy independence for decades to come, protect our freedom, and reduce gasoline prices."

The truth is that the oil companies stand to benefit greatly from such drilling. But the idea that they will profit greatly from the endeavor is not mentioned. The argument could be changed completely by asserting that since the drilling will take place on public land, the profits derived from the activity—all the profits, not just part of the profits—rightfully belong to the public and none of those profits belongs to the oil companies. Once the profits have disappeared, I'll bet drilling advocates will, for the most part, also disappear. Their real interest was their own good and not that of the public.

External reports issued by accountants are intended to provide financial information about the firm audited to outside individuals and businesses. The Security and Exchange Commission (SEC) requires publicly traded firms to file external reports every ninety days and a more complete report every year. Because these external reports are necessary for obtaining loans, establishing credit, attracting investors, and recruiting key employees, most nonpublicly traded firms produce them as well.

SEC requires three types of external reports: a balance sheet, an income statement, and a cash-flow statement. Those three reports constitute the company's "financial statements."

The financial statements are reviewed, audited, and "certified" by accounting firms that are independent of the business being audited. The financial statements required by the SEC must meet what are called Generally Accepted Accounting Principles, or "GAAP" (pronounced "gap"), standards, which are the concepts, conventions, rules, and procedures that together make up accepted accounting practices. One of the main principles of GAAP is that the accountant should use methods that will never overstate the value of assets or income or understate the amount of a debt or expenditure.

Enron listed its income but put its debt off the financial statements. Enron listed its cash flow into the business but concealed its cash flow out.

If I were to list just my assets and none of my liabilities, the picture of my personal wealth would be skewed to present a more favorable view than was justified by the reality. If I listed just my debts and none of my assets, the picture of my personal wealth would be skewed to present a less favorable view than was justified by the reality. So by partial selection of the evidence, I could "prove" that I was rich or that I was broke. By the same token, by partial selection of evidence one can "prove" that religion is great or terrible, that science is wonderful or dreadful, or that a company is doing well or poorly.

Enron and Arthur Andersen partially selected evidence by transferring debt to partnerships that were off the books. Consequently, the picture of Enron available to outsiders, the public, and, in many cases, to the creditors and banks was skewed toward a more favorable picture than was justified by the reality. And as we have learned from the aviation example in the introduction, reality has a tendency to come crashing in on our fantasy world. Reality asserted itself on Enron, just as it always does.

Principle: Truth will out.

From which follows:

Lesson: Concealing the truth from yourself or others tends to give only short-lived temporary benefits. Reality usually asserts itself, often quite harshly. Don't lie.

Accounting, like every profession, is an art in which considerable judgment is involved. By its nature, business activity is exceedingly variable. No single set of accounting rules could ever perfectly describe every situation. In practice, accountants must use their judgment. Good accountants may (and often do) disagree about the specific treatment of certain transactions. Always, however, accountants are expected to be able to justify their decisions, often by reference to GAAP.

By what criteria will the accounting judgments be judged? By the evidence, of course. But what if the evidence has been destroyed? The criminal indictment of Arthur Andersen for fraud would require proof beyond a reasonable doubt, whereas a civil trial on the same issue would require proof by a preponderant weight of evidence. Either way, criminal or civil trials would require analysis of evidence.

But where is the evidence? Nowhere. That was the trouble. The evidence no longer exists. It has been destroyed by shredding. Because the evidence is so important in reaching reasonable conclusions about what happened, destruction of evidence is itself a crime.

Thus, Arthur Andersen was indicted not for poor accounting but for obstruction of justice because it destroyed crucial evidence. All that is now required for conviction is proof beyond a reasonable doubt that the evidence was destroyed with the intention of thwarting justice. The jury concluded that that was true and convicted the firm. Because of the criminal conviction, the firm lost its license to do public accounting. Arthur Andersen is now defunct. Reality, that harsh jade, had her revenge. Arthur Andersen as a licensed public accounting firm is no more.

Recall that a tautology is a circular argument made by repeating the same meaning twice. Repetition of the same statement is even worse and not a reasonable argument. Repetition, rather, indicates the absence of a reasonable argument. Some people like to have their ideas reinforced by repetition. Other people just like to hear themselves talk. Either way, repetitions are ineluctable tautologies easy to spot, often mere assertions like: "That's the rule"; "It's against company policy"; "That's the way we do things around here"; "Like it or lump it"; "It's tradition"; "I talked it over with the staff and we all came to that conclusion"; and so forth.

The full exchange in repetition tautology looks like this:

Nurse: Patients are not allowed out of their rooms during doctors' rounds.
Patient: Why are we not allowed out of our rooms during doctors' rounds?
Nurse: It's the rule.

The nurse's explanation is not a clarification or elucidation of the reasons for the prohibition. It is merely a restatement of the rule in a different form. The nurse's second statement says nothing new and is off the point and tautological. The patient would have a right to reply:

Patient: I asked for the reason for the rule. All you did was tell me the same thing twice. I already know that we are not allowed out of our rooms during doctors' rounds. I want to know why.
Nurse: Ward policy.
Patient: (now exasperated): I asked for a reason. And all you are doing is feeding me bullshit.

Arguing off the point gives the appearance of reason but is really just a rationale thinly disguised. It is an attempt to thicken proofs that demonstrate thinly.

Take the woman who says, "Don't touch me. I'm a Catholic." That the lady doesn't want to be touched cannot be doubted. But that she is a Catholic is not a reason that she should not be touched. Her failure to stick to the point is the mark of a confused thinker who is distracted (or is trying to distract) from the relevant issue. We have already mentioned other forms of diversion arguments that are non sequiturs, including argumentum ad hominem and argumentum ad verecundiam. Both of those assert false reasons and distract us from the truth.

Force is not a reasonable argument because it is not based on evidence.

At this point, I should mention a very common diversionary argument resorted to by the crude at the earliest instant and as a last resort by the more intelligent, an argument that neglects most or all the evidence and is therefore the extreme example of partial selection: **argumentum ad baculum**, the appeal to force.

Violence is off the point and is no substitute for reason. Bloody teeth don't prove anything (except damage). They certainly don't prove anyone right or wrong. Argumentum ad baculum is the gravest error in human thought, wherein the argument has degenerated into a fight. Might doesn't make right, despite the maxim to the contrary. Because someone defeats another person by force, that doesn't mean he was right or wrong, noble or ignoble, supported by God or by the devil, and so forth. It doesn't even mean that he was the strongest, smartest, or luckiest. It merely means he won the battle, no more and no less. Why he won would have to be established by evidence. In general, when someone resorts to violence or the threat of violence, she has thereby admitted that she has lost the rational argument and resorts to desperate measures rather than admit defeat.

> *Principle:* Resort to force is not a rational argument. It is quite the opposite, the epitome of irrationality. War is always an acknowledgment of failure, the worst solution.

From which follows:

> *Lesson:* Use violence as a last resort and only when desperate.

Another form of diversion is to refute some trivial point of an opponent's argument and then suggest that his whole position has been undercut. Whether the argument is undercut by the discovery of some incorrect supporting statement would depend on how much the conclusion depends on the incorrect statement, not on the discovery of the misstated fact per se.

Hecklers rely on humorous objections to discredit speakers. A politician who promises a car in every garage is not really refuted by the interrupter who shouts: "I don't have a garage." Such statements do not contain even a hint of intelligent thought. Yet they do make the speaker look absurd. And they tend to put the speaker off balance. To reply to such stupidities usually diverts the argument off the point. To ignore such stupidities may leave the impression that the heckler is unanswerable because the speaker is deficient in some way.

Despite a vast ignorance about almost everything, people have almost no qualms about spouting off opinions that, when viewed in the cold light, are hogwash. Since almost no one has taken the time or trouble to study issues and understand them, it is highly likely that almost no one has the authority, knowledge, or experience to speak intelligently on those issues, especially at a cocktail party or at a dinner where there has been considerable consumption of alcoholic beverages. It follows that most such publicly voiced opinions are based on inadequate, incomplete, and often erroneous information and are therefore to that extent unreasonable.

"Now that we have done the nasty, Tom, will you marry me?"

"Maybe, Lisa, maybe."

Tom's statement of "maybe" is a diversion away from an intelligent discussion of her question. It is a diversion designed to inspire hope, when it should—if Lisa were trained in detecting hidden meanings as we are—inspire fear.

Arguments that attempt to influence by appealing to popular sentiment such as patriotism, loyalty, tradition, custom, et cetera are known as **argumentum ad populum**, another diversionary argument because whether the group thinks something is not a reason that that something is correct. A group can be right, or it can be wrong. Whether it is right must be determined by evidence, not by consensus. "It's un-American!" "We don't do things that way!" "Most real Americans know . . ." are phrases that distract attention from the real points at issue. It may not be American to have the government own steel mills, as was done in the USSR, but whether it is American has nothing to do with whether it is desirable.

> *Principle:* Any strong opinion firmly held by the public is likely to be wrong at least in part.

From which follows:

> *Lesson:* Public opinion and generally held beliefs are not reasons for or against an issue. Instead of blindly accepting received wisdom, examine the evidence. Act accordingly.

×   ×   ×

Disciplined thought requires that we face facts fearlessly and look disinterestedly at all the evidence, not just part of the evidence; that we not reject evidence because it proves inconvenient or distasteful; and that we not accept evidence because it matches our preconceived opinions. The usual problem that prevents disciplined thought is an emotional vested interest in the outcome of our thinking. The secret workings of the unconscious mind prevent us from facing the truth and dealing with reality effectively. If we are ever to achieve rationality, we must do so by offsetting the influence of unconscious impulses. We must learn what those impulses are and in what context they are most likely to operate. And we must consciously prevent ourselves from partially selecting evidence that we like and rejecting evidence that we don't like.

Therefore, do not lean on arguments as a drunk leans on a lamppost, for support and not illumination. Do not accept arguments because they gratify your ego, advance your position, or help you go along with the crowd.

Pay particular attention to arguments that make you feel uncomfortable or that challenge your traditional beliefs. Therein you are most likely to fall into error.

REVIEW

Review the chapter as you did the previous ones. On the other hand, if you feel you don't need a review, pass on to chapter 6, which discusses the interesting error known as groupthink.

If you are not sure whether you need the drill, work out the following problem. Is there a national debt?

How would you determine whether the United States of America is in debt? Why is the question important? If there were no national debt, should taxes be increased or decreased? Why? Note down your ideas before reviewing mine.

Answer: Whether there is a national debt would depend on the evidence. Currently, the government lists only its liabilities and not its assets. Thus, the calculation of how much is owed is skewed. A more reasonable approach would be to list assets and liabilities, for one would offset the other. The assets of the government are numerous and valuable. They include all federally owned land and buildings; vast amounts of intellectual property; the gold in Fort Knox; production facilities, including Pantex, the factory in Amarillo that makes hydrogen bombs; and so forth. Surely all that stuff must be worth something. Yet those assets are never considered in calculating the national debt. Instead, what is included are the outstanding financial obligations of the United States. Furthermore, much of the public debt in the form of government bonds is actually owned by the citizens of this fair country. Can that be a real debt if Americans owe themselves? Could I list as a debt a billion dollars that I owed to myself as evidenced by an IOU that I have just written to myself?

Why would the government wish to understate its assets and overstate its debt? Has the amount of public debt ever been used to justify the high tax burden currently imposed on Americans? Could a reasonable argument be made that we are taxed to the max?

Taxes are the most important and largest single expense item of most households. This is because you are taxed on what you earn, taxed on what you buy, taxed on what you sell, and taxed on the real property you own, and your estate is taxed when you die. Further, as your pay increases, so does the tax on that pay. Considering the amounts of money involved and the long duration of our taxed life, it is reasonable to state that most people spend a considerable part of their lives working for various government taxing authorities. Now, Americans are taxed at a per capita rate higher than that at any other point in our history. It's true that the marginal tax rate on high incomes (including mine) used to be 90 percent and that it is less now. But the average working citizen still spends more than a third of his time working just to pay his taxes. The current rate of taxation per worker in the United States far exceeds the rates imposed by Charlemagne on his serfs in the eighth and ninth century. Remember that next time you go to vote. If taxes are not a major issue to you, they should be.

Key questions restated and answered directly:

Is there a national debt? Probably not. Reason: Partial selection of evidence only makes it appear that there is a national debt. In fact, a national surplus is likely.

How would you determine whether the United States of America is in debt? Answer: The usual way—liabilities minus assets equals debt. Why is the question important? If there is a national debt, we might wish to address how to pay it off or manage it. If there is a national surplus, we might want to address how to distribute it. If there were no national debt, should taxes be increased or decreased? Decreased. Why? To ease the tax burden.

chapter 6

Groupthink

Social influences normally shape our practices, judgments, and beliefs. A child speaks his parents' language; a member of a tribe in Papua submits to extensive scarification of the back as altogether fitting and proper. Conformity to the group is the way of the world. But good minds working together are not likely to outperform individuals when the group suppresses productive conflict, balanced debate, and careful reasoning. When the compunction to conform to the group goes against the reality principle, away from truth and toward error, purely on the basis of what the group thinks, the phenomenon is called *groupthink*.

Groupthink doesn't work because it is an error in thinking that leads away from reality toward a fake view of issues. Groupthink can lead to disaster, like the Bay of Pigs invasion and the mass suicides at Jonestown and in the Bo and Peep cult of Heaven's Gate.

Social psychologists have identified the multiple ways that groupthink occurs. Usually, the members agree prematurely on the wrong solution. Then they give each other feedback that makes the group as a whole feel certain that it is right, making the right choice. Members discourage each other from looking at the flaws in their thought processes and usually abrogate decision making to a strong leader. As usual, reality comes crashing in and teaches the group the lesson they needed to learn: When our opinions depend on the opinion of others and not on our own considered judgment, chances are that we will be proved wrong.

The name *groupthink* comes from the title of a book by Irving Janis, which analyzed the errors groups make. Cohesiveness, insulation, and stress led the groups to reach consensus early, supporting the leader in whatever he had initially proposed. Usually, the group's leader partially selected evidence that confirmed his and the group's opinions and failed to consider other evidence that did not support the group's position.

In a detailed analysis, Janis reports on the Bay of Pigs fiasco: "How could we have been so stupid?" an irate President John F. Kennedy asked after his invasion of Cuba had failed miserably. The answer is the group didn't fail because its members were stupid as individuals. No way. Not that group. The group failed because of a poor process in making their decisions, in short—groupthink.

The planners of the Bay of Pigs invasion included some of the smartest people in America: Robert McNamara, Douglas Dillon, Robert Kennedy, McGeorge Bundy, Arthur Schlesinger, Dean Rusk, and Allen Dulles. What went wrong?

Item: They all thought they couldn't fail because they knew they were so smart. How could such a smart group not devise a smart action? This illusion of invulnerability caused them to plunge in where more considered judgment might have held back. Smart people can and do make stupid decisions. The Bay of Pigs clearly illustrates that. What counts is not how smart or dumb you are but how right you are. And how right you are depends on how well you reasoned things through. Not opinion, not IQ, not previous experience or reputation, but reason supported by evidence controls the situation. The more cogent the reasons, the more tightly they relate to the conclusion, the more the evidence in support of the conclusion, the more likely the conclusion will be correct and reflect the truth and the reality situation. It's that or disaster. Take your choice.

Let's look at the Bay of Pigs decision more carefully.[1] It teaches many lessons.

Item: Individual members of the group censored themselves from voicing opposing opinions for fear of ridicule or because they did not want to waste the group's time. In a memorandum, Arthur Schlesinger said that he considered the invasion of Cuba immoral. Yet he kept his mouth shut when he attended the meetings of the Kennedy team. Subsequently, we learned that Schlesinger kept his mouth shut because Bobby Kennedy told him to do so: "You may be right or you may be wrong," said Bobby. "But the President has made his mind up. Don't push any further."

Item: Too few alternatives were considered. According to JFK, who tried to explain the mistake afterward, "The CIA gave us only two choices:

Invade or do nothing." Whether this was in fact the case, we don't know. JFK's public statement to that effect certainly made no friends at the CIA. Anyway, that's neither here nor there. The policy could have been framed quite differently by the president himself, for he, not the CIA, was in charge. Multiple options, alternatives, and other objectives could have been considered other than the black-and-white, do-either-this-or-that dilemma allegedly proposed by the CIA. Subsequently, the CIA said that the president's team did not wish to consider or even hear about the risks inherent in the invasion. Nor did the team seem interested in detailed analysis of opposing forces stationed near the Bay of Pigs. Nor did the team want to hear the even more interesting idea that the Cuban people, most of them, supported Castro and were willing to die for his cause.

Item: The head of the group, President Kennedy, early on declared himself in favor of the invasion. That caused the members of the group to feel that they were dealing with a decision already made. To oppose the president might therefore put them in political jeopardy. Groups do better when there is free discussion of all the evidence, not suppression of the opinions of the individual members of the group. In Japanese companies, the lowest member of the group gives his opinion first and so on up the ladder. This prevents the head man from manipulating the group to his own position before the others have had a chance to voice their views.

Item: The importance of the decision, its complexity, and the tight deadline imposed on the group by the president put the members under pressure and duress. Humans under pressure think less well than those who have more leisure for considered thought.

Conclusion: The Bay of Pigs decision is no mystery. The tapes of the sessions are available for review. The group reached the wrong decision because no one was permitted to criticize JFK or his judgment, no disagreement with the majority was tolerated, alternative positions and opposing evidence were not examined, and the group worked in isolation without consulting the public or the public's elected representatives in the Congress. The Kennedy team failed to consider all the relevant and available evidence. Because of their error in thinking they suffered.

Their suffering was not all bad. One good thing that came out of the Bay of Pigs disaster was that Kennedy and his advisers were humbled. They learned the hard way that they could blunder. Bay of Pigs taught them how to better handle the next big problem that came their way, the Cuban missile crisis.

Experiments at the Laboratory of Social Relations at Harvard University asked 123 subjects to compare one line with three other lines, only one of which was the same length as the first line. As individuals, the respondents answered the question with over 99 percent accuracy. In the social group (which consisted of research assistants instructed to give the wrong answer), the same people accepted the wrong judgment of the group 36.8 percent of the time. One quarter of the subjects remained independent of the group throughout the experiment. Once independent, they never went along with the majority when the majority was wrong. Once dependent, they never failed to go along with the majority when the majority was wrong. Among the independents, most had staunch confidence that they were right and the group was wrong. Some independents felt that the majority must be right but that they had to "call it as they saw it." Among the dependents, some felt "they are right and I am wrong." Others yielded so as "not to spoil the result." Some felt that the majority was under an optical illusion. Most of the dependents felt that their differences with the group were signs of general deficiency in themselves, which they had to hide at all costs. All yielding subjects underestimated the number of times they yielded and said it was better to decide for themselves than go along with the group. Yet they did not follow their own advice. They knew what was best. They did what was worst.

Close to one thousand people died at Jonestown. The members of the Peoples Temple settlement in Guyana, near the Venezuelan border, under the direction of the Reverend Jim Jones, fed a poison-laced drink to their children, administered the potion to their infants, and drank it themselves.

How could such a tragedy happen? How could an entire community destroy itself like that?

There is no mystery. Jim Jones founded his church over twenty years before. Initially, he preached racial brotherhood and integration. His group helped feed the poor and find them jobs. As the congregation grew, Jones increased discipline. In 1965, he and about one hundred of his followers moved to northern California. "Father," as he was called, assumed a messiahlike presence and actually became the personal object of the members' devotion. Jones demanded loyalty, enforced a taxing regimen, and delivered sermons forecasting nuclear holocaust and the apocalyptic destruction of the world. In 1977, Jim Jones moved most of his membership to a jungle outpost in Guyana.

One year later, in November 1978, Congressman Leo Ryan visited the site to investigate charges that Temple members were being held against their will. Two families slipped messages to Ryan that they wanted to leave with him. As Ryan's party and these defectors tried to board planes to depart, the group was ambushed and fired upon by Temple gunmen—five people, including Ryan, were killed.

Right after the shootings, Jim Jones gathered the community at Jonestown. He told them that the Congressman's party would be killed and then initiated the final ritual: the "revolutionary suicide" that the members had rehearsed so many times before and now recorded on tape.

> First woman: I feel like that as long as there's life, there's hope.
> Jones: Well, someday everybody dies.
> Crowd: That's right, that's right.
> And later—Jones: Please, for God's sake, let's get on with it. . . .
> This is a revolutionary suicide. This is not a self-destructive suicide. (On the tape, voices praise "Dad." Applause follows.)

Many accounts attest that by the early 1970s, the members of the Peoples Temple lived in constant fear of punishment—brutal beatings coupled with public humiliation, often for trivial or even accidental offenses. Jeanne Mills, who spent six years as a high-ranking member before leaving, wrote, "There was an unwritten but perfectly understood law in the church that was very important. No one is to criticize Father, his wife, or his children."

"Families are part of the enemy system," Jones stated, because they hurt one's total dedication to the "Cause." Besides splitting parent and child, Jones sought to loosen the bonds between wife and husband. He forced spouses into extramarital sexual relations, which were often of a homosexual or humiliating nature. Many of the forced sexual relations were with Jones himself.

Get the picture?

Let's step back for a moment and view it on the wide screen.

All the ingredients of groupthink are there: the cohesiveness preserving the group's harmony, the insulation, the high stress, and the strong directive leadership. All these factors worked together to create the abrogation of clear thought and the denial of the reality of what Jones was—which caused the consequent deaths of 914 people.

There is no need to go through Jones's statements one by one to remind you of the multiple errors in thinking they display. Unfortunately, the horror of this lesson will not end with this group. Others will follow. You can bet on that. Don't be part of it. Don't let it start.

Jeanne and Al Mills were among the most vocal of the Peoples Temple critics following their defections. They topped an alleged "death list" of the Temple's enemies. Mills had repeatedly expressed fear for her life even after Jonestown. Over a year after the Jonestown massacre, Jeanne and Al and their daughter were murdered in their Berkeley home. On the final tape of Jonestown, Jim Jones had blamed Jeanne Mills by name. He promised that his followers in San Francisco "will not take our death in vain" (*Newsweek*, 1980).

Bo (Marshall Herff Applewhite) and Peep (Bonnie Lu Nelson) founded one of the most unusual flying saucer religions ever to emerge out of the New Age concept that ufonauts (astronauts who travel in UFOs) could be channeled (communicated with by telepathy).

Bo and Peep had an experience (in a cave somewhere, probably in Oregon) that convinced them that they were the two witnesses mentioned in Revelation 2 who would be martyred and then resurrected three and a half days later, an event they called the Demonstration. They were surprisingly effective in recruiting devotees to their new religion. The followers adhered to a strict routine, remained isolated from society in general, and immersed themselves in the intensity of a structured lifestyle designed to prepare them for a pick-up by their Space Brothers, who would, after special cloning in a special cloning bank on the UFO, give them new bodies and new jobs gloriously flying the saucer around space.

Under the conditions of isolation and instruction, the followers became more and more convinced that these teachings of the Two (Bo and Peep's alternative moniker) were real.

Later the Two changed their teaching somewhat and began to describe themselves as extraterrestrial walk-ins named Ti and Do. A walk-in is an entity who occupies a body that has been vacated by its original owner. An extraterrestrial walk-in is one from another planet. The walk-in situation is somewhat similar to possession, although in possession the original soul is merely overshadowed rather than completely supplanted by the possessing alien.

Now that you know that background, chart the following narrative, picking out the elements that identify groupthink. From those elements, predict the ultimate clash with reality that will befall the group because of its crooked thinking.

Bo and Peep cult—a group that in the wake of events is probably as familiar to you as Heaven's Gate is—made the news on March 26, 1997, when the bodies of thirty-nine men and women were found in a posh mansion outside San Diego, all volunteers for a mass suicide who had taken barbiturates and placed plastic bags over their heads.

Messages left indicated that they were stepping out of their "physical containers" to ascend to a spaceship that was arriving in the wake of the Hale-Bopp comet. They left behind a video and a Web site explaining that they believed that Hale-Bopp, or a part of it, would crash into Earth and cause widespread destruction. Marshall Applewhite, their leader, predicted that the comet crash would probably signal the end of the world. He further advised that our calendars were off, that the year was not 1997 but 2000. Since he felt that there was a general agreement that the world would end precisely two millennia after the birth of Jesus and that it was 2000 and not 1997, he concluded the end had come.

According to Applewhite, aliens had planted the seeds of current humanity millions of years ago and were coming to reap the harvest of their work in the form of spiritually evolved individuals who would join the ranks of flying saucer crews. Only the selected members of the Heaven's Gate community would be allowed to advance to this transhuman state. The rest of them and us would be left to suffer the dismal fate of living in the poisoned atmosphere of the planet, which would soon be engulfed in cataclysmic destruction caused by Hale-Bopp.

Said Applewhite, "The Earth's present civilization is about to be recycled—'spaded under.' Its inhabitants are refusing to evolve. The 'weeds' have taken over the garden and disturbed its usefulness beyond repair."[2]

If you are interested in the details, the final scenario, and the March 22, 1997, announcement that the Heaven's Gate "Away Team" has returned to level above human in distant space, consult the group's Web site, www.heavensgatetoo.com.

The people of Heaven's Gate, like the people of the Peoples Temple and President Kennedy's cabinet, had a rather high opinion of themselves. Each group envisioned itself as having a central role in some historically important event. Each group "knew" that it was unfailingly right. Each group was isolated from society in general under the direction of a charismatic leader, and highly motivated. Each group denied the evidence that indicated their view might be wrong and felt it had a distinct mission and destiny.

In the case of the cabinet members, they "knew" they were going to rid the Americas of Godless communism. In the case of the Jonestown religious group, the main event was the end of the world in which they would play a key part. In the case of Heaven's Gate, the Space Brothers were, after the pickup, going to end time, destroy the world, and transform the faithful into superior beings who would cruise the galaxies forever.

In each case, reality came crashing down on their heads. The Bay of Pigs invasion failed when the invaders were captured and later ransomed. The Jonestown people died without the world ending. Hale-Bopp continued on its merry way without disrupting Earth in any significant manner. In fact, we're still here! The prophesies proved wrong. The events predicted did not occur. Nevertheless, many people died needlessly, in vain. These people, if not clinically mad, have reached what George Rosen called "The wilder shores of sanity." Their defective reality testing is not as defective as a real-life schizophrenic, but it is close. The more your thinking strays from reality, the more dire the consequences.

NOTES

1. All the information on the Bay of Pigs fiasco comes from Irving L. Janis, *Groupthink*, 2nd ed. (Boston: Houghton Mifflin, 1982), pp. 14–47. Janis cites minutes of the meetings, diaries, memoirs, letters, and prepared statements given to investigating committees. The miracle is that his account jibes with the freedom of information documents released in 1999. The declassified documents on Operation Zapata (the code name for the Bay of Pigs operation) are now available from the National Security Archives (briefing book no. 29) and are featured, in part, electronically on the national security Web site and at http://www.gwu.edu/~nsarchiv/NSAEBB/NSAEBB29/. JFK appointed General Maxwell Taylor to investigate what went wrong at the Bay of Pigs. Arthur Schlesinger Jr. covers the same territory and quotations in his book *A Thousand Days: John F. Kennedy and the White House*, (Boston: Houghton, Mifflin, 1965). For those interested, I highly recommend the CIA's *Oral History of the Bay of Pigs* and the Annenberg Foundation's *Discovering Psychology Series* with host Phil Zimbardo (professor of psychology) where Irving Janis (author of *Groupthink*) is interviewed, segments of the Cabinet sessions are viewed, and then the two social psychologists comment on the errors in thinking.

2. Robert W. Balch, "Waiting for the Ships; Disillusionment and Revitalization of Faith in Bo and Peep's UFO Cult," in *The Gods Have Landed: New Religions from Other Worlds*, ed. James R. Lewis (Albany: State University of New York Press, 1995), p. 163.

chapter 7

Scams, Deceptions, Ruses, Swindles, Hoaxes, and Gaslights

This chapter expands your understanding of reality by telling you about the structure and function of the common frauds and deceptions. By understanding the way con men work, you will understand how to protect yourself from many types of fraud. Along the way, you will also learn how to protect your interests in transactions that (though strictly speaking are legal, nevertheless) fall into a gray zone. Face it: There is no clear dividing line between honest deals and some frauds, and there is an element of deception in most business transactions.

Pedigreed Dog Scam (PDS) is the granddaddy of some of the greatest con games, including boiler room sales of worthless stock, Florida real estate, gold mines, oil rigs, gas leases, and so forth. Here's how it works.

A man comes into a bar accompanied by a dog (usually a mongrel terrier). The man tells the bartender that the dog is a rare breed. Papers might be produced that prove that the dog is a champion. But the man can't stay. He has to meet with his bankers and he can't take the dog to the bank. Would the bartender watch the dog for two hours for ten dollars?

After the dog's owner has left, another customer appears, orders a drink, notices the dog, and comments on how good the dog looks. Out of the blue, the second customer offers $100 for the dog. Of course, the bartender can't sell the dog because he isn't the owner.

"Listen," says customer number two. "I am not going to bamboozle you. That dog is a pedigree. I know dogs. I would be willing to pay $5,000 for it right now. What do you say?"

The bartender now has considerable pain in turning down such an offer, but he does mention that the real owner will soon return. The bartender tells customer number two that he will pass the offer on to the real owner.

Customer two: "See what you can do. I have to go somewhere. I'll be back in three hours. If you can get the dog for me, I'll pay you $5,000 for it, and I will give you $200 for your trouble." Customer number two then exits.

A short time later, customer one returns. He is upset. "I don't know what I'm going to do. My deal fell through. I need some dough."

At that point, the bartender says that he would be willing to take the dog off the guy's hands, say, for $500. But of course customer number one would not hear of parting with such a valuable dog at such a low price. Eventually, the price works up, and the money is paid. Now with the original owner gone, the bartender waits and waits and waits for the prospective buyer, customer number two, to return. Needless to say, the second stranger never comes back. He never returns because he was the shill. He was part of the scam.

Con men use this swindle when they need fast cash. It is thus known in the business as a short con. When the victim is no longer a bartender but a rich businessman, and the property is no longer a mutt but a gold mine, an oil well, some expensive jewels, or swampy Florida real estate, the profits can mount to several hundred thousand dollars. Beware; whatever the property might be, you can bet that in reality it is still a dog.

Principle: All fraud is divided into six parts.

With the pedigreed dog scam in mind, work through and learn the six classical anatomical parts of fraud so that when someone is trying to flim-flam you, you will recognize the pattern and be prepared to resist.

Anatomy of fraud:

Part one: the come-on. The come-on is usually worked by the roper, the person whose job it is to get the victim into the scheme. The roper is a con man who establishes confidence somehow and someway, sometimes by presenting credentials, most times by the sheer force of personality and salesmanship.

Part two: the incentive. The incentive is the reason that the victim would want to place himself in the hands of the fraud artist. In the classic swindle, the incentive is a get-rich-quick scheme, but it can be some other sort of benefit, such as a sexual experience (as in the Murphy game or the badger game). Sometimes it's a good feeling that comes from helping others, as when making a gift to charity. But of course in this case, the charity is fake. The only person who benefits is the grifter.

Part three: the shill. Most swindles employ a shill, a third person, sometimes unwitting but more often part of the scheme, who acts as a disinterested party, reinforcing the victim's participation. The shill is the fake buyer at an auction, serving to bid up the prices. He is the guy who shows how easy it is to win the shell game or three-card monte. The shill is there to ease the mark into the fraud by showing how easy it is to win.

Part four: the switch. Always in the swindle, there is a switch in which a fake thing is substituted for the article of value such that the victim gets real emeralds that were the bottom of a Heineken bottle last night. Or the victim gets a two-thousand-year-old genuine antique Roman coin made yesterday. In the sex frauds, the paid-for object of desire often just doesn't make the scene. Sometimes, as in the badger game, the paid-for object of desire does make the scene, causing worse trouble than the mark ever imagined. She might make it into bed with the mark, but she doesn't make *it*. She doesn't make *it* because her "husband" (a shill) or a "detective" (also a shill) barges into the room just at that crucial moment. The "detective" or the "husband" wants to be paid off or he'll make a stink.

Sometimes the switch is crude, such as substituting a lead brick for a gold brick, a deception that in the 1970s fooled several hundred senior citizens in New York City. More recently, the EDS corporation in Florida fooled hundreds of seniors who paid for not only gold that wasn't there but also storage fees for the same (nonexistent) gold that wasn't stored. EDS routinely sent pictures of gold bricks to the seniors who invested in the gold. What those seniors really paid for was pictures of gold-painted bricks and a nicely engraved (phony) certificate.

In other cases, there is no physical switch involved but an intangible one as in bait-and-switch advertisements where (aw, shucks!) that really cheap Sony sixty-four-inch TV we advertised yesterday was sold out just an hour ago.

Part five: the pressure. Just before or after the switch, there is pressure to hurry the victim along and impede him from carefully considering the transaction. Often, there is a time limit imposed, either by stating the deal is now or never because the offer is about to expire, or the deal may be lost because there is another buyer waiting, possibly with a better offer. This pressure—to do something right now, fast, and often without serious consideration—is so characteristic of those who engage in con games that it is called the *hustle*; those who do the hustle, those who are so skilled at applying the pressure, are called *hustlers*.

Part six: the block. Last but not least is the block, a tactic aimed at stopping the victim from reporting the incident to the police. The block is an essential and carefully planned part of the deception. There are two main types of block: the legal block and the time block.

Legal block. Often the victim can't report to the police because to do so would be to confess wrongdoing as in a smuggling, counterfeiting, or gambling scheme (where gambling is illegal). If the activity is not outright illegal, the block can be shame. Sex schemes play on that shameful angle. How would you like to tell the police or your mother—or worse, read in the paper—that you paid some pimp for the services of a prostitute and then got rolled when you when up to her room?

Time block. Sometimes the block is time. Sometimes time is infinite because the victim never figures out that those diamonds that he bought at bargain prices are actually fake—he never has the fake diamonds appraised. This is because he doesn't want to risk having the supposedly stolen diamonds identified. Sometimes the time block is limited—the victim can't cash in those phony uranium stocks for a specified period of time because there is a "lock up" agreement. Usually, the time block is so arranged so that the con men can skip town.

Remember, most scams succeed because of the desire of the victim to believe that which satisfies his or her ambition, prejudice, or eagerness for gain. There is nothing new under the hoaxing sun, all schemes being but new wrinkles of age-old cons and all consisting of the six classic parts. Thus, the pedigreed dog swindle, which works so well and so often on gullible bartenders, is, in essence, no different from the stock swindle called *pump and dump*, where worthless securities are peddled to greedy people who think they will soon sell the same to someone else at a higher price.

Scams, swindles, and frauds come in so many shapes, sizes, flavors, and colors that no book can cover them all. The best we can do in this short space is to recognize the pattern of deception by identifying the six classic parts of fraud. As you read through the following descriptions of some of the classic scams, do an analysis of each scam to see if you can identify the six classic components mentioned above. Remember the six parts of sham by using the mnemonic CISS (come-on, incentive, shill, switch), followed by P&B (pressure and block). Or ciss, pressure, block. Or CISSPB.

I was doing some medical consulting for a Houston attorney who told me about a great deal that he had just engineered. I can't mention his real name, so let's call him Roger. What do you think of Roger's great deal?

Roger: I had a guy come in here and ask if I was an international lawyer.

Me: You don't know jack about international law.

Roger: I know. But I told him yes.

Me: Roger, that's a lie.

Roger: He needed someone as a go-between to work with someone in Colombia to get permission from the government of Colombia to raise a treasure ship that has been located five miles off the northwestern coast of Colombia. The deal's all set, and the Colombian official has already received the bribe. The ship is known to be holding $86 million worth of gold pieces of eight.

Me: Oh no! You didn't pay anything. Did you?

Roger: It was difficult, but I finally persuaded the client and his business partner to cut me in on the deal. The partner was a real son of a bitch. He didn't want me in on it at all. He said they didn't need me. But I told them if they didn't let me in, I was going to blow the whistle on them and report them to the Colombian government and to the FBI. That convinced them! They had to let me in. They let me in for an 8 percent interest for only $400,000. They needed it in cash.

Me: Cash?

Roger: Yeah, that was the bribe. It had to be in cash.

Me: And now you don't know where they are.

Roger: How did you know? In fact, I haven't seen them since I handed over the cash.

Me: Don't worry, Roger. I know where they are.

Roger: You do! Thank God! That's great. Where?

Me: They are . . . somewhere. Somewhere out there, spending your dough. You have been taken by the hidden treasure scam, a slightly sophisticated version of the pedigreed dog scam.

Roger: Nope! That's impossible. It's not a scam. I have the map. They left the map with me as security. See.

At that point, Roger produced a hand-drawn map of the coast of Colombia. Sure enough, at a point about five miles off the northwestern coast of Colombia, a big red Maltese cross that marked the spot where the supposed treasure was.

Analysis: Treasure hunt scams are as old as the hills. As mentioned, they are like the pedigreed dog scam. In treasure hunt, the come-on is the usual. Someone approaches with a deal that, though a little shady, is interesting and superficially plausible. The incentive is the usual—get rich quick. The shill in the pedigree dog is the potential buyer. The shill in the treasure hunt is the reluctant partner who tries like the devil to prevent Roger from being cut into the profits. The switch is that nothing of value is actually involved. The mutt in PDS is worth five dollars. The treasure map with the big red Maltese cross is worth three dollars. The pressure is to make the deal before someone else gets the chance. The block is the wait and the shame about being fooled plus the shame of trying to do something dishonest. Roger eventually admitted that he had been taken. He didn't tell the police. He was afraid that if he told the police, the word might leak out, and he would catch hell from the person in life whom he feared the most—his wife.

Alchemists used to show the great leaders of medieval Europe how easily they could turn lead into gold. The alchemists did this trick by stirring the molten lead with a hollow iron rod that had a piece of gold held in its hollow bottom with wax. When the rod was dipped in the molten lead, the wax melted, and the gold, being lighter than lead, appeared floating on the top of the mixture. Princes, dukes, and kings supported these alchemist charlatans for decades in the hope that their process of turning lead into gold would make them rich. It never did.

Another form of salting involved the sale of worthless mine property to gullible greenhorns eager to make it big. Before showing the property, gold flakes would be sprinkled around the entrance. When samples were taken by the prospective buyer (now the mark), sure enough, the gold was there. Sure enough, that gold when taken to the assay office proved real.

Chinese immigrants fell for the scam so frequently that the word went out to watch out for gold seeding and to take samples at random from a part of the stake selected, not by the seller, but by the buyer. This perfectly reasonable attempt to get around partial selection of evidence led to the marvelous counterinvention of the dead snake trick.

A snake was killed and kept in the pocket of one of the shills. When the would-be buyer selected an area in the back of the cave, the snake was thrown down in the area and immediately shot at twice by one of the shills in attendance. Since the lead shot in the shotgun shells had been replaced with gold flakes, the area around the dead snake did in fact now yield a large amount of gold, much of it tightly imbedded in the soil the way real gold should be.

Analysis: The come-on is the seller of the worked-out mine. He is usually an older prospector who wants to retire and who thinks it is his retirement right to sell a worthless claim to the gullible. The incentive is the usual, the dream of easy gold. The shill is the seller and his assistant, who are in on the scheme. The switch is the seeding of the selected area by the brilliant technique of the dead snake trick. The pressure is that others are in the wings who are eager to buy the property. The block is that the sellers will be in San Francisco by the time most of the dirt in the claim is sifted and found lacking.

MURPHY GAME SCAM

Murphy approaches a visitor from out of town and suggests that he can get him a woman for the night. Posing as the pimp, Murphy quotes a price to the victim for the sex act that the victim specifies. Murphy then asks for payment in advance because if the victim were to pay the woman directly, there might be trouble with the law, since payment for sex is considered part of the crime of prostitution. The victim pays Murphy, who then leads the mark to a hotel. Murphy asks the victim to wait in the lobby, so that Murphy can go upstairs, conclude the deal with the woman and make sure that the coast is clear of cops. Murphy then goes up the elevator and leaves the hotel by another exit. The victim, like those characters in the 1942 classic movie *Casablanca*, waits and waits and waits.

A variation: Murphy may, to assure the victim, tell the victim a room number and instruct the victim to come up after specified amount of time, say, ten minutes. Of course, there is no woman. Often there is no room either. Or if there is a room, no one is in. Or if someone is in, it's an elderly couple who don't know anything about what's up.

Analysis: The come-on is by Murphy, who is usually on the lookout for businessmen at a convention who are looking for some nooky while away from home. The incentive is forbidden sex. In this game, the shill is also Murphy, who pretends that he is a pimp when actually he is just a con artist acting like a pimp. The switch is that a woman was promised, but she doesn't exist. The pressure is—well, you can imagine what the pressure is. This babe is so hot and so sexy and so good at what she does, she will soon be booked and unable to give her services. The block is the wait in the lobby so that Murphy can make his escape. But the block is also shame. The victim is unlikely to complain to the police because to do so would be to confess his shameful involvement in prostitution.

In a sense, the victim of the Murphy game is lucky that the woman is not there because if she were, then the victim might become involved in the badger game, a much more serious form of trouble.

Badger has the same plot structure as the Murphy game except the woman is there in the room as scheduled. She might actually get into to bed. But she doesn't do *it*, no sir. She doesn't do *it* because the game is interrupted at that crucial moment by the entry of "detectives," the "police," or an irate "husband" who demand payment to keep things quiet. On the darker side, sometimes the game is a blackmail scheme wherein pictures of the victim *in flagrante delicto* are to be sent to the victim's wife unless he pays and pays and pays.

A variation that is played if a customer seems prosperous is to use young girls from age nine to fourteen as bait. Instead of an angry husband storming into the room, it would be the girls "parents." The "mother" would scream at the child and punch her in the face; her blows usually hard enough to cause bleeding from the mouth and nose. The act is convincing and leaves the victim stunned. The alleged "father" would shove his fist menacingly at the victim's face and snarl, "I'm going to put you in prison for a hundred years!" Men so threatened often pay thousands of dollars in hush money. Incidentally, the child's bloody nose and mouth come from the plastic bag of chicken blood that she bites when she is hit.

SHELL GAME AND THREE-CARD MONTE

The shell game and the three-card monte are the most common street swindles today. Because some members of the public have (finally) figured out that monte is a gyp because the marked card is switched before the victim gets to play, the shell game is making a comeback. The shell game has a long history, going back to the second century CE in Egypt, where it was called *cups and balls*. Here's how it works.

Some young men set up a table on the street and start playing with three shells. One or more of the men is a shill (a fake bettor on the side) and the other con man is the dealer. The dealer is also known as "thimble rigger" because as a skilled operator, he can hide the pea anytime he wants. The dealer lets the shills win right and left so that the game looks easy as pie. The victim, attracted to the idea of easy gain, wants to play, too. But as soon as he starts playing, he loses. In fact, he soon finds out that he can't win for love or money because it is rather hard to pick the shell with the pea under it when the elusive pea is under none of them. The basic rule is never to let the victim win, since he might pick up his winnings and leave. So the pea has been removed from the shell it was under. The pea is actually in the palm of the dealer.

Here's the best way to play the shell game.

Lose three times in a row with small bets. Then after the shells have been moved around for the fourth time and all the shells are resting quietly on the table, propose a giant bet. Put up the cash for that bet on the table. When the dealer matches the bet (often assisted by the shills who want to get in on the action, especially since they know this is a sure thing), pull out your gun and place it and your right hand on the table, too. Announce that this time you will not pick up the shell with the pea but that you will pick up the two shells that don't have the pea. Turn over two shells with your left hand (while continuing to hold the gun in your right hand)—no pea. While picking up the money with your left hand, announce, "I reckon there's no need to turn over that last shell. For I'm sure you boys have been honest as hell." Back away while keeping everyone covered. Do not turn your back to the group until you are sure you are safe.

But you may ask, "What should I do if I don't have a gun?" And I reply, "If you don't have a gun, get a gun. Better yet, don't play the shell game at all."

CHAIN LETTER SCAMS

The chain letter urges the reader to send a dollar or some other sum to the name at the top of the list, then retype the letter, deleting the top name and adding the reader's own name at the bottom. The letter promises riches to the people who follow the plan. The chain soon snowballs to a fantastic number of people, but only the originators of the chain letter stand a decent chance of making any big money. The principle of the chain letter is that of the pyramid, with a small top and a large bottom. All money flows toward the top, and the people on the bottom are the payers, not the collectors.

Many other frauds are based on the principle of the pyramid, including referral sales in which someone gets a water softener (or whatnot) free if he steers enough of his friends to the salesman. Another variation is the major effort to build up a network of "dealers" (in dishes, candles, emus, etc.) rather than selling the goods to the public. As in all pyramid schemes, the bubble eventually bursts because there are only a certain number of people, and the scheme, which depends on continued growth, collapses when the limit is reached.

Charles Ponzi, swindler, used a classical pyramid scheme. Ponzi got so famous that his name has entered the English language. Any scheme in which the original investors are paid off with money supplied by a succeeding army of suckers is now known as a Ponzi scheme.

In the beginning, Ponzi discovered that he could purchase international postal-union reply coupons at depressed prices in some foreign countries and sell them in the United States at a tidy profit of up to 50 percent. That was nice, but it was strictly small time. Ponzi wanted something bigger. He came up with telling people that if they invested their money with him, he would return a profit of 50 percent to them in three months. Later, he cut the waiting time to forty-five days. As soon as he started paying out, at least forty thousand people threw money at him. In one day in 1920, Ponzi took in over $2 million from the country's newest gamblers, the little folk who squeezed money out of small bank accounts, mattresses, piggy banks, cookie jars, paper routes, and hot dog stands.

The more money Ponzi took in, the more money he paid out. The more money he paid out, the more money he took in. The chain reaction continued until he had incoming money littering his office, stuffing his closets, and overflowing into his wastebaskets.

One day, the *Boston Post* dug up Ponzi's past record and revealed that he had spent time in prison in Canada for check forgery and in Atlanta for smuggling aliens. That was enough to cause some of the Ponzi investors to hold up. And, of course, as soon as the new money stopped coming in, the scheme collapsed, leaving forty thousand people, many of them poor Italian immigrants, broke.

STOCK MARKET FRAUD

It might be accurate to say the whole market is a fraud, and indeed some people think so. Al Capone, when he was arrested for income tax evasion, said that he was always puzzled that the government was trying to close him down and yet let the stock market continue. Like the insurance business (one of the greatest gyps in history), the stock market is an example of a legitimate business effort evolving into widespread fraud. Don't believe me? Consider the evidence.

Cold-calling brokers from New York, who don't know you from Adam but who tell you they can make you rich as Croesus by next week if you open an account with them and buy some penny stocks, are really out to benefit not you but themselves. If the stocks they tout are so great, why do they need you to buy them? Why don't they just buy them themselves and keep all the profits themselves?

Many penny stocks are fake shares in fake corporations formed by fake brokers who want to dupe the public. And even if you get a nice-looking certificate by return mail, that doesn't mean much. Certificates are easy to print. Chances are the certificate is fake, too.

If you send these cold-calling brokers the money to open the account or to buy shares, chances are you won't see that money again. The cold-calling broker isn't even a broker. He is a fake. He is a con man sitting in a boiler room and reading a script to help him get you to buy into the scam. If you listen to him, you will amuse yourself by recognizing the six classic parts of the swindle, with heavier than usual emphasis on the pressure to do something right now rather than miss the golden opportunity that will soon pass away.

Even if the penny stocks are real, the other thing bad about penny stocks is that they are likely to be owned by people of limited means, who are easily frightened and typically obliged to dump stocks, in times of stress, for what they can get.

Recently, penny stocks have become part of the updated version of the classic market manipulation known as *pump and dump*. As you read about pump and dump, try to figure out how it resembles the pedigreed dog scam.

In pump and dump, someone sets up a free Web site promising investors hot tips on penny stocks. He then buys the stocks in advance of the tips and sells them at a profit as soon as the followers bid up the prices. The stocks then plunge back to earth, causing losses for the unwary investors and profits for the tout. Not only is this not nice, it is also illegal. Yun Soo Oh Park—also known as Tokyo Joe, the Internet's best-known stock guru—according to the Security and Exchange Commission, enriched himself at the expense of subscribers by urging his disciples to buy certain stocks that he was often selling for a tidy profit for himself.

Current FBI and congressional investigations show that Initial Public Offerings (IPOs) were, during the '90s, manipulated in the same manner such that insiders made millions on the first day's run ups, and the public lost millions on the subsequent run downs. Analysis of the situation should have raised the puzzling question of why the stock prices of those IPOs ran up so fast without underlying financial performances to warrant such escalations. It was also puzzling that such rises were often short lived.

Now we know that it had to be like that because the IPOs were being pumped and dumped. The IPOs were part of a bubble artificially inflated with hot air. Participating investment bankers colluded and agreed among themselves—without the knowledge of the regulatory authorities or the investing public—to bid up the IPOs prices for the first few days or so. It was also agreed when the artificial pumping would stop so that the insiders knew when they could safely dump.

Pump and dump and the IPO game resemble the pedigreed dog scam in that they tout as valuable something that is not. What's the lesson?

> *Lesson:* Stay away from pump and dump and from IPOs with the same vigor that you would stay away from that pedigreed dog scam.

By the by, if you have to invest in the stock market, avoid the error of IPO future fact. Stick with companies that have proven, not prognosticated, financial performance. The focus is in the same markets but at a much later, and safer, stage of development.

Did you forget your thinking skills yet? I hope not. Refresh your skills by working out the current examples of how the con men took $8.6 trillion out of the hands of the public. Study the situation and then outline the errors in thinking. Check your answers against mine. My answers are incomplete but suggest some of the ways you might have approached the analysis of the situation described. In each case, the come-on was the same. Because of greed and avarice, CEOs participated in the frauds. The come-on was, "Want to make some real money, really fast?" In each case, a high degree of skepticism would have saved you money. Here's how.

Dynergy. Energy sales are not profitable. But you convince investors that they will be in the future. Then you enter into agreements with other energy traders. Under the agreement, each of you buys millions of kilowatts of energy from each other. Or pretend to buy—no need to go to the trouble of actually moving electricity anywhere. Suddenly, you look like a big player. The stock rises. You cash out at high prices.

Defects. Reasoning contrary to fact: The energy business was lousy. There were no sales. There were no profits. The belief that there might have been sales, profits, or even hope was based on fake evidence, which is not evidence at all—it is the opposite of evidence, leading away from reality to error. Decisions based on fake evidence are likely to be wrong. In this case, they were wrong, dead wrong.

The future is not determined. It can't be predicted with accuracy. Therefore, the so-called projected profits (and the costs of generating those profits) are not determined. In a sense, the projected profits are not real since they don't yet exist. They are certainly not currently real and should not be counted as such on the balance sheet. Future fact is not a fact at all. Future fact is at best contingent. In the case of Dynergy, it wasn't even contingent. It was impossible. In fact, it is highly possible that Dynergy has no future. Stock price, September 2002, $2.07, down from $95. Percent loss: 98 percent.

Adelphia. You sign contracts with customers and get investors to focus on the volume of contracts rather than on their profitability. This time you don't invent imaginary trades, you invent lots of imaginary customers. With your subscription base seeming to grow so rapidly, Wall Street stock analysts give you high marks. The stock rises. You cash out at high prices.

Defects. Reasoning contrary to fact: The business was not growing. The customers were not real. There were no sales; there were no profits. The belief that there might have been sales, profits, or even hope was based on fake evidence, which is not evidence at all—it is the opposite of evidence, leading away from reality to error. Decisions based on fake evidence are likely to be wrong. In this case, they were wrong, dead wrong.

The future is not determined. It can't be predicted with accuracy. Therefore, the profits (and the costs of generating those profits) are not determined and not real since they don't exist. They are certainly not currently real and should not be counted as such. Future fact is not a fact at all. It *might* be a fact in the future. Then again, it might not be a fact in the future. It all depends. We simply don't know because the future is contingent. In the case of Adelphia, because of the egregious nature of the frauds involved, including insider trading, for loans to executives that were tax-free transfers of money never intended to be repaid, fake customers, and so forth, future profits are not contingent. They are impossible. Adelphia current stock price: 1 cent, down from $105. Percent loss: 99.99.

Enron. Sign contracts to provide energy for the next thirty years. Deliberately underestimate the cost. Book the projected profits on those future sales as part of this year's bottom line. Suddenly, you appear to have a highly profitable business. Sell shares and cash out at inflated prices.

Defects. Special pleading. Profits and costs should be handled the same way at the same time. To treat profits one way and to treat costs another way is inconsistent, is special pleading, distorts the reality, and is wrong.

The future is not determined. It can't be predicted with accuracy. Therefore, the profits (and the costs of generating those profits) are not determined and not real. They are certainly not currently real and should not be counted as such. Future fact is not a fact at all. Stock price, September 2002, 18 cents, down from $83. Percent loss: 99.78.

(It is possible that the Enron fiasco included a more involved business fraud called the *bust-out.* Although simple in principle, it often requires months or years to execute. The first point in bust-out is for the con man to get power in the business and direct the money from the business into his own pockets. In the bust-out, there is usually a front man, called the "pencil," an honest or stupid executive who is not in on the fraud. He is the one who runs the routine operations of the company while the fraud artist concentrates his efforts on the scam. The pencil is also the one whose feet will be in the fire after the fraud artist leaves town or bows out or (and this is the usual end of the game) the company goes bankrupt. At that point, the pencil will have a hard time proving that he wasn't a party to the scheme. Ken Lay, former CEO of Enron, could have been the pencil in Enron, and Fastow, the executive who ran off-the-books companies called "raptors" that concealed Enron's costs and debts, might have actually been the con artist.)

WorldCom. Here you don't create imaginary sales. You make real costs disappear by pretending that operating expenses are part of the purchase price of new equipment. The operating expenses are charged off as capital expenses and, therefore, the real costs are shifted to the future. With the costs deflated, the unprofitable business seems on paper to be a highly profitable. Wall Street analysts give you high marks. The stock rises. You cash out at high prices.

Defects. Reasoning contrary to fact: The business was not growing. The profits were not real because the costs were not real. If the costs had been charged to current profits, the profits would have disappeared. Thus, there were no profits. The belief that there might have been profits or even hope of profits was based on fake evidence, which is not evidence at all—it is the opposite of evidence, leading away from reality to error. Decisions based on fake evidence are likely to be wrong. In the case of WorldCom, the decisions were dead wrong and over $7 billion of so-called profits had to be restated because they were not profits at all. This is the largest accounting fraud in the history of the world (so far).

Special pleading. Profits and costs should be handled the same way at the same time. To treat one one way and the other another is inconsistent, is special pleading, distorts the reality, and is wrong. Stock price, September 2002, 13 cents, down from $60. Percent loss: 99.78.

Global Crossing. As mentioned, Global Crossing crossed over to the dark side. As Global Crossing emerges from bankruptcy, Gary Winnick, former CEO, ends up with $936 million while shareholders end up with nothing. Somehow, the fiber optical network that Winnick said was worth $27 billion in June 2002 only brought $250 million at auction in September 2002. This sharp change in evaluation raises the important question: Where did the money go? How could $26.75 billion disappear? Current stock price of Global Crossing stock as of September 2002, 1 cent, down from $61. Percent loss: 99.97.

Recent stock market disasters (Enron, Global Crossing, WorldCom, Adelphia, etc.) involve something more serious than business reversals. They involve misrepresentation of the financial positions, with executives becoming richer as the stock prices soared, and then, when the frauds were exposed, employees and shareholders were left with little or nothing.

In view of the present uncertainty of the true condition of corporate finance, especially in the United States, where government deregulation of business was deliberate, the market price of stocks must factor in that uncertainty to arrive at a price significantly lower than would have been otherwise justified.

Well, what do we do now?

That, my friend, is up to you. It's no fun to lose money. In 2003, Standard & Poor's was down 40 percent from its peak in March 2000. The Bear Market of 1973–74 saw that index decline 48 percent. It took eight years to replace that drop. The Dow Jones Industrial Average was about 9700 in 2003. It could go lower or stay where it is for a while. Or it could go up. Who knows?

I predict a final market sell off. After that, sometime between 2004 and 2008, it might be the time for the intelligent investor, using the know-how gained from this book on basic clear thinking, to make a fortune. In the meantime, investor, those boots were made for walking.

GASLIGHTING HOAX

Gaslighting is a systematic array of techniques designed to destroy the target's mental equilibrium. Most of the techniques are subtle and never clearly point to a malevolent or vengeful other party such that the hapless target never believes things are being done to him; he just thinks he is having a string of bad luck. The term comes from the 1944 Hollywood movie *Gaslight,* starring Charles Boyer and Ingrid Bergman. In the movie, the Boyer character tries to convince his wife that she's going insane by contriving incidents designed to make it appear as if she's forgetful, disoriented, and confused.

We don't have the space or time to discuss more on gaslighting, nor can we do proper justice to other deceptions such as health-care frauds, drug burns, intentional accidents, insurance, gambling dangers, postal fraud, real estate scams, quiz show hoaxes, tangential cons, and so forth. If you are interested, consult *The Rip-Off Book* by Victor Santoro and *Hoaxes and Scams* by Carl Sifakis. My own book *Investment Pearls for Modern Times* discusses stock market frauds. *Fleeced!* by Fred Schulte gives a good discussion of telemarketing rip-offs and how to avoid them.

These books and others and your background in clear thinking will protect you from swindles, but not entirely. When someone sticks it to you, don't take it too seriously. And don't be hard on yourself. Learn from the experience. Do better next time.

REVIEW

See if you can figure out this scam that has been worked successfully several times in Queens, New York, where my father, Bernard M. Patten, was in charge of the Complaint Bureau and Racket Squad of the Queens district attorney's office:

It's Sunday afternoon. A well-dressed man appears at a Lincoln dealership and wants to buy a Lincoln Continental right away. He is willing to pay the sticker price because he wants the car right away. But there's a snag. Because it's Sunday, the dealer won't be able to check with the bank to make sure the well-dressed man's check is good. However, the well-dressed man does have good credit and proper identification, and he insists that he will not wait. "If you don't sell me the car now, I will find another dealer who will." The dealer sells the car, takes a check for $42,000, and issues a bill of sale.

One hour later, the well-dressed man is at another dealer's place. He wants to sell that same Lincoln. He says he needs the cash fast. He is willing to sell for $20,000. Dealer number two is suspicious because he notices the bill of sale is only one hour old. So dealer number two calls dealer one and tells him that he thinks the well-dressed man has passed a bad check and is now trying to make a fast buck. Dealer one is outraged. Dealer one tells dealer two to keep the guy around while he (dealer one) calls the police. The police note the complaint and arrest the well-dressed man.

Question: What is the scam? What is the come-on? What is the incentive? Who is the shill? What is the switch? What is the pressure? What is the block?

Give up?

I don't blame you. This is one of the best-constructed—one might even say most brilliant—scam ever. In the realm of the imagination, it ranks right up there with the great created things of the human mind, for it, too, is a work of art—a work of art, however, without art's usual redemptive qualities.

The scam is that when Monday morning comes, the bank honors the check. That means well-dressed man has been falsely accused and falsely arrested. Furthermore, well-dressed man will explain that he needed the money because he had a hot tip on the third race at Belmont, a tip that happened to pay off at 22 to 1. If he had gotten the money he needed to place the bet, he would have made $440,000! So dealer one, dealer two, and the police are now responsible not only for the consequent damages of the false arrest but also for the economic damages of the lost opportunity.

Usually, dealer one foots the bill with a big settlement, which includes, of course, a free Lincoln.

The come-on is that dealer one will make a big profit from a sale at the sticker price. No one in his right mind goes into a dealer and offers the sticker price. The incentive is the fast buck. The shill is the well-dressed buyer in that he is a con man and not a real buyer. The switch is that the check is real, not fake. The pressure initially is to make the sale and then prevent a big loss by having the sale rescinded and the buyer arrested for fraud. The block is that it is perfectly legal to sell your automobile at a markedly reduced price. Since the race at Belmont is already over and the result registered and official, there is no way of disproving the buyer's contention that he would have put his money on the nag that won.

chapter 8

Begging the Question

This chapter should be an easy and restful chapter for you because it introduces the easy and restful the concept of begging the question, an error in thinking that was touched on in previous chapters.

Implicit assumptions, if they are accepted without proof, derail our thinking away from the truth and toward error. When we assume the point in dispute or take for granted the truth of something that requires proof, we are said to *beg the question*.

Begging the question betrays itself frequently by its emotive language. Calling someone a "dastard" or a "knucklehead" implies condemnation, but unless evidence is produced to support the assertions, they merely beg the question. This is especially true if the words that beg the question are shouted, screamed, or screeched. Name calling, especially when shouted, begs the question.

A common place that question begging shows up is in statements by politicians. And there is no better time to observe such words at work than during election campaigns. This is because people like to feel that they are voting after a rational consideration of the arguments put forward by rival parties. Therefore, candidates pretend to appeal to reason while they know full well that the real vote catchers are emotion and prejudice. Their party is that of the future, the party of progress, peace, and prosperity. The other party is the party of the past, the party of retrogression, war, and economic stagnation, and so forth. These are mere assertions that need to be proven. Otherwise, they beg the question.

In politics the tied suggestions of approval or disapproval make a great difference in the effect they have on the audience. "Republicans are the party of the rich." How many times have you heard that? "Democrats are the party of war." How many times have you heard that? Such sweeping statements might have a nugget of truth attached to them, but they can never be wholly true because they are way too vague and too general.

Tied suggestions (especially in advertisements) beg the question.

The basic principle by which the brain learns things is association. Once two items are firmly associated in the consciousness, each tends to recall the other. This mechanism is responsible for most of the great achievements of the human mind. In a sense, this mechanism is responsible for the richness of associations that make literature, art, and music possible and pleasurable. It is the mechanism that is responsible for all science because it is by association that all scientific laws are induced.

But the same mechanism can derail thinking by making an association that is incorrect, either factually or emotionally. We saw this is in the advertisement for Virginia Slims. *Virginia* is the name of a type of tobacco and the name of a woman. Since the name often appears with a picture of a beautiful young woman, the natural association we will make, the association that the advertisers want us to make, is that that woman pictured is named Virginia.

Slim does accurately describe the transverse diameter of this particular cigarette in relation to the transverse diameter of other cigarettes, but *slim* also is a state meaning small in girth in relation to height.

The employment of some word or expression in two different senses without distinction in the same context is an equivocation. If equivocators know that they are equivocating, then they are deceptive. If they don't know this, then in the most literal sense they do not know what they are talking about.

The use of dual definitions in this Virginia Slims ad bothered the Federal Trade Commission when the cigarette first came out. But the tobacco company was able to persuade the commission that the name reasonably related to the facts that the cigarette was made of Virginia tobacco and was slimmer than other cigarettes. This rationale does not detract from the natural associations we might make, those that the advertisers probably want us to make, that the cigarette, Virginia Slim, somehow made the woman pictured in the ad slim—in fact, slimmer than most—and that by extension smoking Virginia Slims will make any woman who smokes it slim. The claim is not all that unreasonable:

It has been shown that on average, cigarette smokers weigh less than their age- and sex-matched counterparts who do not smoke. But that is beside the point. The point is that by tied associations, the ad wants us to associate the following with Virginia Slims:

"Youth,"
"sexy," and
"slim and trim body habitus."

In the absence of evidence, loads and loads of evidence, such implied claims are unsupported, irrational, and wrong and beg the question.

All tautologies beg the question.

Arguing in a circle is a great way to conceal ignorance. Previously we learned that urine is yellow because it has urochromes, which are yellow pigments. We learned that morphine induces sleep because of its somniferous properties. Both items are mere restatements and beg the questions: What is the yellow pigment? And why does morphine induce sleep?

With this in mind, tell what's wrong with the statement: "Glass breaks because it is fragile."

Circular proofs are tautologies and therefore prove nothing.

Jehovah's Witnesses sometimes try to prove the existence of God by reference to the Bible. Citing the authority of the Old Testament, they claim that the Scriptures are divinely inspired. Otherwise said, God exists because we have a text that has been inspired by God. Such a position begs the question "Is the Bible divinely inspired?" If it is divinely inspired, how do we know that for sure?

In my course on clear thinking, I like to use illustrations from *Alice's Adventures in Wonderland* by Reverend Charles Lutwidge Dodgson, alias Lewis Carroll, Oxford teacher of mathematics and logic. Recall the delightful scene of Alice with the Cheshire Cat:

"In *that* direction," the Cat said, waving its right paw round, "lives a Hatter: and in *that* direction, lives a March Hare. Visit either you like: they're both mad."

"But I don't want to go among mad people," Alice remarked.

"Oh, you can't help that," said the Cat: "we're all mad here. I'm mad. You're mad."

"How do you know I'm mad?" said Alice.

"You must be," said the Cat, "or you wouldn't have come here."

Alice didn't think that proved it at all[.][1]

(She was right. The Cheshire Cat was begging the question.)

Alice went on: "And how do you know that you're mad?"

Good for Alice. She knows that to prove the Cat's statement false, she need only show that one person there is not mad. Alice effectively decided to try the argument with the Cat itself. She is asking for the evidence that proves the Cat is mad. Alice knows that if the evidence is not relevant and adequate, the Cat's statement will not be supported.

> "To begin with," said the Cat, "a dog's not mad. You grant that?"
>
> "I suppose so," said Alice.
>
> "Well, then," the Cat went on, "you see a dog growls when it's angry, and wags its tail when it's pleased. Now I growl when I'm pleased, and wag my tail when I'm angry. Therefore, I'm mad."[2]

The Cheshire Cat's proof is based on more faulty reasoning: A dog that wags its tail when happy and growls when angry is not mad. But this cat wags its tail when angry and growls when it is happy—just the opposite of the dog. Therefore, if the dog is not mad, then the cat that does the opposite of the dog must be mad. The defect in the analogy is clear: A dog is not a cat. What a normal dog does isn't necessarily normal for a cat and vice versa. Dogs and cats may share some features, but they don't share other features because they are different animals. Also notice how Alice questions the Cheshire Cat's definition of *growl* and questions the slight change of meaning in context:

"*I* call it purring, not growling," says Alice.

"Call it what you like," answers the Cat (who needs to opt on the side of flexible definitions for his argument to succeed). The Cheshire Cat, seeing Alice's reasoning getting too close for comfort, changes the subject: "Do you play croquet with the Queen today?"[3]

Diversions are a common trick to derail thinking. When you encounter a diversion, just get that diverter right back on track. Chances are you won the argument.

Flag words often identify question begging.

Lucky for us, the question begger often begins with phrases that flag the problem: "It is undeniable that"; Nothing is more evident"; "Nothing is simpler than"; "It stands to reason"; "Every schoolboy knows"; "As most of us know"; "Every real American believes"; "Every intelligent person wants"(fill in the blanks).

Clear thinking is impossible unless we use words that refer to facts and suspect those that express emotion. When we are told what to believe, what we want, what everyone knows, it is only reasonable to be skeptical and assume the question is being begged.

Leading questions often beg the question. All questions that anticipate a set answer beg the question. "Don't you agree?" "Doctor, isn't it true that. . . ." "Wouldn't you consider it probable that. . . ." "Don't you think it's reasonable to suppose. . . ." Sometimes, the question deliberately baits for the desired answer: "You love me, don't you?" "This wine, which I bought for only three dollars, is great, isn't it?" "Surely, Herman, you don't think that this piece of bent crashed automobile is great art?"

Consider this question: "When we have sex, can I be on top?" She is begging to be on top, but what question is she begging? That question is actually two questions. One question asks to be on top. The other begs a question, for it assumes he will have sex with her. That might not be the case and should be discussed beforehand. Before deciding who will be on top, people should discuss whether they will have sex at all. That is the first question, you know.

> Alice was beginning to get very tired of sitting by her sister on the bank and of having nothing to do: one or twice she had peeped into the book her sister was reading, but it had no pictures or conversations in it, "and what is the use of a book," thought Alice, "without pictures or conversations?"[4]

Alice has already answered the question in her own mind by the form of the question. She doesn't need to state that answer explicitly, but if she did, she would say, "A book without pictures or conversation is no use at all."

In court, such questions as Alice's—questions that presume a certain correct answer or that by implication lead to the answer—are not permitted, and the opposing lawyer (if not sleeping) will object to the "leading" question. A classic example of this is, "Where were you when you saw the headlight broken?"

Objection: Leading. Assumes facts not in evidence. It has not been established that a headlight was broken. At this point, opposing counsel must rephrase the question: "Did you see a broken headlight?"

Here's another classic example: "Have you left off beating your wife?"

Objection: Leading. Complex question. Assumes facts not in evidence. It has not been established that the defendant beat his wife. If the defendant were to answer the question yes or no, by implication he would admit the charge of wife beating.

> *Principle:* Unwarranted or unacceptable assumptions beg the question.

From which follows:

> *Lesson:* Watch out for implicit or unstated assumptions. Typically, although often popular, they are likely to be wrong.

REVIEW

Review this chapter as you did the previous ones. Work out the following:

1. Several years ago, a popular politician switched from the Republican party to the Democratic party, changing the balance of power in the US Senate. The senator came under fire from a number of his critics, especially Republicans.

   One argument that some Republicans thought particularly devastating was that the switch indicated that the senator was not a "true-blue" Republican, else he wouldn't have switched political parties. However, the only evidence cited for his non-"true-blue Republican" status was that he switched parties. His previous voting record was pretty much along Republican party lines.

   Any problem with the Republican reasoning here?

   My answer: This is a case of question begging. The Republicans are defining a "true-blue" Republican (presumably something good) as someone who would never leave the Republican party. Hence, the only matter that is actually in dispute is whether the definition is an appropriate one; no other factual claim is at issue.

2. Mark says to his nephew Herman, who is a high school senior, "Where are you going to college next year?" Any question begging here?

   Answer: You bet. Uncle Mark is assuming Herman wants to go to college. Actually, Herman wants to join the Navy and see the world.

3. "Unless someone wants to add anything further to the discussion of this absurd issue, we will move on to the next topic." Any question begging here?

   Answer: Who said the issue was absurd and why? The form of the statement suggests that the professor is biased against further discussion. Students will take up his offer at their peril because the professor doesn't want further discussion; he wants to move on.

4. In the *Houston Chronicle*, March 26, 2002, an article by Kevin Moran described a Marxist who taught American government and applied for tenure. Many opposed. Among those opposed was former Galveston County judge Ray Holbrook, who said: "It seems clear to me that Dr. Smith espouses a subversive anticapitalist, anti-free enterprise philosophy that I believe is out of place in a public institution of higher learning and is detrimental to the basis of our freedom in this country."

   Problems?

   Answer: Judge Holbrook did not say it *is* clear to me; he said *seems*. That might mean the judge is not sure of what he speaks. Yet, the way he talks suggests that he *knows*. Nevertheless, the indefinite *seems* raises question about whether his view is really correct, since he himself has doubts. Not having had direct contact with Dr. Smith or his course, the judge is in no position to state with certainty what Dr. Smith teaches or doesn't, much less what Dr. Smith espouses. Therefore, the doubt seems justified.

   Marxism is a complex set of doctrines. Which one of those doctrines is subversive? Anticapitalistic? Antifree enterprise? Which one of the many Marxist ideas does Judge Holbrook specifically object to and why? And why would expressing contrary views in a higher educational institution be out of place? What place would be more appropriate? If the judge wants such views excluded from *higher* education, would such views be appropriate to *lower* education? If so, how low? Grade school? Kindergarten? Preschool? What? Of course, the final irony (and contradiction) is that the judge advocates that the professor be restricted in his freedom to say and do what he wants. The implicit assumption is that such restriction of personal freedom, such restraint and limitation on professors of government, is needed in order to protect and promote freedom in general. The judge says that we have a free country but not for professors like Smith, who want to express unpopular ideas. That's a special pleading. And notice that the judge is making himself the judge of what we are free to say and hear.

Fortunately, reasonable people prevailed. The College of the Mainland board of trustees unanimously voted to grant Dr. Smith tenure, with which Dr. Smith got protection from being fired for his political views. The unanimous decision came after a two-hour public hearing.

"What we just witnessed here was a political rally," Judge Holbrook yelled at the board.[5] Holbrook, too, shouted out after students who spoke in favor of Dr. Smith. Another fine example of the principle "When the shouting starts, the reasoning stops."

5. "How did you enjoy the show?" Any begging the question here?

Answer: No doubt. The respondent's range of reply is limited in scope by the form of the question, which presumes the answer will express some form of enjoyment. More information usually will come from more open-ended questioning: What did you think of the show? Or even better, from letting others answer no question at all by our simply remaining quiet and listening attentively to what they have to say.

If you must ask a question, ask one that doesn't presume anything. Hamlet's "How find you the play, Madam?" is open ended. It lets Gertrude, Hamlet's mother, select from the myriad possible responses the one that interested her the most, the one that reflected what was going on in her heart of hearts. Her response was off the point but telling because she never addressed her feelings about the play. Instead, she told Hamlet about what the queen in the play vowed about not remarrying: "The Lady doth protest too much, methinks."

6. "The Unicorn thought Alice a fabulous monster."[6] Any question begging here?

Answer: No doubt, else why would the question be here in this chapter? From the point of view of a unicorn, humans must look pretty funny. It is part of the philosophic dullness of our time that there are millions of rational monsters walking about on their hind legs, observing the world through pairs of flexible little lenses, periodically supplying themselves with energy by pushing organic substances through holes in their faces, who see nothing fabulous whatever about themselves but do think birds, cats, and zoo animals are pretty interesting.

7. From *Alice's Adventures in Wonderland*:

Tied round the neck of the bottle was a paper label, with the words "DRINK ME" beautifully printed on it in large letters. It was all very well to say "Drink me," but the wise little Alice was not going to do *that* in a hurry. "No, I'll look first," she said, "and see whether it's marked '*poison*' or not"; for she had read several nice little stories about children who had got burnt and eaten up by wild beasts and other unpleasant things all because they *would* not remember the simple rules their friends had taught them: such as, that a red-hot poker will burn you if you hold it too long; and that, if you cut your finger very deeply with a knife, it usually bleeds; and she had never forgotten that, if you drink much from a bottle marked "poison," it is almost certain to disagree with you, sooner or later.

However, this bottle was *not* marked "poison," so Alice ventured to taste it, and, finding it very nice . . . she very soon finished it off.[7]

Any problems with Alice's thinking?

Answer: Aside from being hilarious, this passage is chock full of errors in thinking. I'll just mention a few. Because a bottle is labeled "DRINK ME" does not mean Alice should drink it. The label begs multiple questions, among which are "Is it safe?" "What is it for?" "Why should I drink it?" "Who made the sign?" "Why does that person want me to drink the contents of the bottle?" (The Victorian medicine bottle had neither a screw top nor a label on the side. It was corked, with a paper label tied to the neck.)

"Alice was not going to do *that* in a hurry. 'No, I'll look first.'"

Notice Alice had already decided that she would drink the stuff. She will drink it after she looks at it. Thus, she has dismissed the question of "Should I drink?" and substituted the question "When shall I drink?" To the later question she has a ready answer: as soon as I look. Never plunge into any major action without due deliberation.

Alice just needed to go through some rationalizations before acting. Her thinking is way off the point of course and defective in itself. Those nice little stories were not so nice. They were the traditional fairy tales, filled with episodes of horror and usually containing a pious moral. That they told about children who got burnt and eaten up by wild beasts, among other unpleasant things, hardly seems relevant to the issue at hand, which is to drink or not to drink. Furthermore, a red-hot poker has nothing to do with the question of the danger lurking in the bottle. Besides, a red-hot poker will burn you anytime you hold it. You don't have to hold it *too* long to get burned. How long is *too* long, anyway? The same minimization of danger is present in Alice's discussion of the knife: to bleed it is not necessary to cut *very* deeply. Deep will do.

That the bottle is not labeled as poison is neither here nor there, for a poison can be a poison whether labeled or not. Nevertheless, Alice concludes that since the bottle is not labeled poison, it is safe to taste. Stated more formally, Alice's thinking would go: "All poisons are labeled *poison*. This bottle is not labeled *poison*. Therefore, it is not a poison. Therefore, it is safe to drink." Premise one is wrong. Therefore, all conclusions derived from it are wrong.

Even if premise one were correct and the liquid were not a poison, conclusions one and two don't ring true. There are lots of substances that, though not poisons, would not be safe to drink—polluted water, for instance. Other substances are not poisons but would be unpleasant to drink—vinegar, for instance. Other liquids are a food, a poison, or a drug, depending on the definition, and might not be suitable for a little girl to drink—Irish whiskey, for instance.

By focusing on side issues that are off the point, Alice convinces herself that drinking the stuff in the bottle is OK. This is an obvious rationalization to justify the real reason for her action, which is her curiosity as to what would happen.

And speaking of curiosity, I am curious about what the next chapter will be about, since, as I write this, I don't know. And because I don't know, I can't tell you. Let's turn the page and see. I hope the next chapter is not labeled "READ ME," but I have a sneaky feeling it is.

NOTES

1. Lewis Carroll, *Alice's Adventures in Wonderland*, illust. John Tenniel and colored by Fritz Kredel (New York: Random House, 1946), pp. 72–73. All references to *Alice* are to this edition.

2. Ibid., pp. 73–74.

3. Ibid., p. 74.

4. Ibid., p. 3.

5. Judge Holbrook, quoted in an article by Kevin Moran, *Houston Chronicle*, March 26, 2002.

6. This isn't a direct quotation from Carroll. It's actually a misquotation by Martin Gardner, ed. *The Annotated Alice* (New York: Norton, 1990), pp. 228–29. The reference is to *Through the Looking Glass and What Alice Found There*, chapter 7.

7. Paraphrased from Carroll, *Alice's Adventures in Wonderland*, pp. 9–10.

chapter 9

Read Me

This chapter covers the *uniform field theory*, a theory of knowledge designed to help you arrive at the truth. Up to this point, we have concerned ourselves with multiple particular illustrations of clear and crooked thinking. It is possible by induction to generalize about the nature of our activity and arrive at the general principle governing our search for reality. That general principle, the uniform field theory, is that the correct perception of the truth is based on the understanding of all the evidence.

Reasoning itself is a form of evidence because by definition it can be a sign that points to the truth. As a form of evidence, reasoning is subject to correct interpretation. Thus, any and all rules of exact thought, all the guidelines about clear thinking, and all analysis of the named and unnamed fallacies—all the rules, laws, maxims and all the "Pattened Principles" inflicted on you in previous chapters—boil down to the application of the uniform field theory of truth.

But, in a practical sense, all the evidence is rarely available to us. All we can hope for in this, the best of all possible worlds, is a correct interpretation of all the *available* evidence.

Thus, no conclusion can be final because it cannot be based on all the evidence. Future evidence does not yet exist, and the past evidence might be obscured, unavailable to us, missing, or actually fake. Therefore, all conclusions must be based on partial, incomplete, and sometimes erroneous evidence.

Since conclusions can never be based on all the evidence, all conclusions must be considered tentative. If all conclusions are tentative, then they all must be subject to revision and possible change if and when new evidence becomes available.

Thus, in our quest for truth, the most important questions to ask are about evidence. Such questions take the form "Why? What's the evidence? How do you know that for sure?" Questions of that ilk bring out the evidence and lead to correct conclusions about reality and truth.

Sometimes it is helpful to jog our thinking about evidence by using the RA mnemonic: Evidence must be (R)elevant and (A)dequate. If the evidence fails on any significant part of R or A, that is, if it is not relevant or adequate, the conclusion is not supported.

For emphasis and to cement the idea in your memory, please repeat this out loud right now: The uniform field theory holds that our correct perception and understanding of reality is based on the correct interpretation of the available evidence.

From which follows:

> *Lesson:* Analysis of the evidence is crucial. Evidence must be relevant and adequate. Otherwise, a firm or reasonable conclusion cannot be reached.

For the purpose of analysis, it is sometimes helpful to divide correct analysis of evidence into two parts, relevance and adequacy. These parts are similar to each other and in some senses are also different. All relate back to the uniform field theory. The two parts of the uniform field theory relate to analysis of the available evidence, not to the analysis of all the evidence, as mentioned. Each of these two parts bears weight, but the most important part of the initial consideration of evidence is relevance.

Genus definition of *relevance*: Evidence is relevant if it pertains directly and unemotionally to the merit of the position at issue and supports the conclusion. Evidence that does not pertain directly to or does not support the conclusion is irrelevant.

Divisional definition of *relevance*: Evidence is relevant if it

- relates directly to the conclusion.
- provides some reason to believe, counts in favor of, or makes a difference to the perception of the truth of the conclusion.
- is not an emotional appeal.

If the evidence doesn't relate to the conclusion in a reasonable way, it is irrelevant and the conclusion is not justified. Good evidence must have a bearing on, provide support for, or make a genuine difference to the truth or falsity of the conclusion. Otherwise, the evidence is not relevant. All emotional appeals, strictly speaking, cannot directly relate to the truth of any conclusion. Therefore, emotional appeals are suspect because they are likely to be irrelevant.

A red-hot poker is irrelevant to whether Alice should obey "DRINK ME."

We have already looked at lack of relevance in its many varied forms. That a red-hot poker will burn the hand is true, but it is not relevant to the issue that Alice was considering. That the bottle might contain poison was relevant to the issue because one should not drink a poison and Alice was trying to decide whether to drink. Alice's subsequent thinking on this issue got derailed because she concluded that since the bottle was not labeled poison, the liquid in the bottle was OK to drink. Many other liquids besides poisons should not be drunk, and the absence of a poison label doesn't mean that the content of the bottle is not a poison. A poison is a poison whether or not it is labeled as such.

Beware **sound arguments** *or valid arguments that are off the point. They are irrelevant.*

Arguments such as the hot-poker one that Alice considered actually have true premises: Hot pokers do burn hands. Consequently, you should not hold them. But such arguments, in Alice's case, do not directly relate to the question of whether she should drink. They are off the point and therefore irrelevant. Poisons kill. That is true. Such considerations, that one should not drink poisonous fluids, relate directly to the issue Alice considers and are therefore to the point and relevant.

Authority is irrelevant.

Citing an authority is always irrelevant because an authority can be wrong. We might pay more attention to the reasons given by an authority than we would to those given by a nonauthority simply because of that authority's qualifications, but we need not accept those reasons as relevant unless they are. Past experience has shown that an authority acting outside his own narrow field is no authority at all and that some authorities are biased in some way. Of course, citing an anonymous authority, or any authority that cannot be checked and questioned, is irrelevant.

> *Principle:* Accept an authority for the reasons given, not because the authority is an authority.

From which follows:

> *Lesson:* Focus on the reasons, not the authority. Pay no at-
> tention to biased, unqualified, or anonymous authorities,
> for those are, to the extent of those limitations, irrelevant.

A stockbroker, though an authority on the stock market, is biased because he makes his living selling or buying shares for you. Therefore, any recommendation to buy or sell must be viewed as irrelevant unless supported by reasons.

For example, "Did you know that interference from in-laws is the number-one cause of divorce in the United States?"

"How do you know that for sure?"

"I heard it on *The Oprah Winfrey Show* today."

Is the authority cited Oprah herself? If so, why and how is she qualified? Was the authority one of Oprah's guests? If so, why and how is she qualified? Was it an audience member? A writer plugging her new book? An unidentified invited "expert"? If the authority fits any of these categories, the claim is not relevant to the conclusion, and nothing has been proven. Even if the expert were a genuine professor of social work who studied the issue for many years, and, after such study, reached that rather startling conclusion, we would have to see the actual data to determine whether the conclusion related to the data and was justified.

Another example: "A highly placed well-respected public figure said in a recent article in *U.S. News & World Report* that historians will probably describe President Clinton as having developed a very strong, forward-looking, and well-defined foreign policy for the post–cold war years."

Unnamed authorities—cast a cold eye on them. When I read something like this, I just pass over it because the information density and the reliability is mighty weak. It turned out (I learned several weeks later) that the "highly placed, well-respected public figure" was Madeleine Albright, secretary of state under President Clinton. I liked Albright. Some people didn't. Other people were neutral. But whether I liked her—and whether you liked her, whether other people liked her, or whether most people liked her—doesn't matter. Likes or dislikes don't matter because they don't materially relate to any conclusion. What is related to the possible truth of the conclusion is that Albright is a biased source. She is part and parcel of the vaguely described and much-praised foreign policy. So in admiring—some might even say in flattering—Clinton's foreign policy, the secretary of state indirectly and self-servingly praises herself. Furthermore, the secretary of state serves at the pleasure of the president. In view of the power relationships involved, it would be highly unlikely that Albright could hold, would hold, or (if she held different views from Clinton) would voice opinions contrary to those of the president. A biased authority is, to the extent of the bias, no authority at all.

Mere assertions are irrelevant.

Anyway, her bias is neither here nor there, for Albright gave us no reasons for her assertions. She just told us that Clinton's foreign policies were (in her opinion and in so many words) great. She didn't tell us why they were great. Therefore, no relevant reasons were offered to support her conclusions. She herself probably suspects that she is a biased authority. That is why she doesn't cite herself as holding the opinions stated. Oh, no. She doesn't say, "I believe that. . . ." Instead, she cites the unnamed historians of the future: men and women who may or may not hold the opinions that she has stated and who are not available for cross-examination. Thus, the authority cited is not only anonymous but also not yet existent. Maybe those men and women historians of the future would support the secretary of state's self-serving opinion with evidence; maybe they would not.

Therefore, for us to read Albright's statements is mainly a waste of time. Believe none of this ilk.

Groupthink, herd instinct, popular opinions, received standard wisdom, and (so-called) common sense are all usually irrelevant.

Appeals to patriotism, tradition, and common opinion are appeals to highly questionable authorities or to no real authority at all. Such appeals are off the point and therefore not relevant. The bandwagon and consensus mean nothing. That a movie is popular or not is not relevant to the consideration of whether you should see it. Your tastes may differ from the masses, and the masses may be wrong.

How about this claim? "If tanning were really unsafe, millions of Americans wouldn't do it every week."

"Really? How do you know that for sure?"

What large numbers of people think is the truth and what they do are not relevant to what is actually the truth. The benefits and dangers of tanning cannot be deduced from the fact that the activity is popular. Never infer anything from what the majority does or thinks. Remember that a large body of people believe in astrology, psychokinesis, extrasensory perception, out-of-body experiences, creationism, and so forth. At one time, the majority believed the Earth was flat and at the center of the universe. Polls show that the percentage of those believing in ghosts, haunted houses, and communication with the dead has risen in the last decade (News scan data points, *Scientific American* 285 [2001]: 26). That is no reason for us to believe such nonsense.

Even science, some of the time, takes quantum leaps in the wrong direction, as in the (premature) discovery of cold fusion, the Piltdown man hoax, and nonexistent N-rays. How many times have you heard some medical discovery announced in the news only to learn a year later that another study seems to contradict the first? Mammography versus no mammography? PSA screening versus no PSA?

Recent screening tests for the early and exact diagnosis of neuroblastoma in children showed that early and exact diagnosis of such tumors made no difference in survival. In fact, most of the early tumors detected underwent spontaneous involution and therefore required no treatment whatsoever. Estrogen replacement, according to a recent controlled prospective study, caused an increase in fatal heart attacks, not a decrease, as previously reported. Estrogen replacement increases the incidence of dementia, not decreases it, as previously reported.

All fake reasons are irrelevant.

We discussed how people use fake reasons to justify conclusions already accepted. Usually, the conclusion should come after a consideration of the reasons for it, not vice versa. In rationalization, the stated reasons usually bear little or no relation to the conclusion and have been simply made up to justify a questionable position.

For example, "Yes, I subscribe to *Hustler*. But I do it for the great articles."

This is likely a rationalization. I have never seen a great article in *Hustler*, but I have seen plenty of great pictures of beautiful nude women. Besides, even if, from time to time, great articles did appear in *Hustler*, that is not the real reason that he subscribes to *Hustler*. Nor is it the reason I subscribe to *Hustler*. If fake reasons are given in support of a claim, they cannot be relevant to the truth. There are just too many fake things out there. Don't add to them.

All appeals to emotion are irrelevant.

All appeals to tradition or personal circumstance; all innuendo or **obloquy**; all guilt by association; all use of flattery, pity, shame, or charity; all threats of violence, all violence itself, though sometimes effective in getting things that are wanted—are not relevant to the conclusion and are therefore unreasonable.

Emotions may influence us to help or to do something, but that is beside the point. Emotional appeals are not relevant to a reasoned conclusion and are poor substitutes for real evidence. Use of emotions to get to the truth is a poor substitute for reason. Don't do it.

Take this: "Trust me. You have nothing to fear." Unsupported by reasons, the command to trust is irrelevant. When coupled with the above assertion, one might do well to be on guard.

Or this: "You are not going to pass this course unless you sleep with me." Attempting to persuade another by threatening her with some undesirable state of affairs instead of presenting evidence for one's view is irrelevant. There is nothing wrong with pointing out the consequences of a particular course of action, but to use a threat is to use an irrelevant appeal since the threat has no reasoned relation to the conclusion. Sex for a passing grade is a bad argument. To see how bad it is, I'll recast it into standard form. Parentheses enclose the implicit premises:

Since I want to have sex with you,
I want you to have sex with me.
Since I have control over whether you pass,
(And, thus control your future professional life),
(And you wouldn't want to jeopardize your professional life),
(And I will jeopardize it if you don't have sex with me).
(Conclusion:) Therefore, you will have sex with me.

Stated that way, the argument wouldn't convince any reasonable person of the rightness of the action sought. But that argument has probably brought about compliance with the request more often than one might think. It is a potent device to achieve results, but the threatening premise along with the implicit premises (in parentheses) that are employed in such arguments are irrelevant.

Arguments that make you feel bad or feel guilty are irrelevant. "You mean after we flew you down here to Cancun at no cost to you and put you up for three days at the Maya Palace Hotel with all meals and entertainment provided, you are not going to buy even one of our timeshare condos?" This broker is exploiting strong feelings and trying to instill a feeling of guilt in the potential customer for accepting the enticements and not the product. If such enticements were offered, as they usually are, with no strings attached, there is no reason for the customer to feel guilty about anything, much less failure to purchase a condo that he doesn't want. Any attempt to influence an action by an appeal to emotion—in this case, the emotions of guilt and shame—is irrelevant.

A proper response to the broker might be: "We were under no obligation to buy anything. That was one of the original conditions by which you offered us this free vacation, as stated in your brochure. We thank you, but we have no interest in buying the condo." At this point, it wouldn't hurt to give the guy a reason, if you have one: "We don't like the condo because (fill in the blank)."

All bribes and all appeals to the personal interest of officials are irrelevant. "Do me the personal favor of awarding me the McDonald's franchise at Camp David."

President: "No way. I want it here where it belongs—at the White House."

Any attempt to influence a government official by appealing to personal favor or to personal interest is an emotional appeal and therefore not relevant. Use of money to persuade a politician to vote for or against anything is irrelevant and therefore unreasonable. All payoffs and bribes are not reasons that support a conclusion. Therefore, they are wrong.

Many politically incorrect items are irrelevant.

For instance, is ogling OK? Who knows. Some people think it is not OK because it may make a man uncomfortable when women do it. On the other hand, it seems natural enough and is unlikely to hurt anyone significantly. If women ogle me, I don't mind.

One could construct a natural argument to justify ogling: Women are likely to ogle men as a prelude to flirting, which, in turn, might be a prelude to love, which, in turn, might lead to sex, marriage, and reproduction of the species. Therefore, right or wrong, ogling might well be part of the natural landscape, like sniffing the breeze when a steak is cooking. Yes, women will ogle men on this planet until the sun burns out. Therefore, perhaps a better, less prejudicial word for ogling would be "admire." Yes, that's it. Women will admire men until the sun burns out. As that is the reality, it doesn't seem right to argue much against it. A similar natural argument was used by Elizabeth Cady Stanton (1815–1902) in the Declaration of Sentiments: "Resolved, that all laws which prevent woman from occupying such a station in society as her conscience shall dictate, or which place her in a position inferior to that of man, are contrary to the great precept of nature, and therefore of no force or authority."[1] If such an argument in support of women's rights is reasonable, then I would think the argument that women admiring men and men admiring women is also reasonable because it is also natural.

Flattery or any form of praise cannot be reasonably substituted for evidence. Yet because we are so influenced by affirmation, we can be easily manipulated by the cheap trick of flattery.

"I really hate to ask you this because you have been so kind and generous to me in the past, but would you mind loaning me another $100,000? I feel that I can ask you this because, unlike those other stingy bastards, you possess the true spirit of Christian charity." The petitioner has used flattery rather than reason for his request. In fact, other than the dubious moral argument that a true Christian would make the loan, no evidence of need is mentioned.

What about this? "My numbers are behind this month, so I need the sale. Please buy this TV. I need it. My wife needs it. My children need it." Appeals to pity are not evidence of need, nor are they reasonable arguments for us to buy a TV. A discussion of the benefits to us of owning that TV would be more in order. Does the TV in question meet my personal need? Is it sixty-five inches? Does it have surround sound? How about high definition? MicroFine Phosphor CRTs? Is it too big to get into my home? What is the price? Payment plans? Can it be delivered this week? All those things might be relevant to the question of whether I should buy. But the pitiable state of the salesman's numbers that month is (or should be) irrelevant to my decision. His needs, if real and not mere assertions to make the sale, would be relevant reasons for him to make the sale. They are not reasons, though, for us to buy.

Politicians are notorious for using irrelevant evidence.

"Mr. Perot, it seems to me that if you were elected president, the Congress with which you would have to work would not be very cooperative."

"Well, if I were elected, about half of the members of Congress would drop dead of heart attacks. Half of my problem would be solved."

Perot doesn't address the reporter's question. Instead, by using humor, Perot diverts consideration from a real issue. Such diversions are called red herrings after the famous trick used in fox hunting. The partially baked red herring was rubbed over the fox's tail so the dogs would have a good scent to follow. People who disliked fox hunting could divert those dogs by using their own red herring.

During the 1984 presidential campaign, President Reagan's age concerned some people. I remember the TV debate where the issue was raised (again) as the president was running against Walter Mondale, a much younger man.

Reporter: Mr. President, might you be too old to handle a nuclear war?

Reagan: Not at all. And I am not going to exploit my opponent's youth and inexperience.

Reagan did not address the issue (except with a general denial unsupported by evidence) but diverted attention from the issue with humor. The president cleverly pointed out that using age as a sole criterion to appraise the president's ability in handing nuclear war could work both ways.

Sometimes politicians use irrelevant evidence that is not humorous, just stupid. Representative Tom DeLay was recorded as saying that kids should not go to Baylor University or to Texas A&M because "there is sex in the dorms and they don't teach creationism." DeLay is entitled to his opinions. But when he gives reasons for the opinions, then he opens himself to analysis and criticism of the reasons. Selection of a proper college is not simple. Rather, it is a complex, multifaceted task that should include more reasons than the two mentioned by DeLay. To say that Baylor is bad simply for two partially selected small pieces of evidence is to disregard a massive amount of evidence that Baylor is good. Such partial selection of evidence is an error in thinking. Any conclusion based on partial selection is, to that extent, wrong. Furthermore, DeLay implies that because there is sex in the dorms and no creationism taught, Baylor is bad for all students. Some students might thrive in such an environment, as in *The Harrad Experiment*.[2] Therefore, DeLay's statement is overly general. Overgeneralization is an error, and any conclusion based on an overgeneralization is, to the extent of the overgeneralization, wrong. Besides, if educational institutions were to be judged by the two reasons mentioned, then Harvard, Columbia, Princeton, Yale, Stanford, the Sorbonnne, and most of the other great universities of the world would be excluded. Above and beyond those considerations, it's hard to consider the teaching of creationism a standard for evaluation of educational institutions. Quite the opposite is true: Creationism disregards thousands of scientific studies and a fossil record that goes back

2.5 million years. A discipline that disregards massive amounts of carefully gathered scientific evidence is not worthy of attention.

When questioned about this, DeLay said, "The guy who recorded me is a former member of the ACLU." Whether the guy who recorded DeLay's speech is a former member of the American Civil Liberties Union, a present member of the ACLU, or never was a member of the ACLU is irrelevant to whether the statement was reasonable. DeLay is just trying to divert attention from having to defend his own statement by resorting to an irrelevant ad hominen argument of no merit.

Empty consolation is irrelevant.

"Councilman, I am retired and barely making ends meet. If you vote another increase in property taxes, I don't see how I can survive."

"You'll just have to bite the bullet. Things could be worse. You are lucky to live in Taylor Lake Village. Taxes in River Oaks are much higher."

This is a common form of red herring designed to shut up the opposition and to prevent further rational consideration of the issues. What is offered instead of a reason that taxes have to be raised is just a reassertion of the point in question. Instead of intelligent discussion, the retired person gets empty consolation, which seeks to draw attention away from the complaint by claiming that the complainant should be satisfied with an undesirable situation because "things could be much worse" or because the situation with some other group is much worse.

"Things" could almost always be worse. "Things" could almost always be better, too. That is not a real issue. Somewhere and sometimes, chances are that things are worse. Somewhere and sometimes, chances are that things are better. That's a trivial truism, a tautology of no information value.

Drawing attention to such a phony issue is simply a way to avoid dealing with the complaint. One way of countering such diversionary arguments is to point out the obvious: that things could be much worse, but things could also be much better, too: taxes in Deer Park are less than those in Taylor Lake Village. Or one could explain that River Oaks is the wealthiest part of Houston. Comparing its tax structure with Taylor Lake Village is like comparing the value of diamonds with pebbles. In other words, comparing Taylor Lake Village to River Oaks is a false comparison, a false analogy.

Another example: "Please smoke outside, not in here."

"Secondary smoke is no worse than the diesel exhaust of the idling trucks outside. Those fumes can make you sick."

Yes, diesel fumes can make you sick. So what? That is empty consolation for the smoke in the office. The issue that smoking outside would be better for those who work in the office was not addressed. Calling attention to the diesel fumes as a greater wrong is an irrelevant, though psychologically powerful, move that works by contrasting two effects, secondary smoke and diesel fumes, and by that contrast makes the cigarette smoke look better than diesel fumes, which it is. But the point of inquiry was not whether second-hand smoke was better, worse, or the same as diesel fumes. The point of inquiry was that clear air would be better for those in the office than air contaminated by tobacco smoke. That point was not addressed. Anyway, why not get rid of both?

All vague definitions and all linguistic confusions are irrelevant. Use and misuse of vague expressions; wrong definitions, whether broadcast or not; equivocation; ambiguity; and distinctions without a difference are irrelevant:

1. "Max likes tennis better than his wife."
2. "People should not eat fish caught in Illinois twice in the same week because of mercury."
3. Question: "Should I turn left?"
   Response: "Right!"
4. "For us Americans, no setback is a setback."

Ambiguous wording and infelicitous expressions such as those above interfere with reaching the correct conclusion. We don't know whether Max likes tennis better than he likes his wife, or whether Max likes tennis better than his wife likes tennis. People should not eat fish twice in the same week is the more likely interpretation of example two, since it is unlikely that in the same week the same fish would be caught twice. Example three leaves us in the lurch because we don't really know which way to turn because the word *right* has two meanings: "to the right" and "correct." Which meaning applies in the context? You can't tell. And last—a setback is a setback by definition. This billboard slogan on Highway 45 and Dixie Farm Road is designed to unify public opinion despite the setbacks in Iraq. The slogan is a contradiction because a thing can't be a thing and not a thing at the same time. That firm rule applies to setbacks, too, such that a setback can't be a setback and not a setback. That is logically and physically impossible. What is logically and physically impossible is logically and physically impossible even for determined Americans. What I suppose is really meant is that setbacks won't set us back for long or significantly because we as Americans are determined to meet and solve the setbacks. But that, unfortunately, is not what the slogan says. And because it doesn't say that, the slogan implies that the setbacks are not a serious problem that needs to be intelligently and adequately addressed and solved. The slogan, instead of encouraging us to think about the reality situation, encourages us to irrationally dismiss the problem because, after all, "a setback is not a setback for us."

Statements that cannot lead to a correct conclusion are irrelevant.

In general, when things are unclear, ask. Don't be embarrassed to ask about something that you don't understand. Don't be embarrassed to ask about something that you suspect of being improperly phrased. It is better to be a skeptic or risk appearing naive or stupid than to come to a false conclusion.

Distinctions without a difference are irrelevant.

Take, for example, "I wasn't copying, and I certainly wasn't cheating. I was just looking at her paper to jog my memory." This argument tries to distinguish cheating, copying, and looking at someone else's paper to jog the memory. It is based on a fundamental confusion about the definition of cheating versus copying versus jogging the memory. All those distinctions are there, but they don't make a difference. Saying that they do make a difference does not make it so. The student who has been caught cheating is attempting, by offering a distinction without a difference, to avoid the penalty for cheating. Distinction without a difference is a diversionary argument that is irrelevant.

What about this statement from President Nixon: "I'm not a crook!" Whether he was a crook can be debated and would depend on what he did and on the definition of the word *crook*. Let's assume for a moment that he wasn't a crook. That doesn't mean he didn't violate his oath of office to preserve and protect the Constitution. Nixon is attempting to make a distinction between what he ordered men to do in the Watergate break-in versus what real crooks do during other break-ins, a distinction without a difference. Since the distinction is irrelevant to the conclusion, the conclusion is not supported. The implied conclusion was that since he was not a crook, he should not be punished like one.

Here is another example: "I didn't lie to you; I merely told you what you wanted to hear." He did lie. Perhaps he lied for the stated reason.

So what? He is trying to make a distinction between lying and lying for a reason. In this case, he says he was lying to console her. He wants her to conclude that the lie was justified because it gave her what she wanted to hear. However, there is no difference between a lie and a lie for a nice reason. It's still a lie and a distinction without a difference. To deliberately use a distinction that makes no difference is irrelevant to any conclusion.

Begging the question is irrelevant.

Question begging, arguing in a circle, tautology, **pleonasm** (redundant expressions like "pretty much" and "very unique"), complex questions, leading questions, mere assertions, and the like are irrelevant. They were covered (more or less) previously.

By now you should be able to answer the question, "Do you enjoy using crack?" Hint: the answer does not involve a yes or a no. The question must be rejected. A negative reply implies that you use crack but don't enjoy it. When asked questions like this on the witness stand, I usually just sit there and stare in silence at the questioner until the question is rephrased.

All unwarranted assumptions are irrelevant.

Unwarranted assumptions include the fallacy of the continuum and the arguments that appeal to tradition. In a sense, false analogy is based on unwarranted assumptions, as is the fallacy of novelty, that new things must always be better. Under black-and-white thinking, we discussed the fallacy of false alternatives. Under wishful thinking, we discussed the misuse of human hopefulness—because you want something to be true will not make it true. Conversely, because you want something not to be true will not make it not true.

Three closely related unwarranted assumptions are the fallacies of composition, of division, and of the mean. A part is not necessarily the same as the whole, nor is the whole necessarily the same as or even similar to its parts. The mean is just a mathematical abstraction that may or may not relate to the subject under discussion.

What is true of the whole is not necessarily true of the parts of that whole.

To assume that it is true is an unwarranted assumption based on a partial selection of evidence and therefore is likely to be irrelevant to the conclusion: "Mary is wonderful and so is John. Wouldn't it be wonderful to see them get married?" It might be wonderful to see them get married, but the marriage itself might not be so wonderful. The whole called *marriage* is more than the sum of the parts that make it up. Two wonderful people might not add up to a wonderful marriage. In sports, we see that principle often enough. The team has the best players, and yet it doesn't click. Whereas a team that doesn't have the best players might click or might click better.

Water is composed of two parts hydrogen and one part oxygen. Hydrogen and oxygen together are highly explosive. Although its parts are highly explosive, water itself is not explosive at all. Water is water and has properties that are quite different from its component parts, hydrogen and oxygen.

Closely related to this error is the *fallacy of division*, which consists in assuming that what is true of some whole is true of each of the parts of that whole. This, too, is an unwarranted assumption. To get this point, work the water problem backwards: what is true of water is not true of its component parts, hydrogen and oxygen.

"Britney Spears has a beautiful face. Therefore, her nose must be beautiful." It may be true that Spears has a beautiful face, but it does not necessarily mean that the individual parts of her face, such as her nose or ears, are beautiful. This is because the characteristic of the whole is not necessarily a characteristic shared by each of the parts.

The *fallacy of the mean* is the idea that the average rather than the extremes is somehow the best or the correct thing. This is also known as the *fallacy of moderation*. Whether a position is the mean or close to it is irrelevant to the conclusion and should be disregarded. A moderate view might be best, no question about it. But that is not the point at issue here. The point is that the moderate view is not supported as a best view simply because it is moderate. The justification for the moderate view must come from other evidence. It is not wrong to compromise in order to settle an argument, but it is wrong to assume, apart from the evidence, that compromise is the best solution.

For example: "Since you want to pay $2,000 for the TV, and the list price is $2,800, let's split the difference and you pay $2,400." Although such a compromise might seem fair, it may not be the best solution. It certainly is not the best solution if the TV is worth only $1,900. In fact, if the appliance is worth only $1,900, then the offer of $2,000 may have been more than fair. In dealing with salesmen, always consider the possibilities that the store may have built in the anticipated call for compromise, so that the so-called compromise turns out not to be a compromise at all but an advantage to the store.

Another example: "Two plus two is four."

"Nope. Two plus two is six."

"You're wrong. It's four."

"OK. I tell you what. Let's compromise. You say four. I say six. We'll settle at five. OK?"

Two plus two is four, now and forever. Don't forget it. Never compromise a truth like that. The freedom to say that two and two was four was the fundamental truth that Winston Smith (in the novel *1984*) wrote in his diary: *"Freedom is the freedom to say that two plus two make four. If that is granted, all else follows."*[3]

"According to the US Coast Guard Tidal Tables, the mean lower low water depth at Red Fish sandbar is three feet. Since our draft is twenty-nine inches, we can safely pass over the bar without fear of running aground, even though it is lower low tide right now." Whoa! *Mean lower low* means just that. Every day, there are two low tides, one that is lower than the other. The Coast Guard keeps track of such information and computes the mean lower low on the basis of the measurements taken over a nineteen-year period. Because the measurement is a mean, it must indicate that the lower low water was below the stated number on numerous occasions. Therefore, to assume that the tide at present could not be lower than the stated lower low would be an unwarranted assumption that could lead (and has often led) to the catastrophe of running aground.

"The jury, having heard contradictory testimony from the two principal witnesses in the case, concluded that the truth must lie somewhere in between." This is an unwarranted assumption. There is no evidence to suggest that the truth is to be found somewhere between the two testimonies. Simply because the position is between the two testimonies does not mean it is correct. One, the other, or both of the witnesses might be mistaken or lying.

Closely related to the fallacy of the mean is *unwarranted generalization* from statistics. A statistical analysis is at best a mixed experience, and conclusions derived from statistics about particulars are often wrong: "The average appraisal value of homes on Baronridge in Taylor Lake Village is over $300,000. Therefore, everyone who lives on Baronridge is a fat cat." The statistic is correct, but the conclusion doesn't follow because some people who live on Baronridge will have appraisals below the average. Furthermore, the term *fat cat* lacks clear definition, so we really don't know what is meant by the statement.

Nonrepresentative selection results in irrelevant evidence.

Literary Digest closed after it predicted in 1936 that the Republican presidential candidate, Alf Landon, would defeat the Democratic incumbent, Franklin D. Roosevelt, by a landslide. To the complete embarrassment of the *Literary Digest*, the landslide went the other way. What happened was that the *Literary Digest* had taken its poll by telephone. That poll showed that over 80 percent surveyed intended to vote for Alf. The poll did not include people who did not own a telephone. Other Americans, vastly outnumbering the affluent who owned phones, had been hit hard by the Depression. They wanted FDR and not Alf to win the election, and they voted accordingly. The statistical inference was correct only for the group surveyed—telephone owners. Partial selection of evidence, unwarranted assumptions, overgeneralization, biased sample, and so forth struck again and caused a good magazine to reach an absurd conclusion that ultimately damaged its credibility so much that *Literary Digest* had no choice but to go belly up.

How about this statement? "More white men are convicted of crimes than are black men." The intention of this statistic is to make us believe that there is equal justice under law because the blacks are not overrepresented in the population of convicted felons. The statistic is true, but the conclusion does not follow for the simple reason that white men outnumber black men nine to one. Only if the convictions of white men outnumbered those of black men by that ratio might we draw any inferences about social justice. Whether blacks or whites are convicted more or less is off the point anyway. The real question is which racial group commits the most crimes and by how much. The convictions should reflect the number of crimes committed and nothing else.

Another statistic: "There are more married men who have AIDS than there are unmarried men who have the disease."

While this statistic is true, the implication that married men are at greater risk for AIDS is not true. In fact, married men outnumber unmarried men (in the United States) by four to one. The percentage of HIV-positive men in the unmarried group actually exceeds that in the married group by a wide margin. Therefore, although more married men have AIDS than do those who are unmarried, they are not as a general class more prone to develop AIDS. The opposite may be the case: something about being unmarried may have increased the incidence of AIDS in the unmarried group.

Counterevidence, if relevant, must be considered.

The uniform field theory requires us to consider all the available evidence. Consideration of only some of the evidence constitutes a partial selection and may lead to an erroneous conclusion. Especially important is the consideration of counterevidence, which is what mainly protects juries from convicting every time. If you have ever been on a jury, you know what I mean. The DA presents his case, and you are sure the accused is guilty as hell and you wonder why bother to have a trial. Then the defendant's attorney gets up and gives his view of the situation, and you don't know what to think. Now you want to release this poor innocent slob as soon as possible. Later, you focus on and evaluate all the evidence, good and bad, pro and con, and try to reach a reasonable conclusion. To have reached a conclusion without considering the DA's case wouldn't have been reasonable. To have reached a conclusion without considering the defendant's evidence wouldn't have been reasonable, either. Looking at all the evidence is more likely to point to the reality, to the truth of guilt or innocence, than considering only part of the evidence would.

Here is an example from *Alice in Wonderland*:

> "Take off your hat," the King said to the Hatter.
> "It isn't mine," said the Hatter.
> "Stolen!" the King exclaimed, turning to the jury, who instantly made a memorandum of the fact.
> "I keep them to sell," the Hatter added as an explanation. "I've none of my own. I'm a Hatter."[4]

If the Hatter had not offered the additional evidence, the jury might have convicted him of stealing a hat. As it was, the Hatter was under considerable pressure.

Duress, threat, and extortion produce irrelevant evidence.

> "Give your evidence," said the King; "and don't be nervous, or I'll have you executed on the spot."[5]

Intimidation might help you win a squabble, but it doesn't help get to the truth. The best evidence is that which is given freely and objectively without stress or duress. Anything less than that taints the evidence and steers us away from truth toward error.

For example, "I don't care what is in the biology textbooks. I know that I didn't come from a monkey." Since the person fails to consider evidence counter to his belief, his conclusion cannot be justified. Further discussion of the issue with such a person is a waste of time.

Another example: "Motorcycles are uncomfortable in the rain and more than dangerous; no one should be permitted to ride them." Many other factors relate to the desirability of owning a motorcycle: the motorcycle is inexpensive, uses less fuel, is more maneuverable than a car, and so forth. Unless such considerations were looked at in detail, the conclusion that motorcycles are undesirable would not be fully supported.

Contrary-to-fact statements are irrelevant.

All contrary-to-fact statements and all statements about future facts are irrelevant. Such as, "If only Hitler had not invaded Russia, he would not have had to fight on two fronts, and Germany would have won the war." Hitler did invade Russia. Hitler did fight on two fronts. Germany did lose the war. Therefore, the statement is contrary to fact and irrelevant to any reasonable argument. The topic might be of interest in the analogical matrix known as fiction, but an argument contrary to fact neglects established evidence and therefore must be wrong.

Or: "If TV had existed at the time, De Witt Clinton would not have lost the election of 1812 to James Madison." The only thing this statement tells us for sure is that De Witt Clinton lost and James Madison won the presidential election of 1812. TV did not exist in 1812. Clinton lost the election. The argument neglects those two historical facts. Any argument contrary to the evidence is irrelevant.

Or: "If Arafat had been more of a leader and not followed public opinion so much, there would be peace in Israel right now." Since there is no peace in Israel now, any speculation about what past events might have changed that situation would not lead to the factual current situation and therefore are irrelevant.

Similarly, future facts are highly questionable. The future is not determined, and therefore any assertion about what will happen lacks evidence and is therefore irrelevant.

For example, "American prosperity will continue unabated through 2010, and with it the federal surplus will grow tremendously. Thus, tax reductions are fully justified." Statements about what may happen in the future cannot be supported by future evidence because that evidence does not yet exist because the future does not yet exist. Arguments based on nonexistent evidence are irrelevant, as irrelevant as the above statement by a prominent US senator about the federal surplus. His statement proved wrong. Just one year later, the economy, defying most predictions, turned south. The deficit in 2002 exceeded $230 billion, according to the *New York Times*, January 6, 2003.

Predictions about the future are often irrelevant.

To the extent that the foregoing is true, the work of the security analyst—however intelligent and thorough—must be largely ineffective because, in essence, he is trying to predict the unpredictable. When such analysts do seem to connect correctly with the future, the connection is often either heteroclite or, in Dr. Samuel Johnson's famous phrase, "The triumph of hope over experience." So watch out! Today's analysts have been so concerned with anticipating the future that they have already had people paying handsomely for it in advance. Thus, what is projected with so much study and care may actually happen and still not bring any profit. If that profit should fail to materialize as predicted and to the degree expected, the investor may, in fact, be faced with a serious temporary—perhaps even permanent—loss.

Genus definition of *adequacy*: Not only must evidence be relevant to the conclusion, but also it must be sufficient in number, kind, and weight to support the conclusion. Evidence that meets those criteria is adequate. Evidence that does not is not adequate.

Divisional definition: Evidence is adequate if it is sufficient in

1. amount
2. kind
3. weight

to support the conclusion.

The uniform field theory requires that we consider all available relevant evidence and that we examine all relevant evidence for adequacy.

Otherwise stated, relevant evidence is necessary but not sufficient to reach a conclusion about reality, the truth. Some people have trouble with the distinction between *necessary* and *sufficient*. Let's learn it now once and for all. Something is *necessary* if it is needed for something else to happen. That something is also *sufficient* if nothing else is needed for that something to happen. If something else is needed for the something to happen, then what is necessary *is necessary* but not *sufficient*. For example, my Lincoln needs gasoline to go. Gasoline is necessary for my car to take me someplace. But it is not sufficient. The Lincoln also needs spark plugs, oil, a battery, a generator, and many other working parts that I have probably never heard of.

Take the woman who says, "I don't understand why my car stopped. I have plenty of gas." She doesn't seem to understand that fuel is necessary, but not sufficient for the car to work. In the same way, my vacuum cleaner needs electricity to work. Therefore, electricity is necessary for the operation of the vacuum cleaner. But it is not sufficient. The vacuum cleaner also needs an empty bag, the switch turned on, a working armature, and so forth. Only when the necessary and sufficient requirements have been satisfied can I expect the vacuum cleaner to work properly.

Plants need water to grow. But don't expect your plants to grow if all you do for them is provide water. Just watering the plant doesn't guarantee that the plant will grow. Many other things are needed. For plants to grow, water is necessary but not sufficient.

To get my sea captain's license I had to go to sea school for fifty-four hours and had to do four 4-hour laboratories related to navigation, plotting, and deckmanship. The fact that I completed the course does not get me a license. To get the license, I had to pass the sixteen-hour-long Coast Guard written test, the physical examination, the knot-tying tests, the urine drug test, and so forth. Sea school was necessary but not sufficient for the license.

Relevant evidence is necessary but not sufficient.

Correct conclusions require relevant evidence. Therefore, relevant evidence is necessary to reach a correct conclusion. But it is not sufficient. The evidence must also be adequate. It must be adequate in number, kind, and weight to support the conclusion.

But what is adequate evidence?

That is a good question. There doesn't appear to be an absolute answer to that question. What is adequate evidence depends on the time, place, and person considering the evidence.

In law, clear and convincing evidence is needed for an indictment. In criminal law, a jury must find the accused guilty beyond a reasonable doubt. The law, eminently reasonable, recognizes that there is always a doubt. No doubt about that. But the law holds up the criterion of a reasonable doubt as the standard for criminal conviction. If the evidence shows the accused guilty beyond a reasonable doubt, the jury should convict. If the evidence does not show the accused guilty beyond a reasonable doubt, the jury should acquit. In other jurisdictions, Ireland, for instance, the jury can find the accused guilty, innocent, or not proven. If innocent, there is no chance of a retrial. If not proven, then a new trial is possible if new evidence comes to light.

In civil cases, the standard is the preponderant weight of evidence, by which is usually meant 51 percent. So if the evidence weighs in on the plaintiff's side at 51 percent or higher, the jury should find for the plaintiff, not for the defendant.

How much relevant evidence and what type of evidence should I require before I buy something? That depends on the time, place, and person.

In my own case, when I recently bought a CD player for my boat, I considered the color, the quality of sound, the partial waterproofing, and the low price of $14. The decision to buy (a conclusion to spend my money) took two minutes or less. On the other hand, the decision to spend $300,000 on a beach house required lots and lots of investigation, thought, analysis, and expert advice.

Another example: "Jack kissed my hand, told me that he loved me and that he wanted to marry me, so I went to bed with him." For some women, a kiss on the hand might be sufficient. Other women might need the declaration of love and the promise of marriage. Still others might like to see a diamond ring on their finger. Others don't need anything and will go to bed no matter what. Other women still might need a formal prenuptial agreement drawn up by an attorney, witnessed by two people, and notarized and filed with the county clerk. The point is that what is adequate evidence depends on the time, place, and people involved. Since adequacy of evidence is a value scale item, what follows are suggestions on how to appraise the adequacy of evidence. I offer guidelines, not hard and fast rules. What you do is up to you.

Analysis of adequate evidence divides itself into two main categories: causal fallacies and missing evidence.

Oversimplification and post hoc have been covered in previous chapters. Confusion of *necessary* with *sufficient* was covered above. Among other causal fallacies we should know about are neglect of a common cause, confusion of cause and effect, the less the better, the more the better, the ubiquitous gambler's fallacy, and last but not least, the psychological fallacy.

An argument that neglects a common cause is inadequate.

Two seemingly related events may not be causally related at all, but they may relate to a third item that is their common cause. Two events associated in time do not imply cause and effect because they could relate to something else. That's what we learned in the post hoc fallacy. Here we have the same thing. Two events associated in any way do not imply cause and effect because they might better relate to something else. Because lightning seems to precede thunder, many observers were led to believe that lightning causes thunder. It turns out that lightning and thunder are both caused by the sudden intra-atmospheric discharge of electricity. Because light travels faster than sound, the light from the discharge arrives before the sound, even though both were generated at the same time by the same electric discharge.

Another example: "Alcoholics tend to be undernourished. Poor diet must contribute to alcoholism." More likely alcoholics eat poorly because they are too busy drinking. In other words, the malnutrition and the alcoholism relate to a common cause—the addictive effects of ethyl alcohol.

A third example: "Business executives have very large vocabularies. Therefore, if you want to have a successful business career, study words." Here, business executives are linked with vocabularies, and the vocabulary is asserted as the cause of business success. More likely, both business success and the large vocabulary the executives have are two items that both are caused by many other common factors related to business success, including college education, extensive reading, high IQ, and so forth. Since both items relate to a third unmentioned set of items, the evidence is inadequate to support the causal conclusion between success and vocabulary. This means that the evidence is also inadequate to support the prediction that studying words would make for success in business.

A last example: "I wish I had a giant practice like yours. But my patients don't love me the way your patients love you."

"Just return their calls."

The two items, big practice and the love the patients have for their doctor, are related to a third factor, which is more likely to be the controlling factor, as the second physician admits: he returns patient calls.

An argument that confuses cause with effect does not provide adequate evidence for a conclusion.

When I was a Boy Scout at summer camp, every Sunday we enjoyed fried chicken, which was the only decent food served all week. Sunday was visitors' day, and my parents were always impressed at how well we seemed to eat at camp that day. To argue that my parents seemed always to know when we had a good meal and only visited on that day would be to miss the point of cause and effect and to get things backward. The camp served a good meal on visitors' day to impress the parents.

Scene in the Houston unemployment office: "No wonder these people can't get jobs. They are so irritable!" Reversing the cause and effect gives a more plausible explanation. The unemployed are irritable because they have no jobs.

Or: "The reason Bill is so irritable is that the customers haven't been giving him tips lately." It is more likely that the irritability caused the fewer tips than vice versa.

Or: "The homeless are homeless because they have no homes." I'll leave this tautology, which also neglects a common cause, for you to work out. Hint: The homeless are not homeless because they have no homes. The homeless are homeless for another reason. What is that reason?

The less the better and (the closely related) the more the better fallacies are both inadequate.

This was covered partially but deserves elaboration. Less is not necessarily better. Stress is bad, but no stress is bad, too. In high doses, vitamin B6 (pyridoxine) is toxic to nerves. But without small amounts of B6, the nerves can't function. Too much is bad, and too little is bad. What is needed is the correct amount, no more and no less. Therefore, arguments based on extrapolation of less and more without evidence are inadequate.

Take this statement, for example: "Fat is bad. It causes heart attacks and strokes. Therefore, no fat at all is best." Without dietary fat, vitamins A, D, and K can't be absorbed. Since these vitamins are essential to life, a diet without fat would result in serious illnesses.

The *more the better* fallacy is more often committed than the *less the better* fallacy. This is largely because in many cases, the effects of things increase as we increase their quantity. But keep in mind that a pinch of salt may be fine, but twenty pinches can ruin the taste. A lot of *more is better* is an overgeneralization and an oversimplification, proving that a fallacy may overlap several areas of logical interest and bear dual citizenship in the country of boo-boo, blunder, miscalculation, and error.

Drug effects do not often increase with dose, but side effects may.

Always ask for evidence that increasing the dose will increase the benefit without increasing the side effects. Colistin is a great antibiotic for various severe kidney infections. But in high doses, Colistin causes kidney failure. The right dose conforms to the reality principle. The wrong dose does not. Excessive intake of Colistin may lead to death.

Gambler's fallacy is both inadequate and irrelevant.

The gambler's fallacy is a humdinger and if you remember anything from this book, please remember this. The defective reasoning is so common that I believe there is an epidemic of gambling out there accompanied by an epidemic of the gambler's fallacy.

Because a chance event has had a run, the probability of its occurrence in the future is not significantly altered. Those who think the probability is altered commit the gambler's fallacy. The fallacy is named after gamblers who erroneously think that the chances of winning are better or significantly improved because of a certain run of events in the past: "I can't lose because I'm hot"; "My luck has got to change because I've been losing all night." Both these people are unaware that a chance event, such as the outcome of a coin toss or a roll of dice or the spin of the roulette wheel, is totally independent of all the tosses or rolls or spins preceding.

"Honey, let's try again. Since we've had three girls in a row, the next one has to be a boy." Probably not. In fact, the chance of having a boy is almost exactly the chance of having a girl, namely, one chance in two, that is, fifty-fifty. One cannot infer a greater probability of having a boy from the chance events of the past because the evidence supporting such a claim is not only inadequate but also nonexistent.

Take, for example, "I have been playing the Texas state lottery every week for five years. I have to win soon." The implicit premise represents a faulty causal analysis of chance events and provides no support for the conclusion. The chances of winning any particular lottery do not improve as a result of past disappointments.

Or this: "I haven't caught a bluefish in the last fifteen times I have been fishing. Surely, I'll catch one today." Don't hold your breath.

Or this: "The market has to turn around soon because we have had three down years in a row, and that hasn't happened since the 1940s." I have been hearing that for a while. Whether and when the market turns depends not on the duration of the losing streak already experienced, not on the past history of the Dow, but on a host of other realities, including government policy, interest rates, energy costs, CEO psychology, war, and so forth. It is a simplification to conclude that a market in decline for three years must soon turn around. Those who felt that way about the Japanese stock market have been caught in a decline that has lasted over a decade and is likely to continue because the fundamentals that caused the decline have not been corrected.

The psychological fallacy is inadequate justification.

Any conclusion must be supported by evidence and reasons. After that, we can go on to an explanation by citing what we think are probable causes. That explanation can support the conclusion just as the discovery of a motive can support the conclusion for the reason for the crime. But an explanation per se cannot justify an action. Because someone hates his mother-in-law doesn't justify killing her. To justify an action, we must establish the (moral) grounds for believing that the action was right. Ultimately, this justification must appeal to moral principles, self-defense being one such justification for homicide. Thus, moral justification must be radically separated from explanation. No explanation in and of itself justifies a conclusion.

Example: "Why did you [stab that woman to death], son?" asked Frank O'Connor, the district attorney of Queens, New York.

"She wouldn't let go of the pocketbook."[6]

This kid certainly has a reasonable explanation of why he stabbed the woman. It is an explanation that we understand and that we believe is true. But that doesn't justify the killing. In fact, the law has a rather dim view of murders committed during a felony. The Texas law considers such crimes capital offenses punishable by death.

Psychological explanations are not justifications.

It is true that the explanation of an act might give us the psychodynamics, the psychological forces, emotions, habits, unconscious drives, purposes, attitudes, and so on, that drove someone to commit the act. The daunting question, then, is, "Does such an explanation justify the act?" In general, the answer to this question is no. Explaining things just doesn't justify them any more than disclosure of a conflict of interest justifies that conflict of interest. Disclosure and conflict of interest are two different things. Explanation and justification are two different things. Never the twain shall meet. When an explanation is offered as a justification, we are led from the truth to error and therefore commit the psychological fallacy.

Andrea Yates, nurse, honor student, and mother, killed her five children by drowning them in the bathtub. Multiple psychiatrists and psychologists took the stand and explained the complex delusional beliefs that led Andrea to commit this act. The big question, however, was not whether she had reasons for doing what she did (she obviously had reasons—they were crazy, but they were there), but whether her act was morally justified. The case did not turn on why she killed the kids but on the jury finding that Yates knew at some time what she was doing and that what she was doing was wrong. The jury found that her act was not morally justified and sentenced her to life in prison. In so doing, the jury understood the psychological explanation for the crime but did not think that the psychological explanation justified, on moral grounds, the killing of five children. In reaching this conclusion, the jury followed Texas law, which requires that if the person knew what she was doing and that it was wrong, then, regardless of the explanation, including well-grounded psychological explanations, the act is a crime and punishable as such.

Missing evidence is inadequate.

To reach a conclusion on the basis of inadequate or missing evidence is a mistake and will lead away from truth toward error. In this connection, we have already discussed arguing from ignorance, contrary to fact hypotheses, the fallacy of groupthink and popular wisdom, partial selection of evidence, and special pleading. There remain some other things we should mention: insufficient evidence, omission of key evidence, the fallacy of impossible precision, and evidence taken out of context.

Insufficient evidence is inadequate.

To justify a conclusion there must be enough evidence. If there is not enough, the evidence is inadequate and the conclusion is not reasonable.

All contradictions cancel themselves, resulting in zero evidence, which is insufficient to support any conclusion. Therefore, all contradictions produce evidence that is inadequate to justify a conclusion.

Note on the refrigerator door:

I hate you, Mommy.
   Love,
   Jimmy

Well, which is it? Does he hate his mother, or does he love her? Both? Neither? We don't know. The evidence is contradictory. If he hates her, why did he close his note with the words *Love, Jimmy*? If he loves her, why did he say he hated her? The two statements contradict each other and therefore provide no evidence for either conclusion.

What about the man who says, "I don't mind blacks moving into the neighborhood. I just don't want them on my block." Is he prejudiced or not? If he is prejudiced, why does he say he doesn't mind? If he is not prejudiced, why does he say he does mind?

The falsity of these statements arises from the denial of the very statement made. In standard form, it might look like this:

S and not-S

where S is any statement and not-S is the denial of that same statement.

"Experience teaches that men learn absolutely nothing from experience." This quotation, allegedly from George Bernard Shaw, boils down to an implied contradiction. Can you see why?

With this understanding in hand, we are now prepared to answer that immortal question, "What happens when an irresistible force runs up against an immovable object?"

The answer is nothing.

The answer is nothing because an irresistible force and an immovable object cannot exist at the same time in the same place. They cannot exist because they contradict each other. An irresistible force is incompatible with that of an object that can resist any force. This is the equivalent of saying, "There is a force F and an object O such that F can move O and F cannot move O."

"I have no problems with hippies. I just don't approve of their lifestyle."

Contradictions are easy to spot and flag in a most dramatic way the absence of evidence. Absence of evidence may indeed not be evidence of absence. But absence of evidence fails to meet the evidence requirement of the uniform field theory. When there is no evidence, we just don't know. When we don't know, we cannot reach a conclusion about where the truth is or what it is.

Most times, the evidence is not absent, however. Most times the evidence is merely inconsistent or insufficient to reach a conclusion. When the evidence is weak, skimpy, or deficient in number, kind, or weight, we must reserve judgment and not jump to hasty, unwarranted conclusions. Rush to judgment, hasty decisions, and premature actions often are not necessary, especially when the issues are complex. Rushed decisions often result in disaster.

N of one is often inadequate evidence to reach a general conclusion.

"The Italian butcher cheated me on that chuck chop that I bought. When I got home, it weighed 0.8 pounds, not the 1.0 pound I paid for. All Italians are cheats." The evidence (only one case, N=1) is too small to conclude that all Italians are cheats. There is simply not enough data to justify that overly general conclusion. The evidence is relevant because the most likely explanation is that the Italian butcher did cheat. But to conclude from a sample of one instance that all Italians are cheats doesn't follow. One might conclude that that particular Italian butcher is a cheat. The evidence appears strongly in favor of that conclusion. Certainly if he tried to cheat the next time around, the conclusion would be even more firmly established. But there still wouldn't be enough evidence to implicate all Italian butchers, butchers in general, much less all Italians. The flaw has to do with insufficiency of data. The quantity of evidence is just too limited and the sample too small to constitute evidence sufficient to lead to the particular conclusion about all Italians.

Another example: "My ex and I never got along. It was so bad, I don't see why anyone would want to get married." One experience with marriage convinced him that marriage is no good for him, for his friends, or for anyone else. Complete evaluation of the pros and cons of marriage requires much more evidence than the experience of one couple. Perhaps their marriage hit the shoals for reasons other than those that relate to the institution of marriage per se. Perhaps the marriage failed because of flaws in the wife, in the husband, or in both. Perhaps the mother-in-law was at fault.

Unrepresentative data is partially selected and insufficient.

Closely related to insufficient evidence is the error of attributing to a larger group some opinion found in a unrepresentative or biased sample: "A recent survey shows that 98 percent of people support private ownership of machine guns."

The survey might have shown that if it were taken among the licensed machine gun dealers of the United States. But it would be a mistake to conclude that because this group of people feels that way that most people share this opinion. Everyday I am bombarded by opinion data gathered by a political party or by an advocacy group that tells me stuff I know is highly suspect. If one were interested in campus opinions about football, one would not survey just the members of the varsity club. Nor would one survey just the nonathletes.

This book is about seeking the truth. It is not about winning arguments. To get to the truth, we must consider all the evidence and omit none. If evidence that is crucial to the support of the conclusion or that definitively proves the conclusion wrong is omitted from consideration, we cannot get to heart of the matter at the core of the truth. To omit crucial evidence from consideration is not unlike preparing a mixed drink and leaving out the alcohol. You miss the point entirely.

Like this person: "Let's get married. We like to fish together. We share the same tastes in food and movies, and I love your cat." The reasons given might support a proposal to marry your sister or your best friend and live in a kind of platonic relationship. The reasons do not touch on whether there is sufficient love to warrant spending the rest of their lives together, an item of some importance to some people considering marriage and of major importance to most.

Impossible precision is impossible.

When precision is guessed at, when approximate times are treated as if they were precise, or when one uses data that cannot be known or obtained with the degree or precision claimed, the evidence is insufficient and therefore the argument is faulty.

For example, "Humans use only 10 percent of their brain power." Such a scientific-sounding statement must be wrong, though most of us are impressed by it because it seems to indicate that we all are much smarter than we appear. However, it is doubtful that information about such a vaguely described possibility (what the hell is brain power, anyway?) could be available or even precisely calculable. A more reasonable statement that would make a similar claim would be, "Each of us has some brain power that we don't use."

What about the person who says, "His whole life was ruined by the one mistake he made in high school." How many people do you know who made only one mistake in high school? I made plenty of mistakes in high school. In fact, I was expelled from my first high school. Chances are that the guy made plenty of mistakes, as I did, including the one that caused his ruin. That statement was phrased the way it was because the speaker, a lawyer, was trying to get sympathy from the jury. After all, his client made only one mistake and got ruined. Is that fair? Wouldn't you want to do something nice to help correct that unfortunate situation?

What about this? "This table is not perfectly clean. Clean it again." Equally absurd is strict adherence to impossible standards and then blaming someone for not following the standard strictly. That the table is not perfectly clean is probably true. But that may not be relevant in context if the table is a picnic table in the backyard. On the other hand, the close-to-perfect standard should be applied to operating room tables or to tables on which microchips for computers are being assembled.

Or this? "General Patton, your plan for the invasion of Germany is not perfect." To that congressional criticism, Patton replied, "A good plan today is better than a perfect plan tomorrow." After that, he got authorization to take the third army across France and invade Germany.

Or this? "Your book on logic is good, but not perfect. Please revise and resubmit." A more constructive editorial criticism would have been a discussion of the specific areas that need improvement and specific examples on how those improvements might be accomplished.

Or this? "Jimmy, you failed algebra again."

"Nobody's perfect," said Jimmy.

True, nobody is perfect. But that is irrelevant to the issue under discussion. It certainly is not adequate evidence to explain why Jimmy failed algebra.

Out-of-context evidence is a partial selection and, to that extent, is inadequate.

When I was interviewed by *Frontline*, I felt I did a fair job of defending my research on breast implants. My research over the course of fifteen years indicated that the breast implant did not deliver beautiful breasts. Instead, in many cases the breasts were deformed due to rupture of the implant, local spread of the silicone that had been in the implant, and a strong inflammatory reaction to the silicone that in most cases formed a thick, hard capsule of scar tissue that encircled the breast.

When the program about my research was aired, no one was more surprised than I was at the result. By skillful editing and rearrangement of the film clips and my statements, I was made to look like a jerk. In fact, according to the program, I didn't even believe my own research. Of course, that was not true. I believed it all right, perhaps too much.

Example: "Dr. Patten, the president of the International Society of Plastic Surgeons has called you a junk scientist. How do you respond to that?"

"I am a junk scientist."

That's what it looked like I said. But actually I said, "I am a junk scientist because I have been studying a piece of junk. That's what the breast implant is and was and probably will always be—a piece of junk."

By taking my remark out of context and leaving out my spin on the "junk scientist" appellation, the program misled the audience into thinking that I made a terrible admission, which I did not. The audience thought I considered myself a junk scientist. People were not permitted to get the rest of the statement, which would have thrown a different meaning on what I said.

Out-of-context quotations are a favorite trick of TV people. Don't be fooled by TV's out-of-context deceptions, which frequently take the form of sound bites. Please take my advice. Don't watch TV at all. TV is just junk food for the mind.

Principle: Most TV and all sound bites are simplistic partial selections.

From which follows:

> *Lesson:* Never fall for or believe a sound bite for a sound
> bite is the simplest reduction of a simplistic argument

×　　×　　×

Determine truth by evaluating all the available evidence for relevance
and adequacy. Evidence must relate directly to the conclusion and must
be sufficient in number, kind, and weight to support the conclusion.

Before you work on something, make sure it is important. First ask
yourself, "So what?" or "Who cares?" If your answer is that you don't
care and that the information doesn't concern or apply to you (this will
include 99 percent of the filler on TV), forget it. Go have some fun. If
the answer is that you do care, then work on the information using the
summary charts below. Test the evidence for relevance and adequacy.

REVIEW

1. All emotional appeals are irrelevant, including appeals

- to pity
- to force
- to threat
- to special or personal interest
- by bribe, extortion, honor lists,
  or underhanded coercive activities

- to strong feelings including
  charity, love, shame, guilt
- for, to, or by use of flattery

All name calling, innuendo, obloquy, or implications of wrongdoing—
including ad hominem arguments, tu quoque, and the like—are irrelevant because they are emotionally based and cannot relate to the truth
of any conclusion.

2. All appeals to authority per se are irrelevant, including appeals

- to common sense
- to popular opinion
- on the basis of age (or youth)

- to reasons that are not
  reasons but rationales
- to tradition, culture,

- to ignorance (closely related to popular opinion and still wrong)

custom, individuals, and groups—all of which are not immune to error

Appeals to "experts" are frequently irrelevant; this includes textbook writers, teachers, lawyers, politicians, doctors, movie stars, journalists, and especially TV commentators. Who they are doesn't count. Their evidence, if true, does count if and only if that evidence is relevant and adequate to support the conclusion.

3. All linguistic confusions are irrelevant, including

- vague definitions
- ambiguity (including syntactic ambiguity or **amphiboly**)
- broadcast definition wrong

4. All circular arguments are irrelevant, including

- tautology
- pleonasm
- begging the question
- leading questions
- double talk

Closely related but different is supererogation, which tends to raise the question of why the speaker needed to apply more proofs, assertions, or statements than were needed. Another name for this fallacy is "The lady doth protest too much."

5. Unwarranted assumptions are irrelevant, including

- assertions not supported by evidence
- (so-called) self-evident truths
- continuum arguments (including the is-ought mistake—because a thing exists doesn't mean it ought to or should continue to exist)
- the fallacy of novelty (opposite of the continuum but still wrong)
- the fallacy of composition
- the fallacy of division
- the fallacy wishful (or **optative**) thinking
- the fallacy of the mean
- false analogy
- neglect of a common cause
- the less the better fallacy
- the more the better fallacy

6. Attempts to divert attention from real issues are irrelevant, including

- trivial objections
- red herrings
- diversionary humor or ridicule
- extension, distortion, or misstatement of opposing evidence or arguments
- distinction without a difference
- all gimmicky distractions, double talk, chit-chat, patter, and empty talk

If evidence passes muster for relevance, it must then be examined for adequacy.

7. Causal fallacies create insufficient evidence that is inadequate, including

- confusion of *necessary* with *sufficient*
- oversimplification
- post hoc
- confusion of cause and effect
- domino theory
- gambler's fallacy
- psychological fallacy (explaining what happened doesn't justify it)

8. Missing evidence is never adequate, including

- contradiction
- inconsistency (including oxymoron)
- insufficient evidence
- unrepresentative evidence
- future fact presented as if it were certain and not contingent
- contrary-to-fact assertions
- impossible precision
- special pleading
- omission of key evidence
- denying the counter-evidence
- ignoring the counter-evidence
- taking evidence out of context

QUESTIONS

Here are some questions you might ask to try to get at the truth value about situations and statements that come your way.

1. What's the topic? What's the issue or controversy? What's the main conclusion? Does it seem right? If it doesn't seem right, what seems wrong about it?
2. What evidence supports the conclusion? Is the evidence relevant? (If the evidence is not relevant, the conclusion is dubious.)
3. Are there any inconsistencies, contradictions, or tautologies? Is the information from a self-interested or biased source? (If so, the conclusion is dubious.)
4. If the evidence is relevant, is the evidence sufficient in number, kind, and weight to support the conclusion? (If not, the evidence is inadequate, and the conclusion is not reasonable.)
5. Is there a doubt about the meaning of terms or the general significance of what is stated? (All vagueness must be clarified before the conclusion can be understood, much less justified.)
6. What reasons are against the conclusion? (Negative reasons must be shown to be either false or irrelevant to the matter at hand. Otherwise, they must be given their due weight in the net overall justification of the conclusion.)

NOTES

1. The full text of the Declaration of Sentiments is available in June Sochen, *Herstory: A Woman's View of American History* (New York: Alfred, 1974), pp. 415–25.

2. Robert H. Rimmer, *The Harrad Experiment* (Amherst, NY: Prometheus Books, 1990).

3. George Orwell, *Nineteen Eighty-Four* (New York: Penguin Putnam, 1950), p. 69.

4. Lewis Carroll, *Alice's Adventures in Wonderland*, illust. John Tenniel and colored by Fritz Kredel (New York: Random House, 1946), p. 132. All references to *Alice* are to this edition.

5. Ibid.

6. Robert Mindlin, "Boy Killer's Fate Up to the Jury," *Long Island Press*, June 24, 1958, p. 1.

chapter 10

The Logic of Alice

This parting chapter is fun. In it, you will practice what you have learned. The examples below, some new and some by way of review, come from Lewis Carroll's *Alice's Adventures in Wonderland*, henceforth known as AAW.

Charles Lutwidge Dodgson, better known as Lewis Carroll, was a shy, eccentric bachelor who taught mathematics at Christ Church, Oxford. He had a great fondness for playing with mathematics, logic, and words; for writing nonsense; and for the company of little girls, especially one named Alice Liddell (rhymes with fiddle), the daughter of Henry George Liddell, dean of Christ Church, Oxford.

Dodgson's passions somehow fused into two great masterpieces of English literature, the Alice books, immortal fantasies whose fame surpassed that of all Carroll's colleagues at Oxford put together.

If the Alice books had any "porpoise" besides entertaining little girls, it is to send you, the reader, to the pleasures of logic and philosophy and, as Carroll says in the *Introduction to Learners* (1897) "to give a chance of adding a very large item to your stock of mental delights."[1]

Carroll's special genius lies in his ability to disguise charmingly the seriousness of his concerns and to make the most playful quality of his work at the same time its didactic crux. In the case of Alice, we are dealing with a very curious, complicated kind of nonsense, which explores the possibilities of the use and abuse of language and is actually based on a profound knowledge of the rules of clear thinking, informal and formal logic, symbolic logic, and human nature. In fact, most of Carroll's aperçus and jokes are inversions or distortions of the rules of logic or demonstrations of the ambiguities of language. Reason is in service here to imagination, not vice versa.

Oh, yes, those oddball characters. What about them? I like to think that the characters Alice meets are Oxford dons that the real Alice knew well. They certainly sound like dons with their fine mastery of Socratic logic, their crushing repartee, and the disconcerting and totally unself-conscious eccentricity of their conduct.

The wealth of material that Carroll presents for the illumination of philosophy is almost without end. The more I read it and the more I think about it, the more I find. In fact, I have reached the conclusion that AAW is, in actual fact, a story so deep as to yield results in exegesis almost beyond belief.

I urge you to read all of it yourself. Read it at your leisure while sober, and read it at your leisure while drunk, so that both your left and right hemispheres can fully participate in the fun. Along the way, try to capture some of the full wit and wisdom of Lewis Carroll as I try to capture them in the examples that follow.

> Alice was beginning to get very tired of sitting by her sister on the bank and of having nothing to do: once or twice she had peeped into the book her sister was reading, but it had no pictures or conversations in it, "and what is the use of a book," thought Alice, "without pictures or conversations?"[2]

Alice is a child lost in a world not fully understood. Her situation reflects in the microcosm what we (adults and children) experience, more or less, in our everyday lives. That is one of Carroll's main points, of course. But this point aside, let's look at Alice's thinking.

When we assume the point in dispute and take for granted the truth of something that requires proof, we are begging the question. Alice assumes a book without pictures is bad. Thus, Alice begs the question. Assumptions (including those begged) not supported by evidence are irrelevant. Therefore, a conclusion based on them is likely to be wrong.

In her assumption, Alice overgeneralizes because she takes for granted that because she doesn't like books without pictures, others would not like such books, either. Egocentric views of the world are not restricted to little girls in picture books, as we all know.

To prove Alice's generalized statement wrong, we need find only one exception, one book that has no conversations or pictures but is still useful. Since there are literally hundreds of thousands of books without conversations and pictures, it would be highly unlikely that at least one of them wouldn't be useful to someone.

By singling out two of the many criteria that can be used to judge a book, Alice partially selects evidence (trivial evidence at that), constructs a straw man for defeat, and reaches a conclusion that is not justified by the data: She has not read the book. Therefore, she is in no position to make an intelligent judgment about its usefulness or uselessness.

Furthermore, Alice is overlooking factual evidence: Her sister is interested in the book. In fact, her sister is deeply engrossed in reading it. Therefore, the book is already of some use to someone—her sister. So Alice is actually denying the evidence at hand. Denying or ignoring any available relevant evidence is an error in thinking and goes against the principles of correct reasoning.

Alice is being simple and simplistic. Often a book is a complex thing. Writers work long and hard trying to get their books right, fashioning out of chaos, in the torment of their souls, something intricate, intelligent, interesting, and occasionally beautiful. A critic of books should exercise the same due diligence in evaluating books as was exercised in creating them. Without a complex analysis, a reasonable conclusion cannot be reached about a book's usefulness.

Poor Alice! She is using weak-sense thinking. She should be using strong-sense thinking to evaluate all evidence, claims, and beliefs, including her own biased opinions about what constitutes a useful book.

In a certain sense, there is also a linguistic confusion in her conclusion because she is using the word *use* idiosyncratically. Vague definitions preclude logical conclusions. Until we know what she means by a useful book, we can only guess at her definition. I sense that by *use* she means "entertaining and easy to look at and read." Others, myself included, might consider such a book pretty much useless. Regardless, all vagueness must be clarified before the conclusion can be understood, much less justified.

Remember, too, that all circular arguments are irrelevant. In standard form, Alice's reasoning looks circular:

1. Any book without pictures is not useful.
2. My sister's book has no pictures.
3. Therefore, my sister's book is not useful.

Although the argument is formally valid, the conclusion is wrong because the premises are wrong.

The major premise (premise 1), for us to accept it, would need to be proved. In fact, premise 1 is false. There are books that have no pictures or conversations that are useful. Premise 2 is probably true, although we don't know that for sure. Nor does Alice know that for sure. She has not looked at the sister's book in its entirety. She has only "peeped into" the book "once or twice." If the book is the usual run-of-the-mill English book, Alice might have seen only four pages of what is probably a two-hundred-page book. Therefore, she has sampled only four out of two hundred or 2 percent of the actual pages of the book, and there is a reasonable chance that one or more of those pages might have a conversation or a picture. Thus, even premise 2 might be false. We simply don't have enough evidence to say one way or the other.

Whether premise 2 is true hardly matters because premise 1 is false. Any conclusion based on a false premise has to be unsound, meaning not justified—and often just plain wrong.

Danger alert!

Alice is bored. Because she is bored, her boredom is likely to interfere with her judgment and color her observations. That mood likely swayed Alice's judgment about her sister's book. Indeed, Alice is so bored that "she was considering . . . (as well as she could, for the hot day made her feel very sleepy and stupid) whether the pleasure of making a daisy-chain would be worth the trouble of getting up and picking the daisies. . . ."[3]

Understand that if Alice had said that she doesn't like books that have no conversations and no pictures, then there could be no argument. We would have to accept that at face value as her preference. But when she gives a reason for her opinion, then that reason is subject to inquiry and refutation because it is not supported by relevant evidence that is adequate in amount, kind, and weight.

> "Well," thought Alice to herself. "After such a fall as this, I shall think nothing of tumbling downstairs! How brave they'll all think me at home! Why I wouldn't say anything about it, even if I fell off the top of the house!"[4]

Ha, ha, ha! That's very likely because if she fell off the top of her house, she would have likely broken her neck—or worse, be dead—and therefore unable to say anything about her fall or, for that matter, about anything else. The false analogy here is that since one fall has not (so far) seemed to hurt her, all subsequent falls will not hurt her either, not even a tumble downstairs, not even a fall off the roof of the house. All continuum arguments are unreasonable unless supported by relevant adequate evidence.

Furthermore, Alice's focus is off. Instead of concentrating on the point, which is whether she will or will not get hurt when she lands, she is concerned about what she will tell others after similar falls in the future that might happen. And she is concerned what others will think about her when she doesn't say much about her falls: "How brave they will think me at home." What Alice says about the falls or what others say about them is not particularly relevant to the main problem of falls in general and this fall in particular, which is how much damage will occur on impact.

Humor or other diversionary attempts by the ostrich approach of ignoring the real situation are irrelevant because they lead away from the truth to a false idea of reality. Here, Alice focuses away from the real concern about her continued fall, which should be, "Will I get hurt?"

Yes, Alice is in free fall. She should be worried about the consequences of hitting the ground. She should not be thinking about how nice future falls will be if they turn out like this one. Because the future is not determined yet, neither Alice nor anyone else has a right to predict it with accuracy. Hence, Alice is committing the error of future fact. The future doesn't exist. Therefore, the future on which Alice bases her conclusion doesn't exist. Conclusions based on nonexistent evidence are inadequately supported, often mere fantasies, and often wrong.

Anyway, it is the fallacy of the continuum to think that because she did OK after this fall, she would do OK in the next fall. It is an especial error, as this fall has not even been safely completed yet.

Each fall is an independent event. What happens would depend on the details of that next fall. In fact, Alice bases her conclusion of a safe landing on no evidence at all. The usual outcome of such a fall would be expected to be disastrous. Alice should always base her conclusions on what is reasonable and expected. That is the best protection against the unreasonable, the unexpected, and the unexpectable, which has a sneaky habit of turning up now and again. Conclusions based on what is reasonable and expected are the only way of preparing for adverse events in the future and heading off trouble when it looks likely to occur.

Ignoring previous experience and denying counterevidence usually results in catastrophe, except in the fantasy world of children's books—Alice lands quite well and continues (in chapter 2) in her quest for the White Rabbit.

> Soon her eye fell on a little glass box that was lying under the table: she opened it, and found in it a small cake, on which the words "EAT ME" were beautifully marked in currants. "Well, I'll eat it," said Alice, "and if it makes me grow larger, I can reach the key and if it makes me grow smaller, I can creep under the door."[5]

Either/or thinking, black-and-white assessments, and falsely limited alternatives don't work because they exclude multiple other possibilities. Here, Alice failed to consider the very real possibility that eating the cake would neither make her grow nor make her shrink. She failed to consider the most reasonable and expected result of eating cake—which is, and has always been, that there will be no immediate or dramatic change in body size.

> She ate a little bit, and said anxiously to herself "Which way? Which way?" holding her hand on the top of her head to feel which way it was growing; and she was quite surprised to find that she remained the same size.[6]

To be sure, this is what generally happens when one eats cake.

Alice had just finished the first of twelve occasions in AAW in which she alters in size. This first metamorphosis occurred after she obeyed the bottle's sign DRINK ME. But Alice got the erroneous idea that since drinking the stuff in the bottle made her small, eating the cake would change her size in some way or other. Her conclusion is based on inadequate evidence, the case of N=1, an inadequate sample of only one instance. That is hardly sufficient to counter the experiential fact that every little girl should know: one's size doesn't immediately change by eating cake. Over time, if you eat too much cake, you will get fat, but you won't necessarily shrink or expand lengthwise.

Alice's thinking is also a false analogy: Because her size changed after DRINK ME, that doesn't mean there is a reason to think that EAT ME would do the same. Drinking and eating, though similar in some respects, are different in others. Drinking and eating do share the same property of taking things into the body via the mouth and so forth, but that they share some properties does not mean that they would share others as well.

If X has a and b, and Y has a and b, it does not follow that if X has c, Y has c. Whether DRINK ME and EAT ME share the properties in the question of size alteration would have to be proven by more evidence than one trial of DRINK ME.

Post hoc reasoning is often defective, as this episode might prove. Alice knows her size changed after DRINK ME, but she doesn't really know that the DRINK ME was the causative agent. Loads of other data might be required to establish the causal connection. Just because one event follows another does not necessarily mean the second event was caused by the first or that the events are connected in any causal way. Of course, we learn later that the bizarre events with DRINK ME and the other eleven transformations that Alice undergoes have a more rational explanation: Alice is dreaming.

> As she said these words her foot slipped, and in another moment, splash! she was up to her chin in salt-water. Her first idea was that she had somehow fallen into the sea, "and in that case I can go back by railway," she said to herself.[7]

Too bad for Alice that her thinking is elliptic. That is, she has words and a chain of reasoning omitted. She can't go home by railway because she hasn't fallen into the sea. She isn't at Brighton. There is no railway.

First ideas or first impressions to the extent that they are emotionally based and not reasoned are often in error. The error is often compounded when linked to a series of other ideas that seem to follow from the first. Alice's reasoning is elliptic, but if it were spelled out in textual steps, it might be depicted as follows: "The water that I have fallen into is salty. Therefore, I'm in the sea. Since I'm in the sea, I must be near a seaside resort. Seaside resorts always have railroads. Therefore, a railroad must be nearby. Last time I was at Brighton, I came home by railway. Therefore, I shall be able to return home this time the same way, by railway."

Domino theory reasoning like this has to have a separate justification for each item and a separate justification for each link in the chain of connected items. Otherwise, the conclusion will be unreasonable. True, Alice had been to the sea once in her life, and had come to the general conclusion that wherever you go on the English coast, you find a number of **bathing machines** in the sea, some children digging in the sand with wooden spades, then a row of lodging houses, and behind them a railway station. So there was some evidence, however skimpy, for her thinking that fed her emotional need to go home.

However, Alice soon figured out that her imagination had overgeneralized from her limited seaside experience. She was not in the sea. Instead, she was in the pool of salty tears, which she had wept when she was nine feet high. Alice was drowning in her own tears.

> Indeed, she had quite a long argument with the Lory, who at last turned sulky, and would only say "I'm older than you, and must know better." And this Alice would not allow, without knowing how old it was, and, as the Lory positively refused to tell its age, there was no more to be said.[8]

Whether the Lory (a type of Australian parrot) is older than Alice is not relevant to the argument because age does not make a person's argument correct or incorrect. An older person can be right or wrong. Therefore, age is irrelevant to truth. Obviously, the Lory is trying to appeal to authority (argumentum ad verecundiam), in this case, the supposed authority of being older. All appeals to authority are irrelevant because they do not concern evidence. What counts is the relevance, sufficiency, quantity, kind, and weight of evidence, not the age of the person presenting the evidence.

Alice missed the point. She wanted to make her evaluation of the Lory's argument contingent on the Lory's age. Alice's statement shows that she has accepted uncritically the Lory's unsupported and unwarranted assumption that if the Lory is older, then it would know better. Alice should never accept unsupported statements without proof.

Note also that the Lory could have won the argument by telling its age. That it did not suggests that it feared that it was younger, not older, than Alice. How else can we explain its sulkiness and its refusal to tell?

Unless the Lory's age is already known to Alice. That would be a fact if the Lory is Alice's dream representation of her older sister Lorina. In fact, a case could be made that the Duck in this scene represents the Reverend Robinson Duckworth, and the Dodo is Dodgson himself, who had often stammered his name ("Do-Do-Dodgson"). For that reason, the Oxford crowd called Dodgson "the Dodo" after the extinct flightless bird. Crucial evidence: Lewis Carroll inscribed his gift edition of AAW to Duckworth: "To the Duck from the Dodo." Such an analysis would, by reductive elimination, make Edith, Alice's younger sister, the

Eaglet. If this is true, we shouldn't wonder why the Eaglet complains that the others in the party use big words that it doesn't understand!

Notice also that the Lory's statement is truly diversionary because we never learn what it argues about. Therefore, we can't judge anything. Older sisters are like that, I am informed. And that indeed may be Carroll's not-so-subtle point. In effect, he sides with Alice against Alice's older sister, a position likely to gain him some influence and affection from the real Alice. This tactic would curry favor, for most people believe (without supporting evidence) that the enemy of my enemy is my friend.

Carroll may also be savagely parodying the Victorian attitude toward children and the ways in which adults patronize and treat children intellectually. The Lory is a kind of pedant who refuses to come to terms with proper discussion of issues or inform the child of the reasons for things. That sort of pedant insists that we accept what she says without question and at face value merely because she says so. She claims to know best, but she doesn't support that claim with any evidence. In so doing, such pedants show a single, fixed, self-serving, and rigid standard, inimical to children, but characteristic of this type of the pedantic mind.

> "Ahem!" said the Mouse with an important air. "Are you all ready? This is the driest thing I know. Silence all round, if you please! 'William the Conqueror, whose cause was favored by the pope, was soon submitted to by the English, who wanted leaders, and had been of late much accustomed to usurpation and conquest.'"[9]

That passage from the history of the Norman conquest is unlikely to dry Alice, who is still wet from her swim in her tears. The confusion (and the fun) arises, of course, from the two meanings of the word *dry*. The dull, boring, and *dry* history of the Norman invasion has nothing to do with the other meaning of the word *dry*—having no moisture.

Times have not changed. Even today, lots of absurd solutions to problems are proposed to us "with an important air." And with that important air, the Mouse continues:

> "Edwin and Morcar, the earls of Mercia and Northumbria, declared for him; and even Stigand, the patriotic archbishop of Canterbury, found it advisable—"
>
> "Found what?" said the Duck.

"Found *it*," the Mouse replied rather crossly: "of course you know what 'it' means."

"I know what 'it' means well enough, when *I* find a thing," said the Duck: "it's generally a frog, or a worm. The question is, what did the archbishop find?"

The Mouse did not notice this question, but hurriedly went on. . . .

"As wet as ever," said Alice in a melancholy tone: "it doesn't seem to dry me at all."[10]

Good for Alice. She proves that the dry talk has had no effect on wet clothes. Alice had a perfect right, some would say an obligation, to take her own experience seriously. In voicing concern for results, she positions herself in the camp of Charles Peirce, William James, Benjamin Franklin, and Ralph Waldo Emerson, the founders of America's first indigenous philosophy—pragmatism. They thought that reality counts.

Alice tells us that reality counts more than words do and must remain the controlling influence on conclusions. She is not dry. The mouse's dry tale dried her not.

Incidentally, many words besides *it* in English do have confusing referents that depend on context. Take, for instance, *take*, as in "The passengers took the boat upriver." In the ordinary sense, the passengers would pay the captain for their trip, but in another sense, the captain might take after them for theft. This is yet another example of amphiboly.

Carroll makes much of the double meanings of words later on where *knot* and *not* are confused; *draw* (as in sketching) and *draw* (as in water from a well) and *axes* (as in chop off your head) and *axis* (as in what the Earth and other planets rotate on) are mixed up; flamingoes and mustard both have a "bite" (though the bite of each is quite different); and "mine" (the absolute possessive form of *my*) and "mine" (a place where minerals come from) and so forth are discussed. In *Through the Looking Glass*, the Frog can't understand why anyone would answer the door unless it (the door) has been asking something. Pretty stupid! Right? But pretty funny, especially for the entertainment of little girls. And excellent (Carrollian) illustrations of the limitations that language can impose on human thought.

But what's the real point? What's Carroll's point in logic?

His point is that in a bit of reasoned discourse, the terms that occur several times must retain their same sense throughout. They can't keep changing like the Cheshire Cat. Otherwise, confusion arises.

An argument will clearly be cogent and convincing only if in each of its occurrences the word in use retains a fixed meaning with the same name and same reference frame for the same kind of object or idea. The requirement that in a given context a term must be used in essentially the same manner is expressed as the *principle of identity*. When the identity of a word shifts, confusion occurs, as the Alice books so well illustrate.

The problem of double meanings and unclear referents is exploited in that Abbott and Costello skit wherein Abbott "proves" that Costello is not there in the studio in New York City:

Abbott: You're not in San Francisco, right?
Costello: Right, I'm not in San Francisco.
Abbott: You're not in Chicago, right?
Costello: Right, I'm not in Chicago.
Abbott: Well, if you are not in San Francisco and you are not in Chicago, you must be somewhere else, right?
Costello: Right! I am somewhere else.
Abbott: See, I told you![11]

What's the confusion? The confusion is change of context with loss of the identity of the expression *somewhere else*, which is never used in a vacuum or in a contextless way. It always is expressed within a frame of reference. No one can be somewhere else because there is no such place. *Somewhere else* means either not here, where "here" is specifically or implicitly defined, or it means somewhere other than the place explicitly mentioned. Abbott mentioned San Francisco and Chicago, exploring the second meaning. Costello is somewhere other than San Francisco or Chicago. That's true. Abbott then exploits the first meaning, thereby shifting in this context the identity of the phrase *somewhere else*.

Clearly, Costello's admission would in no way imply that Costello is not in New York City, where, incidentally, he was. Costello's admission just means he recognized that he wasn't in San Francisco or Chicago.

"But I'm not a serpent, I tell you!" said Alice. "I'm a—I'm a—"[12]

Part of the hesitation is based on Alice's sudden realization that it is awfully hard to prove anything and even harder to prove a negative statement. For instance, is there any way in the world you can prove that you are not a communist? Someone can prove you are a communist by finding your card. But you can't prove you are not a communist because the absence of evidence is not evidence of absence. In the same way, you can't prove you are not a child pornographer. But someone could prove you are a child pornographer by finding the stuff on your computer, assuming, of course, it wasn't planted there. This is why it was so hard for Iraq to prove that it did not have weapons of mass destruction. Perhaps this is the reason for the presumption at law that you are innocent until proven guilty. It is up to the prosecutor to prove the guilt beyond a reasonable doubt. It is up to the United States to prove Iraq has those weapons. It is not up to Iraq to prove it doesn't have them.

So, sensing the difficulty of proving that she is not a serpent, Alice falls back on a positive assertion of what she is. Alice does this in the hope that that will be sufficient demonstration that, if she is a little girl, she can't be a serpent, as there is no case on record of a little girl being a serpent, too.

But in a larger sense, Alice asks herself, "Who in the world am I?" for she is, after all, the dreamer, and this is her dream. Ah, that's the great puzzle, and it's one of the greatest of philosophic puzzles—the problem of personal identity. The Pigeon explores the question further:

> "Well! What are you?" said the Pigeon. "I can see you're trying to invent something!"
>
> "I—I'm a little girl," said Alice, rather doubtfully, as she remembered the number of changes she had gone through, that day.
>
> "A likely story indeed!" said the Pigeon, in a tone of the deepest contempt. "I've seen a good many little girls in my time, but never one with such a neck as that! No, no! You're a serpent; and there's no use denying it. I suppose you'll be telling me next that you never tasted an egg!"
>
> "I have tasted eggs, certainly," said Alice, who was a very truthful child; "but little girls eat eggs quite as much as serpents do, you know."[13]

The Pigeon's thinking is poor. Obviously, a little girl can have a long neck as well as a short neck. So neck size is no criterion of girlhood one way or the other. Neck size is irrelevant to the issue. Therefore, the Pigeon is wrong to conclude that Alice is not a little girl because of her neck length.

Let's examine the Pigeon's syllogism through which the Pigeon reaches the conclusion that Alice is a serpent. In formal form, that syllogism might appear as:

1. Serpents eat eggs.
2. Alice eats eggs.
3. Therefore, Alice is a serpent.

Recall that in syllogism, there are two assertions, called "premises," and one conclusion that should follow from the premises. In syllogism, the predicate of the conclusion contains the major term, and the subject of the conclusion has the minor term. Thus *is a serpent* is the major term and *Alice* is the minor term. The major premise is that which has the major term, and the minor premise is that which has the minor term. Thus, *Serpents eat eggs* is the major premise, and *Alice eats eggs* is the minor premise. The term that is present in both the major and the minor premise is the middle one. Here the middle term is *eats eggs*.

OK, so let's examine, in a formal way and then in a informal way, the truth of the premises and the truth of the conclusion. Is the major premise true? Do serpents eat eggs?

Answer: Yes.

How about the minor premise? Is that true? Does Alice eat eggs?

Answer: Yes. Probably.

Alice admitted tasting eggs. While it is possible to taste eggs without eating them, it is unlikely that Alice tasted eggs without having eaten them. Alice may have equivocated here, put a little sugar on the dog eat dog, in order to assuage the Pigeon, who seems very keen on this egg-eating issue.

But if the major and the minor premises are correct, why is the conclusion wrong, as we know it must be? Alice is not a serpent. She is a little girl.

Answer: In formal logic, this syllogism is invalid (that is, wrong) because the middle term is not distributed at least once. That is, eating eggs, while done by all serpents, can also be done by other animals as well. Therefore, that Alice eats eggs doesn't exclude the possibility that she is not a serpent. The major premise says *Serpents eat eggs*. It does not say that any animal that eats eggs is a serpent. Alice is quite right in her refutation of the Pigeon: "Little girls eat eggs quite as much as serpents do, you know." That refutation should have stopped the argument dead. Instead of admitting defeat, the Pigeon answers, "I don't believe it . . . but if they do, then they're a kind of serpent: that's all I can say."[14]

This is the Pigeon's confession that the major premise has to be changed in order for the conclusion to be justified. If anyone who eats eggs is a serpent, then Alice is a serpent. But changing the major premise makes it false. Here's the reason. The Pigeon's new statement would look like this:

1. Whatever eats eggs is a serpent.
2. Alice eats eggs.
3. Therefore, Alice is a serpent.

The previous problem of the undistributed middle term has been corrected. Now the middle term is distributed and encompasses all classes that eat eggs. In redistributing the middle term, the Pigeon did correct the problem of the undistributed middle term. But he now changed the major premise so that it is not true. In fact, he changed the major premise to an erroneous broadcast definition. "Whatever eats eggs is a serpent" is not true. Since it is a generalization, we can prove it not true by finding one exception. Since exceptions are legion, the premise is obviously false. Therefore, the Pigeon's conclusion is false, for any conclusion based on a false premise is false.

Therefore, the Pigeon is still wrong. Truth has once again triumphed: Alice is not a serpent. By sheer strength of correct thinking, we have proven that Alice is not a serpent. Furthermore, we know Alice is a little girl. No little girl has ever been a serpent. That is a fact. Therefore, the Pigeon is wrong. He is arguing contrary to fact, which always puts one in a bad position vis-à-vis the truth.

By the way, can you guess why the Pigeon is so hung up on the serpent thing? Deep-seated fears and anxieties are often at the heart of poor thinking, of which the Pigeon's is a typical example. Undoubtedly, at sometime in the past, the Pigeon had had eggs eaten by a serpent. Whenever pigeons (or people) persist in being irrational, suspect a deep, underlying psychological basis adversely working from their heart's core on their perspective capacity, leading them away from truth and toward error.

> At this moment the door of the house opened, and a large plate came skimming out, straight at the Footman's head; it just grazed his nose, and broke to pieces against one of the trees behind him. The Footman continued in the same tone, exactly as if nothing had happened.
> "How am I to get in?" asked Alice again in a louder tone.
> "Are you to get in at all?" said the Footman. "That's the first question, you know."[15]

It was the first question. No doubt, only Alice did not like to be told so.

Alice's question assumed she would get in. Alice was begging the question, and the Footman called her on it.

> "It's really dreadful," she muttered to herself, "the way all the creatures argue. It's enough to drive one crazy!"[16]

Item: We're all mad here. (unsupported assertion)

Item: I'm mad. You're mad. (unsupported assertions consistent with the first item. But more than that, these later assertions are actually subaltern claims that follow directly from the first item. If we are all mad here, then two people who are here [that is, those included in the category encompassed by the first item] are also mad. In a way, the interrelation of the claims of item one and item two point out the usual relation of subaltern claims. The subaltern is implicit and follows directly from the larger categorical claim. Thus, if all S are P, some S must also be P, many S must be P, few S must be P, this particular S that I see washed up on the beach must be P, and so forth.)

Item: Because you're here, you must be mad. (Unsupported conclusion)

"And I wish you wouldn't keep appearing and vanishing so suddenly: you make one quite giddy!"[23]

Alice resorts to an ad hominem argument to give herself time to think of a good reply to the Cat's circular reasoning. Her statement is an attack on the Cat's behavior and has nothing whatsoever to do with the issue under discussion, which was whether they are all mad. Diversionary arguments, whether our own or Alice's, are irrelevant.

"All right," said the Cat; and this time it vanished quite slowly, beginning with the end of the tail, and ending with the grin, which remained some time after the rest of it had gone.[24]

Notice that the Cat unfairly selects part of Alice's request and gives that part of the request undue emphasis and importance. His changing slowly is not what Alice really wanted. Alice wanted him to stop changing and remain constant. But of course she opened herself up to the Cheshire Cat's interpretation by not stating precisely what she wanted. Usually, it's a good idea to say exactly what you want and mean exactly what you say. Usually, it's a good idea to not say what you don't want to say and not say what you don't mean.

> "Well! I've often seen a cat without a grin," thought Alice, "but a grin without a cat! It's the most curious thing I ever saw in all my life."[25]

This shows us that if a statement is true, the converse of that statement is not necessarily true. This same point is hammered in further along during the tea party, where "mean what I say" is not the same as "say what I mean," and "I see what I eat" is not the same as "I eat what I see," and "I like what I get" is not the same as "I get what I like."

> "You might just as well say," added the Dormouse, which seemed to be talking in its sleep, "that I breathe when I sleep is the same thing as I sleep when I breathe!"
>
> "It is the same thing with you," said the Hatter, and here the conversation dropped.[26]

Sometimes the example comes right out of Carroll's lesson book: "All apples are red, but it does not follow that any red thing is an apple." This emphasis on the nonequivalence of converses is important and relates to syllogisms and to if-then statements of the form:

If A (and then) B.

The "if" statement is called the *antecedent,* and the "then" statement is the *consequence.* In more formal logic, this might look like:

If A then B.
A.
Therefore, B.

In practical form, an if-then statement might look like this:

If you take cyanide, then you die.
You take cyanide.
You die.

As a logician, Carroll knew how important it was to understand that converses are not necessarily true. That is why he gives so many examples to prove the point. In fact, disregard of these ideas leads to some common errors in thinking. For instance:

If you take cyanide, then you die.
You do not take cyanide.
Therefore, you do not die.

Or:

If A then B.
Not A.
Therefore, not B.

The confusion here is that cyanide is a sufficient cause of death by itself. It interferes with the cytochrome respiratory chain so effectively that the transfer of electrons to oxygen is prevented and metabolism stops dead. But that does not mean that because you don't take cyanide you will live forever. There are many other causes of death besides cyanide. Cyanide is just one of a large class of poisons that will cause death, and the large class of poisons causing death is part of an even larger class of things (eating too much pie, getting run over by a steamroller, choking on a filet mignon, cancer, stroke, Marchifava-Bignami disease, heart attack, etc.) that can cause death. Not taking cyanide will not prevent one of those other causes from eventually taking its toll. In formal logic, this error is called *negating the antecedent*.

Here's another problem that arises from a similarly defective reasoning:

If you take cyanide, then you die.
You die.
Therefore, you took cyanide.

Or:

If A then B.
B.
Therefore, A.

Affirming the consequent (the name of this fallacy) doesn't automatically imply that you took cyanide, as there are other causes of death. In terms of necessary and sufficient conditions, the error here is the same as the error of denying the antecedent; it is the fallacy of assuming that a sufficient condition is a necessary one. Cyanide is a sufficient condition of dying, not a necessary one.

Back to the Cat: All cats are detached. But the Cheshire Cat is more detached than most. He is probably a very direct symbol of ideal intellectual detachment. He can disappear because he can abstract himself from his surroundings into himself. He can appear as only a head because he is almost a disembodied intelligence. He can appear as only a grin because he can impose an (unsettling) atmosphere without being (entirely) present.

According to Martin Gardner, a former editor of *Scientific American*, the phrase "grin without a cat" is probably not a bad description of pure mathematics. Although mathematical theorems often can be usefully applied to the structure of the external world, the theorems themselves are abstractions built on assumptions that belong to another realm "remote from human passions." Bertrand Russell once put it as, "remote from the pitiful facts of nature . . . an ordered cosmos, where pure thought can dwell as in its natural home, and where one, at least, of our nobler impulses can escape from the dreary exile of the actual world."

Gardner's idea is probably hokum. But I will admit it has endearing features. The origin of the idea of the Cheshire Cat has been discussed ad nauseam, especially by Katsuko Kasai. The origin I like the best is Kasai's interesting conjecture that Cheshire cheese was once sold in the shape of a grinning cat. One would tend to slice off the cheese at the cat's tail and end up with only the grinning head on the plate.

On another level, my idea is probably more basic: Carroll was probably aware of the use of cats in the logical discussion of the principal relations among classes. In dividing the universe of creatures into cats and not-cats, logicians used the defining form

$$x \in cat$$

which defines the class of cats. This, in turn, was seen to determine the class of not-cats, which, I suppose, started with "x is unfeline." If this was used as the class of not-cats, and if not-cats is $\sim C$, then "cats" is C. Using this concept, let's work out the truth tables to see if a cat can logically exist without a smile and vice versa:

Let C = cat

Let S = grin (think of S as a smile, which is a kind of grin. S looks less like a C than a G does, so S will serve better as a symbol for grin than G.)

& is the logical connective signifying conjunction meaning both

∨ is the logical connective signifying disjunction meaning either, or, or both.

Therefore, ~C means not cat; ~S means no grin; (C & S) means a cat with a grin; (C & ~S) means a cat without a grin; (~C & S) means a grin without a cat; and (~C & ~S) means no cat and no grin. Thus, truth tables for such simple and complex statements would be:

	C	S	~C	~S	(C & S)	(C & ~S)	(~C & S)	(~C & ~S)
Case 1	T	T	F	F	T	F	F	F
Case 2	T	F	F	T	F	T	F	F
Case 3	F	T	T	F	F	F	T	F
Case 4	F	F	T	T	F	F	F	T

The table lists all possible combinations of the statements involving the simple terms C and S. There are only four cases. They correspond to the conditions (1) cat with a grin, (2) cat without a grin, (3) no cat but a grin, (4) no cat and no grin. Column 3 is the no-cat column, and its truth values are the opposite of column 1. Column 4 is the no-grin column, which is just the opposite of the grin column (2). The complex statements follow directly. For example, (C & S) is true in case 1 because only in case 1 are C and S true. In the cases 2, 3, and 4, C is false, S is false, or both are false. If either C or S is false, then the conjunction (C & S) must also be false.

So what?

Hold your horses. I do have a point in mind, and that will come out with the analysis of the more complex statements [(~C & S) & (C & ~S)] and [(~C & S) ∨ (C & ~S)].

	(~C & S)	(C & ~S)	[(~C & S) & (C & ~S)]	[(~C & S) ∨ (C & ~S)]
Case 1	F	F	F	F
Case 2	F	T	F	T
Case 3	T	F	F	T
Case 4	F	F	F	F

Thus, we prove that you can't have a cat without a grin *and* no cat with a grin because all the cases of that conjunction are false. Such a statement is a contradiction. But the last column proves that we can have a grin without a cat *or* a cat without a grin. The complex statement reflecting those assertions, [(~C & S) ∨ (C & ~S)], is true in case 2 and in case 3. Situations that are true in some cases and false in others are contingent on the circumstances for their truth and are logically possible, as indicated in the last column.

In the same way with the same tables, I could prove to you that a cat without a grin or a cat with a grin is just a cat, and a grin without a cat or a grin with a cat is just a grin. Carroll probably worked out these tables (just for grins?), and that is why the eminently logical Alice mentions the truth value of [(~C & S) ∨ (C & ~S)], although she claims (contrary to fact) that she has never seen a grin without a cat.

Carroll's point in this is (I believe) to demonstrate that in the analogical matrix known as fiction the grin can exist without a cat and that in the analogical matrix known as logic the same grin can also exist without a cat. In nature such a thing is also possible, if the class of no-cat is defined simply as the class of all things that exist that are not cat. At least I think that's true. Who knows? I do know that my wife, Ethel, has an excellent endearing cat grin, which she puts on when it suits her. In that case, E! (S & ~C) might be justified since the grin in this particular case is attached to a human and not a cat.

In math, $\sqrt{-1}$ exists, but in nature this can't exist.

Grins without cats and math without reality: This is a distinction with a difference, a difference of which we should not lose sight. Math is one thing; the real world is another. Only sometimes do the twain, the two great realms, meet. At other times, the two may be far, far apart. Mathematical proofs can describe or not describe the real world, depending on how closely the assumptions, on which the proofs always depend, relate to the real world.

Math may be the queen of the sciences, but the history of mathematics proves that the queen is often in error (though rarely ever in doubt) because she has been contradicted by reality. The history of mathematics is a graveyard of reasoned "proofs" once thought perfect and later found defective.

> *Lesson:* Do not give undue weight or too much attention to supposed mathematical proofs. Mathematical proofs are only as good as the assumptions that underlie them and may not reflect reality or truth.

Example: When a mathematical analysis by AT&T scientist John Carson was quoted as conclusive proof of that FM radio was not possible, the technical community committed the kind of error then that, unfortunately, continues to be quite common now. Someone proves a statement based on certain assumptions; others forget those assumptions and remember only the conclusions. People then tend to apply such conclusions to all cases, even ones that do not satisfy the original assumptions. This is what had happened to FM, and it was tantamount to a prejudice against FM.

Edwin Armstrong, a Columbia University professor who was always suspicious of mathematical proofs of the impossible, in a brilliant moment of lateral thinking decided to challenge that wisdom and set out to find out what would happen if he used instead a wide band of frequencies for his FM signal. The rest, as they say, is history. Armstrong built an FM receiver and transmitter that was far, far better than any AM setup then available. Having done that, Armstrong was convinced that FM radio would succeed. The only thing that he thought could temporarily slow it down was, in his words, "those intangible forces so frequently set in motion by men, and the origin of which lies in vested interests, habits, false mathematical proofs, customs, and legislation."[27]

"Have some wine," the March Hare said in an encouraging tone.

Alice looked all round the table, but there was nothing on it but tea.

[Look again, Alice. There is a milk jug on the table. We know this because later on in the tea party, the March Hare upsets it. Failure to observe carefully is a cause of incorrect conclusions. Failure to see the obvious is common. Many of our failures result from the mental set governing the search procedure at the time. In this case, Alice is looking for wine, not milk. She sees no wine, but she misses the milk. Milk would have been a more appropriate drink for a girl seven and one-half years old. But perhaps Alice was more interested in wine.]

"I don't see any wine," she remarked.

"There isn't any," said the March Hare.

"Then it wasn't very civil of you to offer it," said Alice angrily.

"It wasn't very civil of you to sit down without being invited," said the March Hare.[28]

In effect, the March Hare is saying because Alice is guilty of doing the same thing that she criticizes him for (i.e., being uncivil), her argument is no good. Thus, with this counterattack on Alice, the March Hare avoids the obligation to explain his uncivil behavior. This is a violation of the relevance criterion. That some other person engages in a questionable practice is irrelevant to whether such a practice merits acceptance. "Practice what you preach" is OK advice but not a logical argument. Two wrongs don't make a right. Shortcomings of your position cannot be defended by pointing out the errors or shortcomings of the opposition. Tu quoque (you do it, too) is a fallacy.

Tu quoque thinking is a common and very powerful psychological response, which most of us have experienced since childhood, to the inconsistent behavior of a critic. We often feel no obligation to respond to criticism under the circumstances. Because such thinking is so emotionally convincing, its fallacious character is usually not fully recognized until it is pointedly brought to one's attention. And that, of course, dear reader, is your job.

"Take some more tea," the March Hare said to Alice, very earnestly.

"I've had nothing yet," Alice replied in an offended tone: "so I ca'n't take more."

"You mean you ca'n't take *less*," said the Hatter: "it's very easy to take *more* than nothing."[29]

True. And an excellent explanation of the null case (the set with no members) known as nothing. It's hard to get less than nothing but easy to get more because nothing is the lowest you can go in the real world of material objects. About nothing, we and Lewis Carroll shall talk more (not less) later.

"You can draw water out of a water-well," said the Hatter; "so I should think you could draw treacle [British for molasses] out of a treacle-well —eh, stupid?"

"But they were *in* the well," Alice said to the Dormouse, not choosing to notice this last remark.

"Of course they were," said the Dormouse: "well in."

This answer so confused poor Alice, that she let the Dormouse go on for some time without interrupting it.

"They were learning to draw," the Dormouse went on, yawning and rubbing its eyes, for it was getting very sleepy; "and they drew all manner of things—everything that begins with an M—"

"Why with an M?" said Alice.

"Why not?" said the March Hare.[30]

The confusions of meanings for *in the well* and *well in* and *drawing pictures* and *drawing treacle* have been covered. Note that it is the March Hare, not the Dormouse, who answers Alice's question. He has a vested personal interest in the matter because his name starts with M and he wants to be part of the story. He wants to be drawn for the same reason that most wealthy and privileged members of Edwardian society in England in the nineteenth century wanted to have their portraits painted by John Singer Sargent. Those aristocrats had a vested interest in seeing themselves well portrayed (pun intended).

Like most people with vested interests (that need defending), the March Hare's defense is irrelevant. In this case, it is an irrelevant appeal to absence of a reason. Failure to know or to have a reason to justify a statement (such as March Hare's "Why not?") is not a reason supporting the statement. Absent evidence, ignorance itself, or no reason whatsoever never justifies anything.

A word about unbirthdays (celebrated by Humpty Dumpty in *Through the Looking Glass*): the concept of contradictions has occupied philosophers from day one. *Unbirthday* is a Carrollian logical extension of *birthday*. If *birthday* exists, then its negation would be *not-birthday*. The day you were born is your birthday. All days that you were not born are your unbirthdays. In this context, *un* is just another way of indicating denial. Yes or no; true or false; 0 or 1; + or –; go or no go; not, and, or; NOT, AND, OR; she loves me, she loves me not. *Unbirthday* is the denial or negation of birthday. It is another way of saying "not birthday." The concept is trivial, but the results are not trivial and underlie much of our Western civilization's quest for logical certainty. You have one birthday a year, and all the other days are unbirthdays. This could be formulated B not B, or we could abbreviate the statement as logicians do by placing the sign for negation, the tilde, $\sim$, before the second B. Thus, $\sim$B stands for unbirthday.

Now, it is obvious that when a statement is true, its denial is false, and when a statement is false, its denial is true. Using the shorthand, we can symbolize this information in a truth table:

B	~B
T	F
F	T

The truth table tells us when it's a birthday, it is not an unbirthday and vice versa, the same thing the Hatter has told us but in symbolic form. Truth tables like this have had a major effect on the development of computerized information processing and underlie most computer logic. The probability of today being your unbirthday is 364/365, and the probability of this being your birthday is 1/365. Therefore, the probability of ~B/B is 364 to 1. By the truth table, it is obvious that any statement of B is inconsistent with its negation, ~B. In other words, B and ~B are mutually exclusive. If it is B, then it can't be your ~B, and if it is ~B, it can't be your B. The Hatter explains this in so many words. But he could have just given Alice the equation, Probability (B or ~B) = 1, and therefore, Probability (1 − ~B) = B.

By the way, the Hatter isn't entirely reasonable. He thinks it is much better to celebrate unbirthdays than celebrate birthdays because there are so many more unbirthdays than birthdays. This reasoning assumes celebrating is desirable. It might be from his perspective or the perspective of the kids, but it might not be true for others, especially adults. The Hatter's reasoning disregards the utility factor, which must be included in any value judgment. Any mother of a two-year-old knows, especially if she has suffered through just one birthday party, that some birthday parties are no fun for adults. In fact, some parties for two-year-olds that I have attended have been pure torture.

Warning! We now pass on to the Queen of Hearts, a character who probably represents the embodiment of ungovernable passion in a person of power—a blind and aimless Fury, a Hitler or Stalin type. Her constant orders for beheading are shocking to those modern critics of children's books who feel that juvenile fiction should be free of all violence. As far as I know, there have been no empirical studies of how children react to such scenes and what harm, if any, is done to their psyche. Absence of evidence, however, is not evidence of absence. So the question must remain open.

My guess is that the normal child finds it all very amusing and is not damaged in the least. However, I do feel that this stuff is not entirely suitable for adults. It especially should not be permitted to circulate indiscriminately among adults who are undergoing psychoanalysis. The depiction of royalty here set forth contains an enormous amount of dignity, arbitrariness, and paraded prestige as necessary to bolster up the absurd pretensions of incompetent leaders, something that has modern resonances, something we should think about when we hear "Hail to the Chief" or read about the shenanigans of the Royals of England.

The reason that the Queen of Hearts and the subsequent trial of the Knave of Hearts can be so terrifying to adults is that most realize that they live in a slapstick modern world under an inexplicable sentence of death. When they try to find out what the castle authorities want them to do, they are shifted from one bumbling bureaucrat to another, receiving no reasonable answers.

Franz Kafka's *The Castle* (which I believe was inspired by AAW) represents the stratified, organized, controlled, completely bureaucratized society, in which the individual is a number and has lost specific and distinct individual dignity, integrity, freedom, and all appearance of such. Yes, Kafka is true, but often we don't recognize Kafka as such because when we go through the Kafkaesque experience, we are kicking, biting, fighting, trying to survive, doing lots of things, but not reading Kafka.

Added to the horror of it all is the ready perception that the arbitrary, bloody Queen of Hearts is an ineffective, abysmally stupid person. Yet she has the power. Her pointlessness is the point. Her gibberish conveys unmistakable meanings to those of us who read hidden messages. But sometimes, I admit, there is nothing but nonsense in nonsense. And sometimes the nonsense is just ridicule of stuffed shirts. Perhaps adults should take consolation in the underlying joyful certainty that they (the leaders) who are trying day and night with unstinted effort to control us are, after all, according to Alice, only a pack of cards.

More than one critic has commented on the similarities between Kafka's other book, *The Trial*, and the trial of the Knave of Hearts and between Kafka's *Castle* and the chess game in Carroll's *Through the Looking Glass*, in which living pieces are ignorant of the game's plan and cannot tell if they move of their own will or are being controlled by invisible strings moved by invisible fingers. This vision of the monstrous mindlessness of the powers that be can be grim and disturbing, especially to those who know history.

> The Queen turned crimson with fury, and, after glaring at her for a moment like a wild beast, began screaming, "Off with her head!"[31]

All attempts to divert attention from real issues are irrelevant. All violence and all threats of violence are irrelevant. A chopped-off head is not a substitute for a logical argument. Nor is a chopped-off head a substitute for a trial on the issues. Official violence and oppression can be much more dangerous and difficult to control than individual private violence. Major checks are therefore required to prevent the major dangers of too much governmental power. That is why we have a constitution. That is why the Constitution must be followed exactly. "Eternal vigilance," said George Washington, "is the price of liberty." Eternal vigilance is probably also the price of everything else that we hold dear.

> "Very true," said the Duchess: "Flamingoes and mustard both bite. And the moral of that is—Birds of a feather flock together."[32]

Note the non sequitur based on confusion of *bite* and the error of concluding that since mustard and flamingoes both bite, and since the flamingo is a bird, mustard must be a bird, too, and therefore must flock with it.

> "Only mustard isn't a bird," Alice remarked.
> [Clever Alice! She defeated the false analogy by stating a fact.]
> "Right, as usual," said the Duchess, who seemed ready to agree to everything that Alice said.[33]

Oh my, my, that Duchess! She is something else. The Duchess is one of the most striking features of the book, especially if one reviews what was standard fare for children of the time. When one sees her in action, one gets a strong reaction against didacticism, which so many of the episodes illustrate. Carroll's parodies of the instructive verse that children were made to memorize and recite is a ridicule of solemnity and a criticism of the practice of inflicting it upon the young.

In the croquet game, the Duchess's motto is "Everything's got a moral, if only you can find it." This, of course, begs the question and is all inclusive, an overgeneralization, and an assertion that needs support by evidence. From that statement, the Duchess becomes more and more extravagant and nonsensical in her application of axioms and proverbs to everything. Alice catches on fast and reacts accordingly. And the moral of that is: Adults—ugh! They aren't consistent, and they aren't fair.

It's true that everyday language is largely arbitrary and unaccountable, but the Duchess's puzzling use of language is one important illustration of adult bullying and condescension. This is, I believe, one of the underlying messages of the Alice books, the rejection of adult authority and the vindication of the rights of the child, even the right to self-assertion, clear instruction, and logical thoughts.

The Duchess continues, "There's a large mustard mine near here. And the moral of that is—'The more there is of mine, the less there is of yours.'"[34]

Another non sequitur as well as a contextual modification of the word *mine*. But despite the change in the meaning of the word *mine* in this context, the Duchess is here describing the zero-sum game, in which the payoff to the winner exactly equals the losses of the loser— "the more there is of mine, the less there is of yours."

Poker is a many-person zero-sum game because the total amount of money won equals the total amount of money lost. Bets on the outcome of chess and checker games are zero-sum. So are some forms of currency trading.

By contrast, a negative-sum game is one in which the total amount won is less than that bet, as in pari-mutuel betting on a horse race. The total amount bet (the handle) is 20 percent more than the total amount paid off because the state extracts 15 percent from the handle and the track takes 5 percent.

Stocks and bonds can be positive-sum games due to the addition of interest to the betted pool in the case of bonds and the addition of dividends in the case of stocks. But stocks and bonds are mainly negative-sum games because of commissions and trading fees, market manipulations, market timing, and withdrawal of money from corporations via fraud.

> The executioner's argument was, that you couldn't cut off a head unless there was a body to cut it off from: that he had never had to do such a thing before, and he wasn't going to begin at his time of life.[35]

Matter of fact: You can't cut a head off when it has already been detached. The executioner's argument is reality based, intelligent, valid, and sound. Why didn't he stop there? Why didn't he just stop while he was ahead?

Instead of resting at the point of irrefutability, the executioner continued (by way of supererogation) with the irrelevant continuum argument: because we never did things that way, we shouldn't start to do them that way now.

Prudence indeed will dictate that things should not be changed for light and transient causes, but experience dictates that they must change if they are required to change by the facts. Otherwise, nothing would change and progress would stop.

> "Yes, we went to school in the sea, though you mayn't believe it—"
> "I never said I didn't!" interrupted Alice.
> "You did," said the Mock Turtle.[36]

The Mock Turtle is telling Alice that she has just said "I didn't." Never means never, and Alice just said "I didn't." Therefore, her statement that she never said what she obviously just did say has to be wrong. That is why the Mock Turtle called her on it.

Verbal traps like this are a significant diversion for Carroll. Humpty Dumpty, in the next Alice book, catches Alice in a similar verbal trap by referring to something that she didn't say. The Mock Turtle continues:

> "We had the best of educations—in fact, we went to school every day—"
> "*I've* been to a day-school, too," said Alice. "You needn't be so proud as all that."
> [Another confusion: Going to school every day and a day school are in fact two different things, though Alice assumes they are the same.]
> "With extras?" asked the Mock Turtle, a little anxiously.
> "Yes," said Alice: "we learned French and music."
> "And washing?" said the Mock Turtle.
> "Certainly not!" said Alice indignantly.
> "Ah! Then yours wasn't a really good school," said the Mock Turtle in a tone of great relief. "Now, at *ours*, they had, at the end of the bill, 'French, music, *and washing—*extra.'"[37]

Out-of-context quotations are unfair and misleading. They partially select ideas or evidence and frequently lead to erroneous conclusions. The phrase "French, music, and washing—extra" often appeared on boarding school bills. It meant, of course, that there was an extra charge for French and music and for having one's laundry done by the school. It did not mean washing was included in the course of instruction.

Near our house in Texas, we have a storefront doctor whose sign reads: "Neurology, pain, and headache control center." Pain and head-ache might need control, but one wonders if the good doctor meant to control neurology as well.

The name *Mock Turtle* is like that, too—a confusion. The (incorrect) reasoning here is that if there is a mock turtle soup (that is, a soup that tastes and smells like turtle soup but is made of nonturtle ingredients), then there must be such a creature as a mock turtle. There must be a mock turtle if there is a mock turtle soup, in the same way as there must be a turtle if there is a turtle soup.

The analogy is false because although turtle soup and mock turtle soup share a certain property, namely, that they are both hot liquids that you drink from a bowl, they differ in that they are not both derived from a 200-million-year-old reptile species that has protective shells called the carapace and plastron. In fact, mock turtle soup was made from veal. An illustrated AAW shows Tenniel's original drawing of the Mock Turtle with a calf's head and hooves for feet, reflecting the actual ingredients that went into Victorian mock turtle soup.

On a deeper level, we are dealing here with a fundamental defect in human thinking called *reification*, or the propensity to convert an abstract concept into a hard belief. Because we can name something or because we have a name for something does not mean that that thing actually exists. It might exist, and it might not exist. It might merely exist in the realm of imagination and not in the real world. Some people think that Yahweh, the God of the Old Testament, was a social-political idea to help organize the Jews out of Egypt, which then became a metaphor reified.

Mock turtles and real turtles—children in the world of adults often exhibit such confusions. For many years, we disciplined our daughter by saying, "Allegra, you're not the only one!" Eventually, she wanted to know who was the Only One and how could she get to be the Only One.

When I worked at the National Institutes of Health, my boss was King Engel. At home at the dinner table, it was always "King said I should do this" and "King said I should do that." King put me on night duty and so forth. One night, my son, Craig, piped up and asked, "Dad, when I grow up, will I have to work for the king?"

Other confusions in the Mock Turtle's story are just pure fun.

"Well, there was Mystery," the Mock Turtle replied, counting off the subjects on his flappers—"Mystery, ancient and modern, with Seaography and then Drawling . . . Drawling, Stretching, and Fainting in Coils."[38]

Of course, Mystery = History; Seaography = Geography; Drawling, Stretching, and Fainting in Coils = Drawing, Sketching, and Painting in Oils.

"He taught us Laughing and Grief."[39]

It is doubtful that there was much laughing in Latin, but the Grief sounds pretty real for Greek as taught in that era.

> The twelve jurors were all writing very busily on slates. "What are they doing?" Alice whispered to the Gryphon. "They ca'n't have anything to put down yet, before the trial's begun."
>
> "They're putting down their names," the Gryphon whispered in reply, "for fear they should forget them before the end of the trial."
>
> "Stupid things!" Alice began in a loud indignant voice. . . . Alice could see, as well as if she were looking over their shoulders, that all the jurors were writing down "Stupid things!" on their slates, and she could even make out that one of them didn't know how to spell "stupid," and that he had to ask his neighbor to tell him."[40]

Here Carroll is playing with the double meaning of the phrase "writing stupid things": You can write the words *stupid things*, and you can also write things that are stupid and, as in the case of the jurors here, you can do both those two things at the same time. It also appears that Carroll is making some sort of comment on the jury system. Its true import escapes me. Have you any ideas?

"Herald, read the accusation!"

> "The Queen of Hearts, she made some tarts,
> All on a summer's day:
> The Knave of Hearts, he stole those tarts
> And took them quite away!"

"Consider your verdict," the King said to the jury.[41]

Wait a second! No, not yet. That's not right. The King is out of sequence. First comes the trial and then the verdict. What kind of court is the King running?

In a legitimate court of law, the accused is entitled to a trial. Mere indictment does not prove guilt. The jury is required to evaluate the evidence to get to the truth, the whole truth, and nothing but the truth. The King of Hearts shows some of the impetuosity of leaders who feel they know the answers without needing to discuss the issues or evaluate the data or (and this is worse) consult with the people. Later on, the king again shows his impatience during the examination of the Mad Hatter: "Give your evidence . . . and don't be nervous, or I'll have you executed on the spot."[42]

As we discussed, evidence given under duress or torture is no evidence at all. According to Charles Mackay, LLD, in his book *Extraordinary Popular Delusions and the Madness of Crowds*, thousands of women confessed to being witches and were burned at the stake during the inquisition. Their confessions said they could fly about, had sexual intercourse with the devil, could change into black cats and other familiars—all the things the torturers wished them to say, they did say. Now we know all those things are impossible. As versatile as some women are, none of them can change into a black cat.

Darkness at Noon by Arthur Koestler discusses how, during the Stalin era in Russia, this problem led to confessions of guilt from perfectly innocent Communist Party members. *The Rise and Fall of the Third Reich* by William L. Shirer handles the same subject in great detail during the Nazi era in Germany, and the novel *1984* (written by George Orwell) depicts a totalitarian society gone further awry by being able to extract any confession from anyone about anything, often for no real reason except to exert power and control or to maintain power and control or both.

> "I'm a poor man," the Hatter went on, "and most things twinkled after that—only the March Hare said—"
> "I didn't!" the March Hare interrupted in a great hurry.
> "You did!" said the Hatter.
> "I deny it! said the March Hare.
> "He denies it," said the King: "leave out that part."[43]

Whether the Hatter is poor is irrelevant to the evidence that he is giving. Appeals to pity are emotionally based and irrelevant. All emotional appeals are unreasonable.

And what the devil does "and most things twinkled after that" have anything to do with anything, much less this trial? The Hatter is confused and nervously speaking nonsense.

Notice the March Hare is so eager to deny things that we never get to know what he is denying. The king doesn't care, however, and tells the jury to "leave out that part," an impossible task, since they don't know what "that part" was.

Respect for all the evidence must be the cornerstone of trials at law. We don't see much of that respect here. The King believes that he is special, that somehow the rules do not apply to him or that he can just make them up ad hoc. Obviously, he is mistaken.

Denying counterevidence and ignoring any evidence produce inadequate evaluations and lead away from truth and toward error. Missing evidence is never adequate. The King of Hearts, as a judge, as a leader, is, like so many of our government officials, clearly inadequate, a failure.

> Here one of the guinea pigs cheered, and was immediately suppressed by the officers of the court. They had a rather large canvas bag, which tied up at the mouth with strings; into this they slipped the guinea pig, head first, and then sat upon it.[44]

Why they picked on the guinea pig and not the others in the courtroom who were also out of order is not clear. This may have been another example of the arbitrary exercise of power, it could have been the manifestation of a prejudice against the guinea pig, or it could have been both those things or neither. Who knows?

Alice did have a thought about the matter, but it wasn't particularly sympathetic or nice: "I'm glad I've seen that done. . . . I've so often read in the newspapers, at the end of trials."[45]

Suppressed evidence and sealing of files is common at the end of trials, especially civil suits. But what Alice is probably referring to is *quash*, meaning to set aside or annul, as in, "The court quashed the indictment." Some supposedly educated attorneys say *squashed* instead of *quashed*, and that I suppose is the origin of what happened to the guinea pig.

> "What are tarts made of?"
> "Pepper, mostly," said the cook.
> "Treacle," said the sleepy voice behind her.
> "Collar that Dormouse!" the Queen shrieked out. "Behead that Dormouse!"[46]

Ignoring, denying, and suppressing counterevidence results in biased appraisals that are likely to be wrong. Here, the cook is giving false testimony. The Dormouse tells the court so. Yet it is the Dormouse, not the cook, who is punished. "Power corrupts and absolute power corrupts absolutely," said Lord Acton. Authorities can be wrong. Kings can be tyrannical. Queens ditto.

> At this moment the King, who had been for some time busily writing in his note-book, called out "Silence!" and read out from his book, "Rule Forty-two. All persons more than a mile high to leave the court."
> Everybody looked at Alice.
> "I'm not a mile high," said Alice
> "You are," said the King.[47]

Here we have a dispute about fact. Is Alice a mile high, or is she not? It should be easy to settle this issue by objective measurement. "Measurement began our might: Forms a stark Egyptian thought, forms that gentler Phidias wrought," wrote the Irish poet William Butler Yeats in his *Last Poems*. Yeats was right: Measurement began our might. Numbers are nice. I like them, too. Numbers (if correct) often lead to truth. "I have always believed in numbers," said John Nash, who won the 1994 Nobel Prize in economics.[48]

In the case of the King versus Alice, why not get some numbers here? To prove Alice's height, we need only measure her and report the result in a number and a unit of extent. In this case, the unit of extent will probably be feet, and the number will probably be four. That height (four feet) would be considerably smaller than 5,280 feet (one mile), proving the king wrong.

Direct measurement is one form of verification. Verification is nice. Verification leads to truth because it is a procedure designed to confirm or deny a stated view of reality. As such, verification is at the heart of scientific inquiry and the reason for experiments. Verification was at the heart of the dispute between Iraq and the United Nations. Iraq said it had no nuclear or biological weapons of mass destruction. But Iraq did not fully submit to inspections to prove it. The failure to fully submit led to suspicion that Iraq was hiding something, which led to war.

If the King of Hearts permitted the measurement of Alice, he would be proved a liar. Without measurement to know the reality situation for sure, we have to rely on probabilities. The probabilities are that the King of Hearts is wrong. It would be unheard of to have anyone a mile high. The king knows that. So does Alice. But getting official recognition of the fact is another question. For years, suffragettes claimed that the Declaration of Independence indicated that women must have the right to vote, otherwise they were taxed without representation. The suffragettes claimed that the Declaration of Independence clearly states that government must derive its powers from the consent of the governed. Since women were governed without having a voice in the government, the government was proven wrong by its own admission. It took many years and many long battles, frequent imprisonments of women and so forth before that simple fact was recognized by the Nineteenth Amendment to the United States Constitution.

This misstatement of fact, the problem of Alice's height, was of course caused by the king himself. He had just written rule forty-two and made it so excessive he thereby gave himself away. In the secret workings of his unconscious mind, he wrote a rule that is so blatantly absurd that its irrational origin became obvious.

"Nearly two miles high," added the Queen.[49]

Denying the obvious, stonewalling, as in the Watergate fiasco, does no good because truth will out. If a person a mile high is absurd, then a person two miles high is twice as absurd. The Queen is wrong, twice wrong. She is wrong to support someone who is obviously wrong, and she is wrong about the fact under discussion.

"Well, I sha'n't go, at any rate," said Alice: "besides, that's not a regular rule: you invented it just now."[50]

Good for Alice!

Is it possible that, in some way or other, Alice has been "improved" by her adventures? Is it possible that the Queen of Hearts, the Cheshire Cat, the Hatter, and the rest of them have been working out her redemption? She seems moral, honest, and, at this point, just—especially in contrast with those around her, who appear to be immoral, dishonest, and unjust.

Not only has Alice become moral, honest, and just, but also she has become fiercely logical, subversive and revolutionary, destructive and terrible, and merciless to privilege, established institutions, and comfortable habits. She is now indifferent to authority, careless of the well-tried wisdom of the ages. She fearlessly contradicts the King!

Alice looks into the pit of hell and is not afraid. She sees herself a child, a little girl, a feeble speck, surrounded by unfathomable emblems of power and control, yet she bears herself proudly, as unmoved as if she were lord of the universe and as unmovable as if she were the immovable object of classical logistics.

Callie, my two-year-old granddaughter, often behaves the same way. "(I don't care what you say.) The moon is following us." "(I don't care what you say.) It looks like steam and it is steam." "No nap! I don't want to get out of the pool. I want to play more." "I am angry at Mommy and Daddy because they put me in time-out." Good for Callie. And good for Alice. Callie and Alice are thinking as individuals and are thinking well.

Though all that is true about Alice (and Callie), various internal evidences still make me suspect Alice of having a "past"—of having been naughty, of being naughty the way Callie is naughty sometimes. With Alice and Callie, as with us all, there is room for improvement. Later on, we see in the *Looking Glass* book that Alice improves and has even developed a kind of (primitive) social conscience:

> "I like the Walrus best, said Alice: "because he was a *little* sorry for the poor oysters."
> "He ate more than the Carpenter, though," said Tweedledee.[51]

Wow! That reply is a more delicious indictment of sentimentalism than was ever made.

> "It's the oldest rule in the book," said the King.
> "Then it ought to be Number One," said Alice.
> The King turned pale.[52]

As well he should. Alice caught the King in a lie. And the moral of that is: People in power do make up rules to support themselves and friends. In the literature of the Western world, rule forty-two has become the emblem of arbitrary rules and regulations. As a kind of inside joke, Douglas Adams considered forty-two the secret of the universe. If you understood forty-two, you understood life.

Although arbitrary behavior is common enough, it is not reasonable and it is not right because it is not based on a promotion of the general welfare. The King of Hearts, the poor fellow, like so many of our present leaders, is over his head. The King, like some of our past presidents (Clinton and Nixon), has lied to the public and therefore has lost face.

Next, we have the discussion of the written evidence against the Knave. Identify the errors in the King's thinking as they occur.

> "What's in it?" said the Queen.
>
> "I haven't opened it yet," said the White Rabbit; "but it seems to be a letter, written by the prisoner to—somebody."
>
> "It must have been that," said the King, "unless it was written to nobody, which isn't usual, you know."[53]

This is the null class (a set with no members) problem again. From medieval times to the present, philosophers have debated the existence or nonexistence of nobody, nowhere, nothing, and the like. Does nothing exist, or is it nothing? Treating a null class as though it were an existing thing is a rich source of Carrollian logical nonsense. We saw the March Hare offer nonexistent wine; the King of Hearts thinks it unusual to write letters to nobody; Alice wants to know where the candle flame goes when it goes out; the Gryphon tells Alice, "They never executes nobody"; and we subsequently encounter the unexecuted Nobody walking along the road; and so forth.

The confusions engendered about nothing have a long and honorable history in literature. Recall that Ulysses deceived the one-eyed Polyphemus by calling himself Noman. When Polyphemus cried out, "Noman is killing me!" no one took this to mean that someone was actually attacking him.

So what is Lewis Carroll's position on the null set problem? Carroll is a nominalist. Nominalists think that some terms exist as mere necessities of thought or convenience of language. Nominalists think such terms do not have an external real existence. There is a name, that's true, but more importantly, there is the thing itself. Sometimes the name is just there to fill in the blank, to indicate the absence of a real thing, and to denote that absence. The most elementary principle of semantics is that agreement about the use of signs rather than the signs themselves enables us to communicate. Thus, *nobody* exists in name only. The thing itself is no person and is not real. *Nobody* has a general reality that corresponds to it. *Nobody* is only a way, a short cut, for saying no person. *Nobody* is just a shorthand way of saying there is no real person under discussion. The White King (in the statements below) admits the nonexistence of *nobody* when he contrasts *Nobody*, whom he can't see but whom he thinks Alice sees, to a real person whom he can't see either.

By the same token, *nothing* means no thing and *nowhere* means no where. Therefore, *nothing* has no existence. *Nothing* merely designates nonexistence. *Nowhere* designates no existence in any place or no place that is existent. An understanding of this concept would have prevented the White King's confusion, which is caused by his confounding what a thing is called with what a thing is.

> "I see nobody on the road," said Alice.
> "I only wish I had such eyes," the King remarked in a fretful tone. "To be able to see Nobody. And at that distance too! Why, it's as much as I can do to see real people by this light."[54]

Notice Nobody's reification is confirmed by the capital *N* when the king refers to him. When Alice does the talking, *nobody* is a nobody with a small *n*. Later (or is it earlier, for time is reversed in the looking glass?), the King asks the messenger:

> "Who did you pass on the road?"
> "Nobody," said the messenger.[55]

(Here, we don't know if the messenger is reifying *nobody* or not. The capital *N* might be there simply because the sentence needs to start with a capital.)

> "Quite right," said the King. "This young lady saw him too. So of course Nobody walks slower than you."
> "I do my best," the Messenger said in a sullen tone. "I'm sure nobody walks much faster than I do!"
> "He ca'n't do that," said the King, "or else he'd have been here first."[56]

Note the apparent contradiction: Can nobody walk both slower and faster than the messenger? Also note the contextual change. The King is talking about Nobody as if he were a real person, and the messenger is talking about nobody as if he were the absence of a real person. Hence the confusion and the fun. The difficulty is partly the result of one of Lewis Carroll's favorite devices in entertaining children, the play on words and exposition of the failings and difficulties of language.

By the way, nobody should conclude that the honorable author of this book is denigrating the concept of the null class. Quite the contrary. I have an inordinate respect for nobody, since I know that I am a nobody.

And the concept of nothing has applications: the Hindu discovery of nothing, symbolized by the zero (0), enables any grade school child to make calculations that our ancient Greek and Roman ancestors could do only on an abacus.

The null class, 0, is defined by negating any defining form of the class one (1). So it follows that the universe class and the null class are each other's complements. Every element that is not included in "everything" is "nothing." Nothing includes all the interesting characters in AAW as well as square circles, secular churches, married bachelors, and anything else that doesn't exist.

> "Who is it directed [addressed] to?" said one of the jurymen.
> "It isn't directed at all," said the White Rabbit: "in fact, there's nothing written on the *outside*." He unfolded the paper as he spoke, and added "It isn't a letter, after all: it's a set of verses."
> "Are they in the prisoner's handwriting?" asked another of the jurymen.[57]

Note the two jurymen have decided to have a go at getting some real evidence. They want to know who the letter is addressed to and they want to know whether the Knave wrote it. Both might bear an important relationship to the significance and weight that should be attached to the letter. It turns out the letter is not a letter at all but a poem that only by contorted analysis can possibly relate to the theft of the tarts, much less to the prisoner, the Knave of Hearts.

> "No, they're not," said the White Rabbit, "and that's the queerest thing about it." (The jury all looked puzzled.)
> "He must have imitated somebody else's hand," said the King. (The jury all brightened up again.)[58]

Here, the King assumes a fact not in evidence. Whether the Knave forged the handwriting of another would have to be proven by evidence that is relevant and adequate. So far, that assertion is certainly not proven; it is merely an assertion, the King's assertion, that of a proven liar. The other fault, which is common enough, is that the King is too quick to arrive at unwarranted conclusions. The desire to decide things quickly is incompatible with the detailed and full evaluation of complex situations. We saw the same kind of rush to judgment in the year 2000 presidential election. People claimed the country was in danger, or undergoing some kind of unnecessary angst, because the election results were equivocal. Due diligence and due process are more important in deciding the true result of an election than is speed.

> "Please your Majesty," said the Knave, "I didn't write it, and they ca'n't prove that I did: there's no name signed at the end."[59]

Ho, ho, ho. That is pretty funny. It reminds me of the fairytale about Reynard the fox. When it was announced that a chicken had been stolen, Reynard screamed, "Don't look at me. I didn't eat the chicken!"

Who said he did? Why is he being defensive? And how does he know, if, in fact, he didn't eat the chicken, that the chicken had been eaten? The only thing that had been announced was that the chicken had been stolen.

If the Knave didn't write the note, how did he know it wasn't signed? Furthermore, the absence of a signature is neither here nor there. It certainly doesn't prove the Knave didn't write it. And it doesn't prove he did write it, either. The Knave sounds defensive. He would have to explain how he knew the poem was not signed. If his explanation were not relevant and adequate, the jury would be correct to assume the Knave did write the poem.

> "If you didn't sign it," said the King, "that only makes the matter worse. You must have meant some mischief, or else you'd have signed your name like an honest man."
>
> There was a general clapping of hands at this: it was the first really clever thing the King had said that day.[60]

Here the King's argument is reasonable but off the point. The question is whether the Knave wrote the poem. And if the Knave did write the poem, so what? How does it relate to the case in point? The King would have done well to question the Knave on how the Knave knew the poem was not signed. Instead, the King launches a general discussion about anonymous notes, which, in general, do mean mischief and do reflect adversely on the character of the writer. Whether this anonymous note means mischief and reflects adversely on the character of the writer must be determined by an evaluation of the particulars of the note itself. My analysis indicates that the poem in this note, like the

Lobster Quadrille of chapter 10, the Hatter's rendition of "Twinkle, Twinkle, little bat!/How I wonder what you're at," as well as the "Jabberwocky" of *Looking Glass*, is pure, unmitigated nonsense—placed here at our disposal for pure, unmitigated fun.

> "That proves his guilt, of course," said the Queen: "so, off with—"
> "It doesn't prove anything of the sort!" said Alice. "Why, you don't even know what they're about!"
> . . . "No, no! said the Queen. "Sentence first—verdict afterwards."[61]

That last statement by the Queen epitomizes the major problem in this final chapter of *Alice's Adventures in Wonderland*. As I see it, that problem is that the King and Queen, not having read my book on clear thinking, both obsessed with their power and position, do not know how to evaluate evidence for relevance or adequacy. As a result, none of the evidence presented has anything whatsoever to do with the crime of stealing the tarts. Even if it did, it would have been inadequate to convict the Knave. None of the evidence implicates the Knave in any direct way. Even Alice, a seven-and-one-half-year-old little girl, has figured that out.

Another view, and one I believe is correct, is that it is now time, at age seven and a half, for a little girl like Alice to begin questioning the adult world's organization, thinking, customs, ethics, and procedures. Each generation does that. Each generation has to, for each generation must work out its own salvation.

Alice is growing up, and as a maturing human, she is beginning to assume the set of thinking so necessary for the forward progress of our race: critical inquiry. Alice has reached the end of her hero's journey, from innocence to experience, from preconscious acceptance to conscious questioning. In telling off the King and Queen, Alice becomes child-as-judge. And as judge, in the fierceness of her now-independent thought, she dismisses them all as a meaningless pack of cards. Alice—child heroine—asserts in the face of a primitive, threatening universe the reasonableness of her own (and the Knave of Hearts') right to exist and actively to rebel against the social order that sentences to death ("off with her head") all those who demur from its mad decrees. Alice concludes that grown-up stupidity is imposing. That grown-up culture is nothing but ridiculous bombast and, to quote her directly, "stuff and nonsense."

This raises the same question raised in Kafka's *Castle*: Why do we adults accept all those useless rules with so much conviction? Why do we, with such acquiescence, follow moronic governments and politicians? Why do we obey the rule forty-twos of our time?

But notice that Alice's fury was ignited by the King's attempt to exclude her from the court (that is, from the company of adults). Children don't like that, especially when it means going to bed early or not being privy to family secrets. There's where children draw the line and react accordingly, often with a temper tantrum like Alice's.

But on a higher plain, let's not forget that the creatures she has met, the whole dream, are Alice's. Those things reflect the psychology of herself, for she is the dreamer. They are Alice's personality transmuted, but they reflect the words and attitudes of her teachers, family, and pets as they appear to her, a little girl. The verisimilitude comes from the full understanding of the reactions of a child's mind to academic training, particularly to instruction in logic and mathematics, where often the work was too hard and the books—unlike this one that you have in your hand—too difficult to understand.

In that context, Alice's reactions seem right because they are based on reality because Carroll drew upon the comedies and tragedies of the schoolroom for his fun. Like all good writers, Lewis Carroll wrote what he knew. Like all good teachers, he knew and loved his students well.

NOTES

1. Lewis Carroll, *Symbolic Logic*, in *Mathematical Recreations of Lewis Carroll* (New York: Dover, 1958), p. xv.

2. Lewis Carroll, *Alice's Adventures in Wonderland*, illust. John Tenniel and colored by Fritz Kredel (New York: Random House, 1946), p. 3. All references to *Alice* are to this edition.

3. Ibid.

4. Ibid., p. 5.

5. Ibid., p. 12.

6. Ibid.

7. Ibid., p. 19.

8. Ibid., p. 25.

9. Ibid., p. 26.

10. Ibid., pp. 26–27.

11. This is the way I remember the skit, and I have a fairly good memory.

12. Ibid., p. 59.

13. Ibid., p. 60.

14. Ibid.

15. Ibid., p. 64.

16. Ibid.

17. Ibid., pp. 71–72.

18. Quoted in Martin Gardner, ed. *The Annotated Alice* (New York: Norton, 1990), p. 65.

19. Carroll, *Alice's Adventures in Wonderland*, pp. 72–73.

20. Ibid., p. 73.

21. Ibid.

22. Lewis Carroll, *The Diaries of Lewis Carroll*, ed. Roger Lancelyn Green (London: Cassell, 1953), p. 42.

23. Carroll, *Alice's Adventures in Wonderland*, pp. 74–75.

24. Ibid.

25. Ibid., p. 75.

26. Ibid., p. 78.

27. The original story came from an article in *Columbia College Today*.

28. Carroll, *Alice's Adventures in Wonderland*, p. 77.

29. Ibid., p. 84.

30. Ibid., pp. 85–86.

31. Ibid., p. 93.

32. Ibid., p. 106.

33. Ibid.

34. Ibid.

35. Ibid., p. 101.

36. Ibid., p. 112.

37. Ibid., p. 113.

38. Ibid., p. 114.

39. Ibid.

40. Ibid.

41. Ibid., pp. 129–31.

42. Ibid., p. 132.

43. Ibid., pp. 133–34.

44. Ibid., p. 135.

45. Ibid.

46. Ibid., p. 137.

47. Ibid., p. 141.

48. From the movie *A Beautiful Mind*.

49. Carroll, *Alice's Adventures in Wonderland*, p. 141.

50. Ibid.

51. In Gardner, *Annotated Alice*, pp. 187–88.

52. Carroll, *Alice's Adventures in Wonderland*, p. 141.

53. Ibid.

54. Gardner, *Annotated Alice*, pp. 222–23.
55. Ibid., p. 225.
56. Ibid.
57. Carroll, *Alice's Adventures in Wonderland*, p. 142.
58. Ibid.
59. Ibid.
60. Ibid.
61. Ibid., pp. 143, 146.

Vale (Farewell)

Although Lewis Carroll was quick to point out that unlike the fairy tales (à la the Brothers Grimm or Hans Christian Andersen), his stories have no moral, I think he might have been hinting in that direction when he showed the general pandemonium in *Alice's Adventures in Wonderland* at the end of the trial at the book's conclusion.

That bedlam is the result that we can expect when thinking stops and emotions ride fierce and unrestrained. That mayhem and anarchy are the opposite of what Carroll loved so dearly—clear, rational thinking and right behavior. His moral, if there were one, might have been that bad thinking results in chaos. Whether that was his moral is not particularly important.

What is important, what really counts, is that it is the truth.

Glossary

amphiboly: A double meaning, especially when it arises from a faulty grammatical construction. Examples: "Wanted: High school student for baking." Or "We dispense with accuracy." (Don't trust a pharmacist who can't express clear thoughts.) Or how about the advice of the Delphic oracle: "If Croesus goes to war, he will destroy a great empire." Croesus did attack Cyrus of Persia who destroyed Croesus' empire, Lydia.

argument: Originally "proof" or "evidence." Now often a reason or reasons offered for or against something. In this book, *argument* is used in the traditional sense. As it is usually used in logic, however, a better term would probably be *demonstration*.

argumentum: Latin for proof, argument, subject, contents, or matter related to proof.

argumentum ad baculum: Appeal to force—a grave error, wherein the argument has degenerated into a fight. Might doesn't make right, despite the maxim to the contrary. Because someone defeats another person by force doesn't mean that the winner was right or wrong, noble or ignoble, supported by God or by the Devil, and so forth. It means merely that he won the battle. Resort to force is not a rational argument. It is quite the opposite.

argumentum ad hominem: An error wherein a person, not his or her argument, is attacked.

argumentum ad ignorantiam: An error wherein the argument appeals to ignorance, asserting that something must be true because it has not been proven false.

argumentum ad populum: An error wherein persuasion is attempted by appealing to a popular sentiment, such as patriotism, loyalty, tradition, custom, and such. Argumentum ad populum is diversionary because whether the group thinks something is not a reason why that something is correct. A group can be right or wrong, and this must be determined by evidence, not by consensus. In most cases, the argument ad populum doesn't even reflect the view of the cited group as determined scientifically. Instead, the argument more likely reflects the speaker's view.

argumentum ad verecundiam: Latin for "proof based on respect for." This is an argument that cites authority as the reason that a speaker should be believed. In most cases, the respect is for authority. The argumentum ad verecundiam is based (irrationally) on a proof (argumentum) based on respect for authority (verecundiam). Arguments based on authority are not reasonable arguments because there is no special reason that an authority would be right. In fact, the argument ad verecundiam is often a diversionary technique that distracts from the facts in evidence and toward potential error.

bathing machine: Bathing machines were small locker rooms on wheels. Horses pulled them into the sea to the depth desired by the bather, who then emerged modestly through a door facing the sea. A huge umbrella in back of the machine concealed the bather from public view.

begging the question: An error in clear thinking and in informal logic wherein something is asserted as true but needs to be proven.

conceit: A fanciful, witty notion that is often a striking metaphor that is strained and arbitrary. A conceit is a false analogy gone further awry.

contradiction: A statement that is false for all possible circumstances. Philosophers like to put this by saying that contradictions are necessarily false. A sentence S is logically false, therefore a contradiction, if, and only if, every row of its truth table assigns the value F (false). Two contradictory statements cannot be simultaneously true. For example:

It is raining.
It is not raining.

1 and 2 contradict each other. Compare this with **contraries**.

contraries: In logic, the situation where two statements are so related that only one can be true but both can be false. For example:

The present king of France is bald.
The present king of France is not bald.

If there were a present king of France, the two statements, 1 and 2, could not both be simultaneously true. As there is no present king of France, both statements are false, and therefore, 1 and 2 are contraries and not contradictions.

deduction: Proceeding from the general to the particular to reach a conclusion supported by evidence.

distributed: A term is distributed if, and only if, it refers (as either subject or predicate) to the whole class that it names.

fallacy: A false or mistaken idea or opinion, an error in reasoning, or a defect in argument, especially one that appears to be sound but isn't.

falsify: To show to be false.

generalize: To infer that what has been found true in all known cases is true of all cases, even including those that have not yet been observed. In most scientific reasoning, the scientist makes a "leap of faith" from the particular to the general; this is the basis for the tentative nature of scientific hypothesis. Not all generalization is refutable, however, especially when the generalization covers all the known and all the possible observations. For instance, I am generalizing when I say all the people in my immediate family are doctors. Since my wife, my son, my daughter, and I are all doctors, and since I have no other people in my immediate family, my assertion is true of all the possible cases and can't be refuted. Thus, generalizations about true particulars can be and often are absolutely true and should be defended as true absolutely.

inductive: Proceeding from the particular to the general to reach a conclusion supported by evidence.

logic: Scientifically, the study of the strength of the evidential link between the premises and the conclusions of arguments. In this book, logic is sometimes loosely used as the art of correct and reasonable thinking. Either definition makes logic a form of evidence itself, if evidence is defined as a sign that leads to truth. However, in the contemporary field of academic logic, logic and truth are disjoined at a fundamental level. Logic, according to this academic view, tells us the degree of reasonable confidence that we can have in the truth of an argument's conclusion, were the premises true. It cannot tell us which or if the premises are true. For that reason, logic is a theory of truth preservation, informing us how truth can best be preserved across inferential links but not how to determine what is true to begin with. One consequence is that any full evaluation of argument requires both logical and factual analysis. The validity idea is not a shortcoming of logic any more than factual disciplines' dependence on logic is their shortcoming. The benefit of the disciplinary arrangement enables logic to contribute distinctively to the rational evaluation of arguments. According to the academic view, logic's task of truth preservation must be clearly defined and distinguished from the task of truth determination. Hence, academics will not call an argument true, as they believe arguments cannot be true (or false). In this view, arguments can only be valid or invalid, sound or unsound.

logical deduction: Reasoning from the general to the specific individual cases or particular facts or from premises to a logically reasonable conclusion (as opposed to logical induction). Remember this by this mnemonic: *De* is Latin for "from"; *duc* is a Latin root meaning "leads." Therefore, deduction is that which leads away from the general and to the specific particular.

logical induction: Reasoning from individual cases or particular facts to a general conclusion (as opposed to logical deduction). Remember this by this mnemonic: *In* is Latin for "into"; *duc* is a Latin root meaning "leads." Therefore, that which leads into the general from the particular is inductive.

major premise: That which contains the major term that is the predicate of the conclusion of the syllogism.

middle term: In a syllogism, that which appears in both premises.

minor premise: That which contains the minor term that is the subject of the conclusion of the syllogism.

obloquy: Verbal abuse of a person or a thing; censorious vituperation, especially when widespread or general.

optative: The grammatical form in Greek that expresses desire or a wish. Hence, wishful thinking.

pleonasm: The use of more words than are necessary for the expression of an idea. Examples: "plenty enough" and "very unique." If a thing is unique, it is one of a kind by definition and doesn't need the word "very" to emphasize its uniqueness.

positivism: A system of philosophy basing knowledge solely on data of sense experience. Originated by Auguste Comte (1798–1857), it was based on observable, scientific facts and their relations to each other. Positivist philosophy strictly rejects speculation about or search for ultimate origins. Comte is best known for his "law of the three stages"— the theological, the metaphysical, and the positive. In stage one, humans saw processes as the work of supernatural powers. In the second stage, humans explained them by means of abstract ideas. In the last stage, humans accumulated data (observed facts) and determined relationships among them. Comte believed that astronomy, physics, chemistry, and biology had already evolved through these three stages.

premise: A previous statement that serves as the basis for the advancement of reasons in an argument, or either of two propositions of a syllogism from which a conclusion is drawn. Remember this by the mnemonic: Premise comes from the Latin *praemittere* (*prae* = before, *mittere* = send, *praemittere* = to send before). When an argument is cast in standard form, the premise is always sent before the conclusion. In a syllogism, the major premise contains the predicate of the conclusion; the minor premise contains the subject of the conclusion.

rub: "There's the rub" means "there's the catch," and it also means "there's the essence"—the meanings can be close but not identical. Shakespeare implies both senses but paints a concrete picture that would have been familiar to his audience. "Rub" is the sportsman's name for an obstacle that, in the game of bowls, diverts a ball from its true course. Shakespeare was fond of the sport. He played not on lanes but on lawns, where obstacles were common.

sorites: From the Greek *soros*, meaning "a heap." In logic, a series of premises followed by a conclusion, arranged so that the predicate of the first premise is the subject of the next, and so forth, the conclusion uniting the subject of the first with the predicate of the last in a series of syllogisms.

sound argument: When an argument is valid and its premises are all true, then the argument is sound. When an argument is valid but at least one premise is false, the argument is unsound. The ideal argument is a sound argument, as that is most likely to have a conclusion that matches reality.

special pleading: To use an argument when it supports our preconceptions and reject it in another context when it fails to do so.

statement: A sentence that makes a definite claim. For instance, "Socrates is bald" claims that Socrates exists and that he is bald. The statement "Socrates is bald and Socrates is wise" makes one claim (aside from the existential claim) that encompasses both bald and wise.

subaltern: Something ranked below or inferior in some way, usually in status, quantity, or both. "Some S are P" is a subaltern categorical particular statement whose truth claim follows directly from the universal categorical affirmative statement "All S are P," with "Some S are P" ranked below the more universal claim because it encompasses less.

supererogation: More than is required or expected.

syllogism: An argument or form of reasoning in which two statements or premises (which are usually generalizations) are made and a conclusion is drawn from them. Classical logic has three types of syllogism—categorical, conditional, and disjunctive.

tautology: A circular argument usually made by repeating the same thing twice. Circular arguments become more plausible (or seem more plausible) and less easy to recognize if developed at length, as in the Coast Guard collision regulation discussed in chapter 4. A statement that is always true says nothing new and is also a tautology. A sentence S is logically true, and therefore tautological, if, and only if, every row of its truth table assigns it the value T (true).

truth: What is (as opposed to what is not).

tu quoque: Latin meaning "you, too." This fallacy consists in rejecting a criticism of one's argument or action by accusing one's critic or others of thinking or acting in a similar way.

unsound argument: When an argument is valid but at least one premise is false, the argument is unsound.

valid argument: Any argument that doesn't violate the rules of logic—that is, not invalid. It is important to note that valid has a highly specific, technical use in academic logic that differs from several colloquial uses, such as "You made a valid point," where valid means "true," or at least worthy of consideration; "Her argument is not valid," where valid means "compelling"; "This coupon is no longer valid," where valid means "active, applicable, or properly functioning." In the technical definition as opposed to the colloquial, validity is a property of arguments, a property of an interrelated set of propositions. It is not a property of any one or more of the propositions themselves. Hence, it would be nonsensical to say that a claim, premise, or conclusion is valid in the technical sense. Premises, claims, statements, and conclusions can be true or false, but they cannot be valid, for only their interrelationships can be valid. Logicians consider those interrelationships valid if they are not invalid. The policing of the interrelationships is

part of the truth-preserving duty of logic as opposed to the truth-dis-
covering duty of science.

verify: To show to be true.

verecundiam: From the Latin *verecundia*, meaning "modesty," "diffi-
dence," or "bashfulness." With the genitive, it means "respect for" or
"scruple about."

Select Bibliography

This annotated list contains only those books that the author recommends for the general reader. More in-depth reviews by the author can be found on Amazon.com.

CLEAR THINKING

Browne, M. Neil, and Stuart Keeley. *Asking the Right Questions*. Upper Saddle River, NJ: Prentice Hall, 2001. This guide to critical thinking uses abundant examples and a cross-cultural approach to teach important skills on how and when to ask crucial questions. The focus on evidence-based decision making is directly in line with the reality principle.

Cannavo, Salvator. *Think to Win*. Amherst, NY: Prometheus Books, 1998. Lesser sense reasoning is that used to boost one's argument and support one's beliefs. Greater sense reasoning is that used to discover truth. Although the title of this book suggests that it is concerned with lesser sense arguments, its actual mission is to help people think better—thus, a greater sense logic book.

Capaldi, Nicholas. *The Art of Deception*. Amherst, NY: Prometheus Books, 1987. The work is uneven and lacks focus and definitely misnamed. Without having a background in logic, I think some of the author's points would have passed me by and others probably would have been just downright confusing. One wonders about a book on the art of deception deceiving people to believe that that is what it is about when it is really about clear thinking and logic.

Crusius, Timothy, and Carolyn E. Channell. *The Aims of Argument*. Mountain View, CA: Mayfield, 2000. Most texts on the subject are too formalistic and prescriptive, but this brief and effective rhetoric is designed to help people plan and deliver their arguments. Particularly important is the analysis of pictures and the deconstruction of visual arguments.

Damer, T. Edward. *Attacking Faulty Reasoning.* Belmont, CA: Wadsworth/Thomson Learning, 2001. One of the best books on the subject. More than sixty fallacies are attacked according to general principles of clear thinking. Particularly interesting is the discussion of the answers to the exercises.

Flew, Anthony. *How to Think Straight.* Amherst, NY: Prometheus Books, 1998. A good introduction to critical thinking by an expert in the field.

Russo, J. Edward, and Paul J. H. Schoemaker. *Decision Traps.* New York: Doubleday, 1989. Light reading and a little simple and simplistic but worth a look for those interested in direct applications of clear thinking to practical problems and business decisions.

Skyrms, Brian. *Choice and Chance: An Introduction to Inductive Logic.* Belmont, CA: Wadsworth/Thomson Learning, 2000. This is a good introduction to logic, both inductive and, to a lesser extent, deductive. It probably serves better as a textbook than as an aid to individual learning, but under the proper conditions and with the proper reader, it could serve both. I like it best when it explains truth tables (chap. 1) and the rules of the calculus of probability (chap. 6). Particularly interesting are the practical applications in the exercises, especially in cards, dice playing, and horse racing.

St. Aubyn, Giles. *The Art of Argument.* New York: Emerson Books, 1962. This is a little book, but does it pack a wallop! Especially interesting is the appendix on the "Good Old Days" and how a political speech may be taken to task for its errors in thinking.

GROUPTHINK

Janis, Irving L. *Groupthink*, 2nd ed. Boston: Houghton Mifflin, 1982. This classic of social psychology is based on the idea that people in groups might think differently (and by implication) less well than they would have thought as individuals on the same issue. Most of the evidence in this book supports the idea that group thinking, like thinking in general, goes awry when there is a failure to evaluate all the available evidence for relevance and adequacy.

Lewis, James R. *Doomsday Prophecies.* Amherst, NY: Prometheus Books, 2000. Wonderful documentation of the outer reaches of sanity in some of the most nefarious doomsday cults, including the Happy Hookers for Jesus, Heaven's Gate, AUM Shinrikyo, and Millerites (Adventists).

LOGIC AND REASON BOOKS
NOT FOR THE FAINT OF HEART

Aristotle. *Nicomachean Ethics*. Harmondsworth, UK: Penguin Classics, 1976. This little book has had an enormous impact on moral philosophy, particularly in the West. It may surprise you to know that Aristotle regarded ethics as a practical, not a theoretical, science.

Langer, Susanne K. *An Introduction to Symbolic Logic*. New York: Houghton Mifflin, 1937. Symbolic logic is an instrument of exact thought, both analytic and constructive; its mission is not only to validate scientific methods but also to clarify the semantic confusions that beset the human mind. This book is probably the clearest book ever written on symbolic logic, and no special knowledge is needed to understand it. Read the chapter on the assumptions of the *Principia Mathematica* before you attack the *Principia* directly.

Smullyan, Raymond M. *First-Order Logic*. New York: Dover, 1995. The work is self-contained and serves as an introduction to quantification theory and analytic methods. The material on trees is difficult but necessary for an understanding of the tableau method.

Thomas Aquinas, Saint. *On Laws, Morality, and Politics*, edited by William P. Baumgarth and Richard J. Regan, SJ. 2nd ed. Indianapolis: Hackett, 2002. Absolutely brilliant in form and content, this work clearly shows Saint Thomas a master of logic and reasoned argument.

Whitehead, Alfred North, and Bertrand Russell. *Principia Mathematica*. 1910. Reprint, New York: Cambridge University Press, 1997. This great three-volume work is deservedly the most famous ever written on the foundations of mathematics. It aims to deduce all the fundamental propositions from a small number of logical premises and primitive ideas to prove that mathematics is a development of logic.

WORTH A LOOK FOR THOSE
WITH INQUIRING MINDS

Crews, Frederick. *Postmodern Pooh*. New York: North Point Press, 2001. Should be required reading for anybody who wants to understand the absurdity of culture-theory ideas and the damage they inflict. The logic is brilliant and fun.

Howard, Philip K. *The Death of Common Sense*. New York: Random House, 1994. How law and its applications often results in misadventure and irrational actions. Multiple examples prove that government often acts like some extraterrestrial power, not an institution that exists to serve us, and almost never deals with real-life problems in a way that reflects an understanding of the reality.

Kelly, Fred C. *Why You Win or Lose: The Psychology of Speculation*. 1930. Reprint, Wells, VT: Fraser, 1962. The logic and psychology of stock market speculation in a 177-page nutshell. Vanity, greed, wishful thinking, neglect of reality, and the will to believe are the major reasons that you lose.

Mackay, Charles. *Extraordinary Popular Delusions and the Madness of Crowds*. Amherst, NY: Prometheus Books, 2001. The public is repeatedly duped, and this book explains how and why. Want to know why the Dow in October of 1929 went from 381 points to 41? Want to know what happened in the tulip mania and the South Sea Bubble? Human nature never changes. Here are the details—read 'em and weep.

Paulos, John Allen. *Innumeracy: Mathematical Illiteracy and its Consequences*. New York: Vintage, 1990. This entertaining book argues that our inability to deal rationally with numbers or with probabilities results in misinformed government policies, confused personal decisions, and an increased susceptibility to pseudosciences of all kinds. Innumeracy is the mathematical counterpart of illiteracy, another disease that also ravages our technological society.

Quinn, Daniel, and Tom Whalen. *A Newcomer's Guide to the Afterlife*. New York: Bantam Books, 1997. This interesting book is a discussion of, and in many cases a refutation of, the religious logic of an afterlife. Many of the implications of living forever are addressed with wry wit and intelligent thinking, leaving a pretty dim view of the traditional concept of life after death.

Salk, Jonas. *Anatomy of Reality*. New York: Columbia University Press, 1983. The book is a part of the Convergence series that looks at the deep philosophical and scientific issues of our time. Salk has come up with the general idea of how nature works, and he seems to be on the right track.

Santoro, Victor. *The Rip-Off Book*. Port Townsend, WA: Loompanic Unlimited, 1984. This book outlines the basic principles of fraud and gives a good picture of how fraud artists bilk the public. It should be required reading in every high school economics course.

Schiffman, Nathaniel. *Abracadabra!* Amherst, NY: Prometheus Books, 1997. Excellent in telling how the human mind is so easily deceived by spatial and time misdirections.

Schulte, Fred. *Fleeced!* Amherst, NY: Prometheus Books, 1995. This is an excellent account of telemarketing rip-offs and how to avoid them. Too bad this book has not had a much wider readership—it might have prevented some of the great frauds of our time.

Sommerville, C. John. *How the News Makes Us Dumb*. Downers Grove, IL: Inter-Varsity Press, 1999. Beautiful discussion of the topic and proof of his point by showing the contradictions in the daily flow of so-called news.

LEWIS CARROLL AND THE ALICE BOOKS

Carroll, Lewis. *The Annotated Alice: The Definitive Edition*. Introduction and notes by John Tenniel. Edited by Martin Gardner. New York: Norton, 2000. *Alice* was written for a British audience of another century. To fully capture its full wit and wisdom, we need to know a great many things that are not part of the text. Read this after you have read about the life and times of Alice and her creator by Stephanie Lovett Stoffel, referenced below.

———. *The Hunting of the Snark*. 1876. Reprint, London: Chatto and Windus, 1969. "The bowspirit got mixed with the rudder sometimes." Want to read real Carrollian nonsense? Read this.

———. *The Political Pamphlets and Letters of Charles Lutwidge Dodgson and Related Pieces*. New York: Lewis Carroll Society of North America, 2001. These are the political pamphlets and letters of Charles Lutwidge Dodgson (Lewis Carroll), compiled and annotated by Francine F. Abeles. We see in Carroll's letters and pamphlets his inventive mind at work. Particularly interesting are the discussion of how to place winning horse racing bets and his plea for a more intelligent system of voting and election.

———. *Symbolic Logic and the Game of Logic*. Mineola, NY: Dover, 1958. Two books in one, and both are great treats. His solutions to the syllogisms by using visual methods and his profound knowledge of category theory deserve to be better known. Carroll's symbolic logic is a way of expressing logic in unique diagrams of propositions and conclusions.

Fisher, John. *The Magic of Lewis Carroll*. London: Nelson, 1973. A mass of logic and mathematical games lies behind the scenes in the Alice books. Some of these come out here in the full light of brilliant illustrations.

Rackin, Donald. *Alice's Adventures in Wonderland and Through the Looking Glass: Nonsense, Sense, and Meaning*. New York: Twayne, 1991. Some of the discussion is itself nonsense, but it is an interesting demonstration of how far one can get carried away.

Stoffel, Stephanie Lovett. *Lewis Carroll in Wonderland: The Life and Times of Alice and Her Creator*. New York: H. N. Abrams, 1997. Beautifully illustrated handbook about Carroll and friends by a scholar and collector who works for the Lewis Carroll Society of North America. Start here if you want a bird's-eye view of Carroll.

Index